Irene Mandl a recognized leader in European Born Globals (EBGs) job creation research has an interesting book with Valentina Patrini, which may well start a major game change. Rapidly expanding EBG firms are markedly impacting entrepreneurial leadership thinking, and skilled personnel job creation. The authors research methodology of independently studying different EU countries shows EBGs require developmental help, and also can help growth of firms in other networks. A 'must-read' that should elicit greater support and encourage multifaceted research.

> Manek Kirpalani, *Distinguished Professor Emeritus, John Molson School of Business, Montreal, Canada*

Firms, which internationalize early and fast in their life, have been considered a challenge for international business theory and for the practice of management. Their growth also has a potential impact on economic systems and the creation of new jobs. The latter issues represent a gap in studies. This book addresses this gap and represents a relevant contribution to the field. Companies internationalizing early and fast are likely to require talents in order to develop quickly a competitive advantage. They can also stimulate the rise of other similar enterprises and encourage people to start their own international new venture. The European economy is particularly in need of new drivers of economic and social growth and this book sheds light on one the possible drivers.

> Antonella Zucchella, *University of Pavia, Italy and Anglia Ruskin University, Cambridge, UK*

This is an important book that sheds further light on a vital phenomenon. Since we initiated the European research on the Born Global phenomenon in the mid 1990s it has been demonstrated that an increasing number of such firms are established, but our knowledge about their growth and job creations is still sparse. This book contributes new knowledge in that respect and demonstrates the importance of these firms for the economic development in Europe. It also adds to our insight into what motivates entrepreneurs to establish such firms and how different institutional settings may support their survival and growth. I welcome this book and its contribution.

> Tage Koed Madsen, *Professor, University of Southern Denmark, Denmark*

European Born Globals

In the aftermath of the global recession, job creation is a policy priority. While it is a well-accepted fact that the majority of jobs are created by small and medium-sized enterprises, not all SMEs are rapidly growing, or even intend to expand. With limited public budgets, business models within the SME population that do show high job creation potential become very attractive.

One of the business types identified as major engines of job creation are 'born globals', characterised as firms which engage intensively in internationalisation activities shortly after start-up. They are high on the entrepreneurship research agenda but so far little attention has been devoted to their potential as job creators, the processes they apply when hiring, or the barriers they face.

Combining secondary data analysis, literature reviews and international case studies, *European Born Globals* sheds new light on the motivations and processes of job creation in born global firms. By contributing to understanding the 'why' and 'how' of job creation in born globals, this book will be essential not only for policy makers, but also for academic research and management education.

Irene Mandl is Head of Unit 'Employment' at Eurofound and has worked in policy-oriented research on employment and the labour market as well as entrepreneurship for more than 15 years. Some of her major research topics refer to SMEs, internationalisation, specific forms of entrepreneurship or new forms of employment.

Valentina Patrini is a researcher at Eurofound. Valentina mainly focuses on entrepreneurship, internationalisation and innovation, and their relationship with employment and job creation. She has ten years of experience in the field of socioeconomic research, including policy evaluations and comparative studies at European level.

Routledge Studies in International Business and the World Economy

For a full list of titles in this series, visit www.routledge.com/Routledge-Studies-in-International-Business-and-the-World-Economy/book-series/SE0358.

European Born Globals

Job Creation in Young
International Businesses

**Edited by Irene Mandl and
Valentina Patrini**

Routledge
Taylor & Francis Group

LONDON AND NEW YORK

First published 2018
by Routledge

2 Park Square, Milton Park, Abingdon, Oxfordshire OX14 4RN
52 Vanderbilt Avenue, New York, NY 10017

Routledge is an imprint of the Taylor & Francis Group, an informa business

First issued in paperback 2019

British Library Cataloguing in Publication Data
A catalogue record for this book is available from the British Library

Library of Congress Cataloging in Publication Data
A catalog record for this book has been requested

ISBN: 978-1-138-71395-6 (hbk)
ISBN: 978-0-367-88429-1 (pbk)

Typeset in Times New Roman
by Wearset Ltd, Boldon, Tyne and Wear

Contents

**8 More than job creation: employee engagement in knowledge
sharing and learning advantages of newness** 128

MARÍA RIPOLLÉS, ANDREU BLESA, MIGUEL A. HERNÁNDEZ
AND IÑIGO ISUSI

**9 Conclusions: policy relevance of born globals for job
creation in Europe** 148

IRENE MANDL

Figures

Tables

Contributors

Svante Andersson is Professor in Business Administration at Halmstad University.

Andreu Blesa PhD is Associate Professor of Marketing in the Department of Business Administration and Marketing at Universitat Jaume I, Castellón, Spain.

Jessica Durán is Researcher in IKEI, and she holds Bachelor degrees in Tourism, and in Humanities and Business, both obtained from the University of Deusto (Spain), in addition to several qualifications from specialised courses.

Andrea Dorr studied psychology at the University of Vienna.

Natasha Evers is both a full-time Lecturer of International Marketing and Exporting and a Researcher at the Whitaker Institute of Innovation and Policy, National University of Ireland, Galway.

Majella Giblin is a Lecturer Above the Bar in Management at the J. E. Cairnes School of Business and Economics, National University of Ireland, Galway.

Miguel A. Hernández holds a Bachelor's degree in Business Administration and Management and a Master's degree in International Marketing from Universitat Jaume I.

Iñigo Isusi holds a Bachelor's degree in Regional Economics from the University of the Basque Country and an MSc in Regional Planning from the University of Wales College, Cardiff, in addition to pursuing several specialisation courses at the University of Leuven (Belgium).

Irene Mandl is Head of the Research Unit 'Employment' at the European Foundation for the Improvement of Living and Working Conditions (Eurofound).

Jaan Masso PhD is a Senior Researcher at the University of Tartu.

Thomas Oberholzner has graduated from the Vienna University of Economics and Business Administration, having studied business management and specialising in regional economics and economic geography.

Valentina Patrini is a Researcher in the Research Unit 'Employment' at the European Foundation for the Improvement of Living and Working Conditions (Eurofound).

María Ripollés PhD is Associate Professor of Management in the Department of Business Administration and Marketing at Universitat Jaume I, Castellon, Spain.

Tiia Vissak PhD is a Senior Researcher at the University of Tartu. Her main research interests are internationalisation processes, networks, management issues, transition and emerging economies.

Forewords

We are living in times of intense change, not least linked to rapid technological development. Utopian and dystopian pictures are drawn, with a particular focus on the future of work, which go so far as to question whether work has a future at all.

Some predict a society where most routine work is performed by robots and artificial intelligence, while a sizeable portion of the workforce, maybe supported by a universal income, dedicates more of its time to creativity and leisure. Others point to the polarisation of labour markets and warn of increasingly unequal societies, with many in poor quality jobs and a growing number of unemployed and socially excluded. Many bear in mind that technology-driven changes have already been with us for a long time and make less radical predictions; their concern is the transitional social costs associated with larger, deeper and faster structural change.

In any scenario, it is clear that economic growth and job creation are not necessarily tied to each other. Much policy focus has traditionally been placed on the former. In fact, an emphasis on productivity can push a sort of job-poor economic growth and an expectation that substantial job creation can result only from exponential growth.

However, driven either by philosophical reasons ('To work is … an indispensable duty of social man', quoting Jean Jacques Rousseau) or by social evidence (unemployment is the main reason for dissatisfaction with one's life, as well as for social exclusion and poverty), job creation has remained a central policy goal in Europe. Proof of this can be found in initiatives from the Lisbon Strategy's aim of 'more and better jobs' to Jean-Claude Juncker's 'Agenda for jobs, growth, fairness and democratic change' to the 'job-rich recovery' supported by the Europe 2020 growth strategy.

Most research has focused on macroeconomic issues, but if evidence is to enlighten policy action, we need more knowledge on the specific drivers of actual job creation. Jobs are created, in fact, through thousands of individual decisions, the vast majority of them taken within SMEs that create real jobs in Europe. This happens in a territory somewhere between economic and human considerations, between behavioural reasons and the business environment, between innovation and expectations and actual results, among other factors.

The context for the individuals making these decisions in these organisations has also changed in recent years. The traditional business model of an SME created locally, which slowly expands regionally and reaches the global level only after having realised growth to a certain size is no longer the only model. A number of companies are actually 'born global'. Thinking globally and acting locally is part of their strategy from day one. They have shown high potential in direct and indirect job creation, as they combine a large number of the elements identified in Eurofound research as factors that influence companies to create jobs.

I welcome the publication of this book as it aims to provide more information on the less known field of job creation in born global companies. This fills a significant knowledge gap, thereby contributing to the policy goal of creating jobs and enabling the meaningful inclusion of individuals in society through such jobs.

I want to congratulate Routledge for its initiative to publish the book, Irene Mandl and Valentina Patrini from Eurofound for editing it, and Svante Andersson, Andreu Blesa, Natasha Evers, Majella Giblin, Miguel A. Hernández, Iñigo Isusi, Jaan Masso, Thomas Oberholzner, María Ripollés and Tiia Vissak for their valuable contributions that made the publication possible. They have pioneered valuable research, and I hope the knowledge provided in the book will inspire policy action and act as an impetus for more academic work and further policy discussion in the field.

Juan Menéndez-Valdés
Director of Eurofound

Examining Eurofound's volume on 'European Born Globals' reminded me of an exploratory stroll through a region to learn about a newly developing neighbourhood. This analogy places the topic of born globals within the broader perspective of economic geography.

When observant, not in a hurry, and in search of meaningful information strolling through the region looking for the new developments, one begins to appreciate many distinct, but different, features and gets to know, and even like, some neighbourhoods within that region; but these are not the developments one was seeking. In the early instances, not much seems new or too distinct on the surface. There are some high-, low-, and medium-rise buildings, some larger and some smaller, with some green space between them. Some of these buildings are home to large corporations and have familiar names on impressive bronze plaques on ornate façades and much in-and-out traffic, indicating active interactions locally. Finding newness, new façades and new structures, expected of new developments, seems difficult. After some time, effort and careful examination, unfamiliar corporate names on new plaques on smaller buildings appear, pointing to smaller firms without eye-catching traffic or ornate façades that are not that easy to locate. These visible external attributes, however, convey very little about the high level of activities inside to attract one's further in-depth examination. This is the analogical story of highly active smaller firms called 'born globals' that are obscured by the shadow of larger traditional firms.

After persistent and further examinations, the stroller decides to explore a few of the smaller buildings, that seemingly house small and medium-sized enterprises (SMEs). Upon entry into one such SME, one finds a very busy firm quietly creating jobs, income, wealth and social benefits (revenues, profits and taxes), from national and international sources, through innovative products, processes and strategies. These are a relatively new class of firms in unassuming structures, with a variety of connotations used to refer to them, such as born globals, International New Ventures (INVs) and High-Growth Enterprises (HGEs). They are active within the commercial and industrial region dominated by traditional large firms with well-known corporate names and impressive corporate headquarters – but are often somewhat 'invisible'.

In the absence of a directory with detailed information to provide incisive local information on these locally-based internationalised enterprises, this book functions nearly as the 'Google Map' that not only provides the address, the location and portrays such business structures, but also allows for peering through their unassuming façades to see the rich diversity of in-progress international and local activities within the buildings housing such born global enterprises.

Collectively, these firms quietly grow at relatively high rates – for example, HGEs have achieved impressive growth and internationalisation – that result in increasing incremental employment, income, tax base and wealth, mostly at a time when larger firms do not strongly contribute to such. The book examines the state of these impressive firms in a selected number of European countries and the focus of the inquisitive examination, or strolling through these corporate regions, is that the distinguished SMEs bear various relatively lesser-known titles such as born globals, INVs and HGEs, among others. In spite of their attractive names and impressive achievements, only occasional news clips cover their accomplishments and contributions. Preciously little is known about these firms' potent activities, offerings and strategies that are veiled behind their indistinguishable corporate names and structures. Although the veils of their solid structures protect them from the penetrating gazes of global competition, it also deprives interested citizens from learning about their noble activities contributing to their social and economic wellbeing.

Eurofound's edited volume removes the veil and fills the information void on country-specific born globals with a comparative analysis at the end. This class of SMEs merit in-depth examination for their accomplishments and potential for further contributing to their home and host countries; and this volume provides substantive information about them, from which all readers, including scholars, management and policy makers, can learn, and on which they can build further.

Hamid Etemad, PhD, MSc, MBA, M.Eng.
Editor-in-Chief, *Journal of International Entrepreneurship*
McGill University
Montreal, Canada

Acronyms

AG	Aktiengesellschaft
BG	Born global
CBG	Classical born global
CEO	Chief executive officer
COO	Chief operating officer
CSP	Concentrated solar power
CTO	Chief technology officer
CV	Curriculum vitae
EBG	Eurofound's born global
EU	European Union
FDI	Foreign direct investment
GDP	Gross domestic product
GEM	Global Entrepreneurship Monitor
GmbH	Gesellschaft mit beschränkter Haftung
HR	Human resources
IAESTE	International Association for the Exchange of Students for Technical Experience
ICT	Information and communications technology
IDA	Industrial Development Agency
MBO	Management buyout
MNC	Multinational corporation
NACE	Nomenclature statistique des activités économiques dans la Communauté européenne
NAFTA	North America Free Trade Agreement
R&D	Research and development
SCADA	Supervisory control and data acquisition
SME	Small and medium-sized enterprise
UV	Ultraviolet

1   Introduction

Irene Mandl

Europe is recovering from the most severe economic crisis experienced since World War II, which for most Member States resulted in considerable reductions in economic activity and important increases in unemployment. In order to tackle the challenges related to the effects of the downturn, but also to face more general and long-term trends such as globalisation, demographic trends or environmental developments, the European Union and its Member States launched a strategy of 'growing to a sustainable and job-rich future' (European Commission, 2012). The strategy aims at creating a business, labour market and social environment that is conducive to 'smart, sustainable and inclusive growth' (European Commission, 2012), which also refers to job creation.

In this context, it has been acknowledged that small and medium-sized enterprises (SMEs), that is companies with fewer than 250 employees, not only provide about two thirds of private sector employment in the EU, but have created around 85 percent of the new jobs in the aftermath of the recession.[1] However, bearing in mind the large number of SMEs in Europe and the resulting heterogeneity among them, it becomes obvious that not all SMEs are equally dynamic job creators (Eurofound, 2016; European Commission, 2015) – and some of them do not even intend to grow in terms of employment at all.

In spite of the fact that the topic of growth and job creation ranks rather high on the political and academic agendas, surprisingly little research has been conducted so far to explore the characteristics of companies which contribute more to employment growth than their counterparts. Similarly, limited attention has been paid up to now to the framework conditions that need to be in place to constitute an environment conducive to job creation.

Nevertheless, two issues which are repeatedly addressed in discussions on dynamic job creators are the company age and market orientation. Thereby, it is widely acknowledged that young firms as well as those active internationally show better employment development. However, these two characteristics are rarely discussed jointly.

Traditional entrepreneurship theory establishes that firms start-up locally, orientate themselves at the regional or national market, and only after settling well there, consider international activities. Nevertheless, for about the last two decades, academia has been exploring the business model of enterprises which, shortly after their inception, engage intensively in global markets (for example, Taylor and Jack, 2013; Cavusgil and Knight, 2009; Madsen *et al.*, 2000). These companies are discussed under a variety of names, with 'born globals' and 'international new ventures' probably being the most common (Eurofound, 2012).

Hence, while this type of enterprises enjoys increasing attention among research, policy interest is only slowly picking up in Europe. One reason for this could be that the potential these firms have as regards their contribution to economic development and innovation is not well known. Discussions on the employment effects of born globals are even more scarce – and this not only among policy, but also from a research perspective.

This book aims to contribute to closing this knowledge gap by providing a range of views from different EU Member States exploring job creation in born globals and related employment aspects. The contributions shed light on the motivations and processes of hiring in such young international businesses, but also discuss the main challenges these enterprises are confronted with in their growth endeavour, in order to discover how they could be (better) publicly supported for the European labour markets to benefit from their employment potential.

The first part of the book focuses on the European level. Chapter 2 provides an overview on the relevance of SMEs in Europe and explores their employment contribution in recent years. It also discusses the main characteristics of SMEs that have a higher job creation potential than others, as well as company-external aspects that need to be in place to make employment growth happen in SMEs.

Chapter 3 introduces the business model of 'born globals' by summarising their main characteristics and highlighting their contribution to the European economy and the labour market. This is followed by a more specific discussion on the drivers and constraints for job creation by born globals, as well as by an overview of the processes followed by these companies when hiring staff.

The second part of the book provides some national perspectives. Chapter 4 illustrates the prevalence of born globals in Sweden, their employment contribution and growth ambitions. Similar information is explored in Chapter 5 on Austria, which also discusses born globals' recruitment practices, barriers encountered and external support required while hiring. Chapter 6 analyses the sustainability and employment development of Estonian born globals, including some indications of job quality in these firms. In Chapter 7, the example of an Irish cluster explores the interrelationships between local companies, large multinational enterprises and born globals, and the resulting effects on innovation activities and employment growth in the region. Chapter 8 illustrates the relevance of knowledge sharing practices within Spanish born globals and their effects on employment development.

The book concludes, in Chapter 9, with a comparative analysis of the individual contributions, and also provides some policy pointers derived from the research.

Note

1 https://ec.europa.eu/growth/smes_en.

References

Cavusgil, S. T. and Knight, G. A. (2009), *Born global firms: A new international enterprise*, Business Expert Press, New York.

Eurofound (2012), *Born global: The potential of job creation in new international businesses*, Publications Office of the European Union, Luxembourg.

Eurofound (2016), *ERM annual report 2015: Job creation in SMEs*, Publications Office of the European Union, Luxembourg.

European Commission (2012), *Europe 2020: Europe's growth strategy*, European Commission, Brussels.

European Commission (2015), *Annual report on European SMEs 2014–2015: SMEs start hiring again*, Publications Office of the European Union, Luxembourg.

Madsen, T. K., Rasmussen, E. and Servais, P. (2000), 'Differences and similarities between born globals and other types of exporters', in Yaprak, A. and Tutek, H. (eds), *Advances in International Marketing*, Vol. 10, Emerald, Bingley, pp. 247–265.

Taylor, M. and Jack, R. (2013), 'Understanding the pace, scale and pattern of firm internationalization: An extension of the "born global" concept', *International Small Business Journal*, Vol. 31, No. 6, pp. 701–721.

2 SMEs and job creation in Europe

Irene Mandl

2.1 Introduction

The European economy is characterised by a dominance of small and medium-sized enterprises (SMEs), that is companies employing fewer than 250 staff (European Commission, 2003). SMEs constitute over 99 per cent of European business and are increasingly recognised as a job engine for Europe, being responsible for a large share of employment and job creation. Nonetheless, given the heterogeneity of the SME population, not all of them contribute equally to employment growth. Several company external and internal elements influence the job creation behaviour of SMEs. This chapter discusses the economic and labour market contribution of European SMEs (Section 2.2), the individual determinants of their employment growth (Section 2.3), and concludes with a 'Profile of the job creating SME' (Section 2.4).

2.2 Economic and labour market contribution of European SMEs

In 2015, the about 23 million SMEs in the non-financial business sector in the EU represented 99.8 per cent of all enterprises (Muller *et al.*, 2016). On average, there were 4.5 SMEs per 100 inhabitants in the EU28. However, the density of SMEs shows some heterogeneity across Member States: while there were 9.4 SMEs per 100 inhabitants in the Czech Republic and between 7 and 8 in Sweden, Slovakia and Portugal, SME density was lower than 3 per 100 inhabitants in the UK, Germany and Romania.

The vast majority of SMEs (92.8 per cent) are micro enterprises (fewer than 10 employees) (Muller *et al.*, 2016). Small (10–49 employees), medium-sized (50–249 staff) and large firms are much less widespread in the EU28 (6 per cent, 1 per cent and 0.2 per cent respectively). SMEs generated €3.9 trillion of value added, accounting for 57.4 per cent of the respective EU value in 2015.

With about 90 million people, SMEs were responsible for 66.8 per cent of the employment in the EU in 2015 (Muller *et al.*, 2016). Micro enterprises offered 30 per cent of the jobs, small firms accounted for 20 per cent of employment and medium-sized firms provided 17 per cent of employment in the EU28. On average, an EU SME employs about four staff members. See Figure 2.1.

Since 2013, the SME sector in the EU28 shows a moderate, but steady recovery from the global economic and financial crisis. In 2014, SME employment grew by 1.1 per cent compared to the previous year, and in 2015 an employment growth of 1.5 per cent was observed (Muller *et al.*, 2016). In 2015, micro enterprises were responsible for more than half of the employment growth within the SME population, and for 37 per cent of overall employment growth. Muller *et al.* (2016) identify that the recovery was mainly driven by exports, highlighting the potential of economic and labour market contribution by born globals (which are found to be micro enterprises, see Chapter 3). This importance of born globals is supported by available data showing that in 2013 only 1.2 million of the EU SMEs conducted exports (Muller *et al.*, 2016) and the SMEs' share of total imports was limited to 20–50 per cent across the EU Member States (OECD, 2015).

Furthermore, some heterogeneity regarding job creation dynamism across sectors can be observed. A few sectors, such as advertising and market research, legal and accounting services, office administration and support and other business services, services to buildings, landscaping and employment activities show an employment growth of more than 5 per cent in 2014 and 2015 (Muller *et al.*, 2016). However, these sectors are accountable for a limited share of total employment. Larger sectors (for example retail or wholesale trade and construction) realised a more moderate employment growth.

An analysis of the development patterns of job characteristics in SMEs during the crisis shows an overall trend towards job polarisation – which is in line with

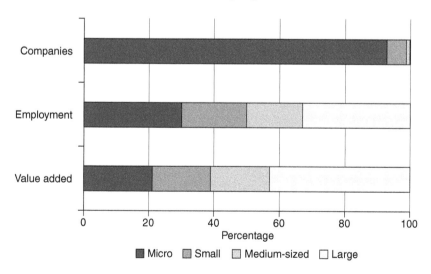

Figure 2.1 Distribution of share of enterprises, employment and value added by size class, EU28, 2015.

Source: Muller *et al.*, 2016 (author's presentation).

the general economic development during this period (Eurofound, 2014). The only sizeable job creation could be observed in workplaces with 11–49 employees, related to the lowest paid job category. While establishments with 11–19 employees realised a net creation mainly for part-time jobs, those with 20–49 employees are also characterised by a net increase in full-time jobs in the lowest paid job segment. After the crisis (2011–2013), workplaces with up to ten employees continued to suffer net job destruction, notably in the lower-paid jobs. In contrast to that, workplaces with 20–49 employees showed a more positive trend, with net job creation realised particularly in the lowest and highest paid job categories (including a net increase in full-time positions in the latter). See Figure 2.2.

While the recent job creation results in SME employment are still below the pre-crisis level, the forecasted outlook gives some justification for cautious optimism. For both 2016 and 2017, an employment growth in the EU SME population of 1.1 per cent (compared to the respective previous year) is expected (Muller *et al.*, 2016).

2.3 Determinants of job creation in SMEs

2.3.1 Overview

From the above discussions it becomes obvious that even if a considerable share of job creation in Europe is to be attributed to the SME sector, employment

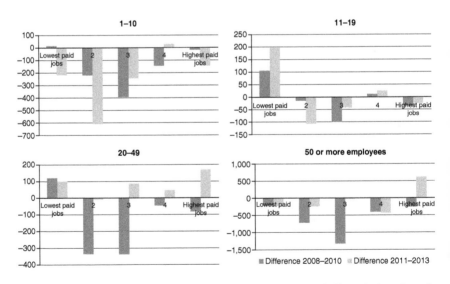

Figure 2.2 Employment change, in thousands, by job-wage quintile and size of workplace, EU25, 2008–2010 and 2011–2013.

Source: Eurofound, 2016 (based on EU-LFS annual data, Eurostat).

Note
Croatia, France and Slovenia were excluded from the analysis.

growth cannot be considered 'as a given' in terms of happening continuously and in every case. The developments during and after the global economic and financial crisis show that certain company external framework conditions need to be in place to enable companies, including SMEs, to retain existing and hire additional staff.

Similarly, and taking into account the vast SME population and the resulting variety among the businesses, it should be clear that not all (types of) SME are equally dynamic in job creation. It is striking, however, that neither policy nor research pay a lot of attention to the characteristics of SMEs that contribute to employment growth (Burke *et al.*, 2002; Ichou, 2010). Respective discussions are rare, and if they happen, are limited to a few structural elements such as company age, size or sector (also see above).

Eurofound (2016) compiled the factors influencing job creation in SMEs in a more systematic and comprehensive way than the more scattered approaches taken so far. The findings show that employment growth is directly and indirectly determined by a combination of comparatively many, and mutually influencing, different elements. Some of these factors relate to the SMEs themselves, while others concern the company external environment – with limited opportunities by the SME to influence them. Figure 2.3 provides an overview of these determinants which will be discussed in the following sections. It has to be noted that while this 'bundle of elements' have been identified to generally influence job creation in SMEs, they are not equally important to the individual company. Accordingly, it can even happen that a factor which is a driver for employment

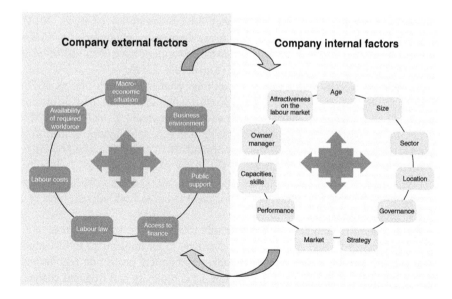

Figure 2.3 Determinants of job creation in SMEs.
Source: Eurofound, 2016.

growth for one SME hampers job creation in another, due to the specific characteristics of the firm and its interaction with its environment.

2.3.2 Company external determinants

Since the recent recession and its observable effect on SMEs, it is widely recognised that the overall macroeconomic situation affects the economic performance and development of businesses (European Commission, 2009 and 2014; OECD, 2013; Ichou, 2010; Muller *et al.*, 2015). In the current climate, the national or sectoral economic situation is found to hamper employment growth in the majority of Member States due to decreased demand, delays in receiving payments from customers, increased difficulties in accessing finance or competition through the shadow economy (Eurofound, 2016). The exceptions to this are countries which have not been overly affected by the crisis, or specific, generally prospering sectors (such as IT, creative industries and sectors related to 'greening').

Similarly, the administrative and institutional business environment is often highlighted as a determinant for the economic development of SMEs, thereby indirectly influencing their job creation behaviour (Napier *et al.*, 2012; OECD, 2010; Criscuolo *et al.*, 2014; Accenture and Oxford Economics, 2011). Unfavourable or frequently changing regulations and taxation (business and employment related), time consuming administrative requirements and red tape as well as inefficient administrative procedures and institutions, put a burden on SMEs and hinder them from investing time and resources in more productive activities – which delays or hampers job creation (Kaarna *et al.*, 2012; BDI, 2013; Šukytė, 2010; Carroll *et al.*, 1999; Swedish Agency for Growth Policy Analysis, 2014). In contrast, government initiatives to improve framework conditions for SMEs, as well as targeted public or social partner-based support, have been identified as a driver of employment growth in SMEs (Eurofound, 2016).

In addition, access to finance is a common challenge which affects SMEs more than larger companies (European Commission, 2009 and 2014; Muller *et al.*, 2015) and, therefore, indirectly influences employment growth (UEAPME, 2013). In the majority of Member States, limited access to finance is identified as a barrier to job creation in SMEs (Eurofound, 2016). This is caused by either a lower level of credit available since the crisis (Ardic *et al.*, 2011; Infelise, 2014; De Kok *et al.*, 2011; Bornhorst and Arranz, 2014) or by credit conditions offered to SMEs that are unfavourable for them (such as high interest rates or a high level of collateral required).

Quite naturally, company external factors related to the labour market more directly influence SMEs' employment dynamism. In the majority of EU Member States, SMEs perceive labour law – notably employment protection regulations, but also the lack of flexibility of legislation, its complexity and frequent changes – as a barrier to job creation (Eurofound, 2016).

Also labour costs – referring to both wage levels and non-wage labour costs – affect SMEs' decision to hire. While they are widely seen as a barrier (European

Commission, 2005 and 2014; Lugger, 2014; Aaltonen *et al.*, 2009; Statistics Lithuania, 2009), there are a few examples of them positively affecting employment growth. In Estonia, for example, SME exporters experience a competitive advantage due to low labour costs, and the subsequently enhanced internationalisation activities boost job creation (Eesti Pank, 2010). In Portugal, there is some optimism that recently established public initiatives to reduce payroll costs drive SME job creation while, for Sweden, available data show that a similar initiative has already resulted in employment growth (Egebark and Kaunitz, 2013).

As a final element to be discussed in this section, the labour supply should also be mentioned. The availability of sufficient workers with the skills required by SMEs is a precondition for hiring. Available data indicate that this is not only a considerable problem for SMEs (Ernst & Young, 2015; UNIZO, 2014; Kaarna *et al.*, 2012; SAERG, 2014; Vehmas, 2014; Aaltonen *et al.*, 2009; Federation of Finnish Enterprises, 2014; BMWi, 2014), but it also becomes increasingly important. While in 2011, 14 per cent of European SMEs reported finding skilled staff and experienced managers as a challenge, the share increased to 17 per cent in 2013 (Muller *et al.*, 2015). Furthermore, there are some indications that notably small, young, innovative and growth-oriented enterprises suffer most from this shortage (Reinstaller *et al.*, 2010) – flagging a particular challenge for born globals.

2.3.3 Company internal determinants

While company external factors influencing SMEs' job creation behaviour are at least indirectly discussed in research and policy debate – as drivers and barriers to the firms' economic growth – company internal aspects are hardly considered. This seems to be an important omission, taking into account the specificities of SMEs, often highlighting how influential internal aspects are for the company's performance.

This introduces the first factor to be discussed in this section: the influence of the SME's economic development on its job creation behaviour. In line with what was discussed above for the effect of the macroeconomic development, the SME's performance can be considered as one of the most important determinants for employment growth. In most cases, SMEs will only hire staff if they have secured a sustainable level of demand that requires additional workforce in the medium to long run, as well as a sustainable level of liquidity and profitability which is sufficient to cover the emerging HR costs in the future. This can be evidenced by data from the European Company Survey: SMEs which experienced an improved or at least stable financial situation between 2010 and 2013 were almost three times more likely to increase their employment numbers than SMEs that suffered from financial deterioration. See Figure 2.4.

However, a good business development is not a sufficient guarantee for an SME to also realise employment growth. The inherent business strategy is also decisive. SMEs following an explicit growth strategy, including, for example, internationalisation and innovation pathways, are characterised by higher

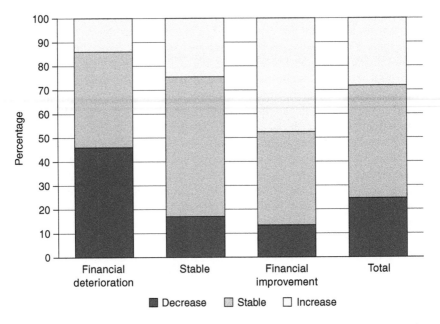

Figure 2.4 Change in employment between 2010 and 2013, by SMEs' financial situation, EU28.

Source: Eurofound, 2016 (based on the Third European Company Survey).

Note
Data excludes the public sector and companies established after 2010.

employment growth than their counterparts (De Kok *et al.*, 2011; Calvo, 2006; Falk, 2013; Istat 2013 and 2014; Dörflinger *et al.*, 2013; KPMG, 2010; De Wit and Timmermans, 2008; Onkelinx and Sleuwaegen, 2010; DGPYME, 2006). These findings are highly relevant for the discussion on born globals' job creation potential as it will be shown in Chapter 3 that these businesses are characterised not only by high levels of international activities, but also by innovativeness and growth ambitions. This also highlights the relevance of the business model. In addition to the example of born globals, in terms of governance it is widely acknowledged that family businesses (that is, companies where the majority of ownership and decision-making is done by the family of the founder) are growing more modestly, due to their orientation on long-term sustainability rather than striving for quick growth.

Also the SME's endowment with resources is identified as a determinant of job creation. In addition to the above-mentioned access to finance, the capacities and skills also available in the firm affect its growth potential. The OECD (2002 and 2010), for example, mentions a company's capacities to internationalise and innovate as important characteristics of high-growth SMEs. Other relevant in-house competences influencing employment growth are management skills (related to both business aspects and human resources), flexibility and adaptability of the management, staff and the organisation as a whole (raising the issues of, for example, organisational structure, work processes or internal communication), and the ability to access, analyse and make use of information on market developments, funding, external support, legislation, taxation and related topics (Eurofound, 2016).

Considering the central role a single owner/manager has in many European SMEs, it becomes obvious that many of the factors discussed so far in this section strongly depend on this person. Accordingly, Eurofound (2016) highlights the strong influence that the personality, motivations and attitudes of the owner/manager have on the SME's job creation behaviour. In general, if the owner/manager is opportunity-driven, confident in future developments and has a reasonable level of risk-taking behaviour, the SME is more likely to contribute to employment growth (Van Praag and Cramer, 2001; Ichou, 2010; De Kok *et al.*, 2010). On the contrary, necessity-driven entrepreneurs or those who expect negative future developments fear the consequences and stigma of failure and are highly risk-averse or do not want to give up full control and independence, are found to be more reluctant to create additional jobs (Vlach *et al.*, 2013; Poschke, 2010; Ichou, 2010; De Kok *et al.*, 2010; European Commission, 2005; Starczewska-Krzysytosyek, 2012; Mandl *et al.*, 2009).

As a result of many of the above-mentioned elements, the capacity of an SME to attract the workers it needs affects its recruitment activities. SMEs often suffer from a negative image as an employer as they are perceived to offer lower wages, limited career prospects and more unfavourable management practices than their larger counterparts – with whom they enter into competition in the labour market. Furthermore, due to their smaller size and more limited resources in the recruitment process, they might be less visible as a potential employer for workers looking for a new job.

From a more structural point of view, one of the few company characteristics that policy and research discuss as influential for job creation in SMEs is firm age. In general, it is recognised that start-ups and young firms create more jobs than older companies (relative to their employment numbers) (Criscuolo *et al.*, 2014; Aaltonen *et al.*, 2009; Ibsen and Westergaard-Nielsen, 2011; KfW, 2006; Lawless, 2013). Available data from the European Company Survey supports this opinion (see Figure 2.4). This is widely explained by the phase of the company life cycle, with young companies developing and then growing while older firms are more likely to have settled in a maturation or saturation phase and therefore require fewer additional staff (Eurofound, 2013). In contrast to this common understanding, in Hungary and Romania it is seen that younger enterprises are not as dynamic in job creation as older ones. This is argued to be because of their struggle to survive during the first years of existence, resulting in less emphasis on employment growth before reaching a consolidation phase (National Council of Private Small and Medium Enterprises in Romania, 2014). See Figure 2.5.

In spite of the above-mentioned European data indicating that employment growth among SMEs is mainly to be attributed to micro enterprises, national

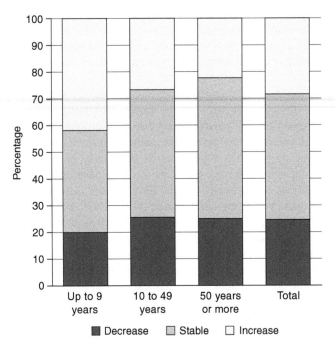

Figure 2.5 Change in employment in SMEs between 2010 and 2013, by age of establishment, EU28.

Source: Eurofound, 2016 (based on the Third European Company Survey).

Note
Data excludes the public sector.

data do not allow for such a straightforward assessment. Indeed, a large variation in employment contribution of the different SME size classes can be observed across the Member States (Eurofound, 2016). Micro enterprises are found to be the most dynamic job creators in Croatia, Finland, Ireland, Lithuania and Slovenia. Small companies show the highest contribution to employment growth in Austria, Cyprus, France, Greece, Portugal and Romania. Medium-sized firms are dynamic job creators in Poland and Sweden. In spite of these differences, a widely shared finding is that a large share of one-person enterprises (that is, companies without any dependent employees other than the owner/manager) are hesitant about hiring (Dörflinger *et al.*, 2011; Aaltonen *et al.*, 2009; SAERG, 2014).

Similarly, there is little that is specific that can be said regarding economic sectors. Overall, the service sector is characterised by more pronounced employment growth while construction and manufacturing contribute less (Eurofound, 2016). However, in some Member States, at least some industries within the manufacturing sector show an important contribution of SMEs to job creation (such as the chemicals and pharmaceutical industry; automobiles, IT and electronic equipment in Austria; or the food industry in Italy, Latvia, Slovenia and Romania). In Latvia, Lithuania and Luxembourg, construction SMEs contribute to employment growth at an above-average level.

Finally, for about one quarter of the Member States of the European Union there is evidence that the location of the SMEs influences their job creation potential. Urban SMEs tend to be more dynamic, probably due to better access to clients, suppliers and business partners, workforce, institutions and infrastructure (Eurofound, 2016).

2.4 Concluding remarks: the profile of the job creating SME

Both at European level and within the Member States, there exists the common recognition that SMEs are not only responsible for the major share of employment, but also contribute considerably to job creation. However, while it is quite obvious that – due to the huge variety among the vast SME population in Europe – not all SMEs equally contribute to employment growth, this issue is hardly discussed in policy-making or covered in research. More specific information would, however, be useful to better target public support fostering job creation in SMEs – notably as, since the global economic and financial crisis, several Member States experienced public budget cuts and are, therefore, forced to search for ways of spending the available funds in the most efficient and effective method.

In the limited discussion on job creation in SMEs, mainly company external influence factors are discussed – as elements affecting the companies' economic performance and development and thereby indirectly influencing employment growth. This is without question an important discussion that should be continued in order to further improve the business environment for SMEs.

However, company characteristics also impact on the job creation behaviour of SMEs and might be even more relevant, particularly as they could be influenced by the owners/managers if they were aware of them. In spite of this, such elements are hardly ever considered in public or policy debate and, if they are, only in a fragmented way.

The research to hand, in contrast, clearly shows that job creation in SMEs is influenced by a collection of company internal and external factors. As they are interrelated and might affect each other, they should be jointly discussed and addressed in terms of policy and support.

The 'direction' in which the determinants of job creation affect employment growth in SMEs might differ from company to company, depending on the individual characteristics of the firm and the environment it acts in. Nevertheless, the analysis conducted in the framework of this research allows a 'profile of the job creating SME' to be derived, pinpointing the characteristics of the company and its environment, which in general result in a higher potential for an SME to hire additional staff. While this 'profile' is assumed to be an important orientation for European policy makers, it has to be kept in mind that it summarises an ideal situation that might not be fully achievable in practice. Accordingly, a recommendation could be to aim at achieving all the below-mentioned characteristics, while at the same time not neglecting the employment potential of those SMEs characterised by many (or even just some) of those elements, but not necessarily all of them.

Profile of the job creating SME

SMEs which tend to create jobs are:

- Young
- Innovative
- International
- Located in urban areas
- Well performing due to sufficient market demand
- Competitive due to an attractive product/service portfolio
- Well financed in terms of having sufficient access to finance and applying diversified funding strategies
- Willing and able to invest
- Ambitious and prepared to grow
- Run by sufficient and qualified managers
- Attractive to the labour market, so that they can equip themselves with the staff and skills required.

These factors need to be supported by an external business environment with:

- Sufficient demand
- Feasible competition
- A supportive image of entrepreneurship
- Favourable legislation and taxation
- Feasible labour costs
- Effective and efficient public administration
- Suitable public support
- Sufficient provision of finance
- Labour supply that matches the SMEs' needs.

Source: Eurofound, 2016.

References

Aaltonen, S., Heinonen, J., Kovalainen, A. and Luomala, K. (2009), *Työllistämisen esteet, mahdollisuudet ja aikeet pk-yrityksissä*, Employment and entrepreneurship 49/2009, Ministry of Employment and the Economy, Helsinki.

Accenture and Oxford Economics (2011), *Driving public entrepreneurship: Government as a catalyst for innovation and growth in Europe*, Study conducted on behalf of the Government of the Future Centre.

Ardic, O., Mylenko, N. and Saltane, V. (2011), *Small and medium enterprises: A cross-country analysis with a new data set*, Policy Research Working Paper 5538, World Bank, Washington DC.

BDI (Bundesverband der Deutschen Industrie) (2013), *BDI-Mittelstandspanel, Ergebnisse der Online-Mittelstandsbefragung Frühjahr 2013*, IfM Bonn and TNS Emnid, Bonn.

BMWi (Bundesministerium für Wirtschaft und Energie) (2014), *Engpassanalyse 2014*, Fachkräfteengpässe in Unternehmen, in vielen Berufsgattungen bestehen seit Längerem Engpässe, Berlin.

Bornhorst, F. and Arranz, M. R. (2014), *Growth and the importance of sequencing debt reductions across sectors*, International Monetary Fund (IMF), Washington DC.

Burke, A. E., FitzRoy, F. R. and Nolan, M. A. (2002), 'Self-employment wealth and job creation: The roles of gender, non-pecuniary motivation and entrepreneurial ability', *Small Business Economics*, Vol. 19, No. 3, pp. 255–270.

Calvo, J. L. (2006), 'Testing Gibrat's law for young, small and innovative firms', *Small Business Economics*, Vol. 26, No. 2, pp. 117–123.

Carroll, M., Marchington, M., Earnshaw, J. and Taylor, S. (1999), 'Recruitment in small firms: Processes, methods and problems', *Employee Relations*, Vol. 21, No. 3, pp. 236–250.

Criscuolo, C., Gal, P. N. and Menon, C. (2014), *The dynamics of employment growth: New evidence from 18 countries*, OECD Science, Technology and Industry Policy Papers No. 14, OECD Publishing, Paris.

De Kok, J. M. P., Ichou, A. and Verheul, I. (2010), *New firm performance: Does the age of founders affect employment creation?*, EIM research report, Zoetermeer, the Netherlands.

De Kok, J. M. P., Vroonhof, P., Verhoeven, W., Timmermans, N., Kwaak, T., Snijders, J. et al. (2011), *Do SMEs create more and better jobs?*, European Commission, Brussels.

De Wit, G. and Timmermans, N. G. L. (2008), *High-growth SMEs. Evidence from the Netherlands*, research report published under the SCALES-initiative (Scientific Analysis of Entrepreneurship and SMEs), Zoetermeer, the Netherlands.

DGPYME (Dirección General de Industria y de la Pequeña y Mediana Empresa) (2006), *Análisis de crecimiento en la Empresa Consolidad Española*, Fundación Banesto e Instituto Universitario de Empresa, Madrid.

Dörflinger, C., Gavac, K., Hölzl, K. and Talker, C. (2011), *Ein-Personen-Unternehmen (EPU) in Österreich: Ein- und Ausblicke*, KMU Forschung Austria, Vienna.

Dörflinger, C., Dörflinger, A., Gavac, K. and Vogl, B. (2013), *Familienunternehmen in Österreich: Status quo 2013*, KMU Forschung Austria, Vienna.

Eesti Pank (2010), *Rahapoliitika ja Majandus: Hetkeseis ja ettevaade 2/2010*, Bank of Estonia, Tallinn.

Egebark, J. and Kaunitz, N. (2013), *Do payroll tax cuts raise youth employment?*, IFN Working Paper No. 1001, Research Institute of Industrial Economics, Stockholm.

Ernst & Young (2015), *Mittelstandsbarometer Österreich und Europa*, Jänner 2015, Befragung von 6.000 mittelständischen Unternehmen in Europa, Vienna.

Eurofound (2013), *Restructuring in SMEs in Europe*, Publications Office of the European Union, Luxembourg.

Eurofound (2014), *Drivers of recent job polarisation and upgrading in Europe: European Jobs Monitor 2014*, Publications Office of the European Union, Luxembourg.

Eurofound (2016), *ERM annual report 2015: Job creation in SMEs*, Publications Office of the European Union, Luxembourg.

European Commission (2003), *Commission recommendation of 6 May 2003 concerning the definition of micro, small and medium-sized enterprises* (2003/361/EC), Official Journal of the European Union L124/36.

European Commission (2005), *First employee: Obstacle to growth – Recruiting the first employee*, report of the expert group, Brussels.

European Commission (2009), *Overview of family-business-relevant issues: Research, networks, policy measures and existing studies*, final report of the expert group, Brussels.

European Commission (2014), *Employment and social developments in Europe 2014*, Publications Office of the European Union, Luxembourg.

Falk, M. (2013), *Innovation und Beschäftigung. Neue Ergebnisse auf Basis der Innovationserhebung verknüpft mit Leistungs- und Strukturerhebung*, Austrian Institute of Economic Research (WIFO), Vienna.

Federation of Finnish Enterprises (2014), *PK-yritysbarometri 2/2014*, Helsinki.

Ibsen, R. and Westergaard-Nielsen, N. (2011), *Job creation by firms in Denmark*, IZA DP No. 5458, Institute for the Study of Labor (IZA), Bonn.

Ichou, A. (2010), *Modelling the determinants of job creation: Microeconometric models accounting for latent entrepreneurial ability*, EIM Business and Policy Research, Zoetermeer, the Netherlands.

Infelise, F. (2014), *Supporting access to finance by SMEs: Mapping the initiatives in five EU countries*, ECMI Research Report No. 9, Centre for European Policy Studies, Brussels.

Istat (Istituto Nazionale di Statistica) (2013), 'Il sistema delle imprese italiane: Competitività e potenziale di crescita', in *Rapporto annuale 2013: La situazione del paese*, Rome.

Istat (2014), *Rapporto annuale 2014: La situazione del paese*, Rome.

Kaarna, R., Masso, M. and Mari, R. (2012), *Väikese ja keskmise suurusega ettevõtete arengusuundumused*, Poliitikauuringute Keskus Praxis, Tallinn.

KfW (2006), *Mittelstand: Jobmotor der deutschen Wirtschaft*, KfW-Mittelstandspanel 2006, Frankfurt.

KPMG (2010), *Les PME qui grandissent: Comment ces virtuoses de la croissance se sont adaptées pour traverser la crise*, Paris.

Lawless, M. (2013), *Age or size? Determinants of job creation*, Research Technical Paper, Central Bank of Ireland, Dublin.

Lugger, M. (2014), *Senkung der Lohnnebenkosten: 7 von 10 Betrieben würden mehr Personal einstellen*, press release, Vienna, 26 September.

Mandl, I., Gavac, K. and Hölzl, K. (2009), 'Ein-Personen-Unternehmen in Österreich', *Wirtschaft und Gesellschaft*, Vol. 35, No. 2, pp. 215–236.

Muller, P., Caliandro, C., Gagliardi, D. and Marzocchi, C. (2015), *Annual report on European SMEs 2014/2015*, European Commission, Brussels.

Muller, P., Devnani, S., Julius, J., Gagliardi, D. and Maryocchi, C. (2016), *Annual report on European SMEs 2015/2016. SME recovery continues*, European Commission, Brussels.

Napier, G., Rouvinen, P., Johansson, D., Finnbjörnsson, T., Solberg, E. and Pedersen, K. (2012), *The Nordic growth entrepreneurship review 2012*, final report, Nordic Innovation Publication 2012, No. 25, Oslo.

National Council of Private Small and Medium Enterprises in Romania (2014), *White paper for SMEs in Romania*, Bucharest.

OECD (2002), *High-growth SMEs and employment*, OECD Publishing, Paris.

OECD (2010), 'Issues paper 1: Innovative SMEs and entrepreneurship for job creation and growth', conference paper, *'Bologna+10': High-level meeting on lessons from the global crisis and the way forward to job creation and growth*, OECD Working Party on SMEs and Entrepreneurship (WPSMEE), 17–18 November, Paris.

OECD (2013), *Skills development and training in SMEs*, OECD Publishing, Paris.

OECD (2015), *Entrepreneurship at a glance 2015*, OECD Publishing, Paris.

Onkelinx, J. and Sleuwaegen, L. (2010), *Internationalization strategy and performance of small and medium sized enterprises*, Working Paper Research No. 197, National Bank of Belgium, Brussels.

Poschke, M. (2010), *Entrepreneurs out of necessity: A snapshot*, IZA Discussion Paper No. 4893, Institute for the Study of Labor (IZA), Bonn.

Reinstaller, A., Hölzl, W., Janger, J., Stadler, I., Unterlass, F., Daimer, S. *et al.* (2010), *Barriers to internationalisation and growth of EU's innovative companies*, INNO-Grips II final report, European Commission, Directorate-General for Enterprise and Industry, Brussels.

SAERG (2014), *Förutsättningar för konkurrenskraftiga företag*, Företagens villkor och verklighet 2014, Stockholm.

Starczewska-Krzysztoszek, M. (2012), *Szanse i zagrożenia dla rozwoju mikro, małych i średnich przedsiębiorstw*, Polish Confederation Lewiatan, Warsaw.

Statistics Lithuania (2009), *Smulkiojo ir vidutinio verslo sąlygų tyrimas 2009*, Vilnius.

Šukytė, D. (2010), 'Barriers for SMEs development in Šiauliai', *Konferencija ekonomikos ir vadybos aktualijos*, Vilnius, pp. 604–610. Available at: http://etalpykla.lituanistikadb.lt/obj/record/LT-LDB-0001:J.04~2010~1367173651839.

Swedish Agency for Growth Policy Analysis (2014), *Sänkt moms på restaurang- och cateringtjänster*, Stockholm.

UEAPME (Union Européenne de l'Artisanat et des Petites et Moyennes Entreprises) (2013), *SMEs in Europe: Interest representation and access to finance in the past, present and future*, Brussels.

UNIZO (Union of Self-Employed Entrepreneurs) (2014), *Groei in de KMO*, Brussels.

Van Praag, C. M. and Cramer, J. S. (2001), 'The roots of entrepreneurship and labour demand', *Economica*, Vol. 68, pp. 45–62.

Vehmas, T. (2014), *PK-yritykset ja työvoiman kohtaanto*, Employment and entrepreneurship 47/2009, Ministry of Employment and the Economy, Helsinki.

Vlach, J., Průša, L., Szabo, J. and Pavlíček, T. (2013), *Sociální a ekonomické postavení osob samostatně výdělečně činných v ČR v roce 2012*, VÚPS, Prague.

3 Born globals' job creation dynamism – the European perspective

Valentina Patrini, Iñigo Isusi and Jessica Durán

3.1 Introduction

Traditional internationalisation theories, like the Uppsala model (Johanson and Vahlne, 1977 and 1990) describe the internationalisation path of firms as gradual, sequential and evolutionary (the 'stages theory'). Firms are observed to initially invest in the home market where, after a process of maturation, they eventually reach a phase of saturation (Oviatt and McDougall, 2005). This is when they begin sporadic sales abroad, to geographically and culturally close foreign markets. Over time and with increasing experience in international activities, the firms expand from a few closer target markets towards a larger number of more distant ones. Similarly, they tend to begin their internationalisation process with less risky entry modes, such as ad hoc exporting activities and exporting through independent domestic intermediaries. As international sales increase, they engage in direct exporting and domestic agents are replaced by the firm's own foreign sales subsidiaries. Rising sales levels might also allow firms to engage in further foreign direct investment (FDI).

The traditional internationalisation theory was challenged about 25 years ago by the identification of a new model, the 'born global' internationalisation pattern (Rennie, 1993). Studies show that, in a context of globalisation and technological advances, some firms begin to export within a few years from their inception (Cavusgil and Knight, 2009; Eurofound, 2012a), avoiding some of the steps characterising the traditional stages model.

3.2 The business model of born globals

So far, there is no universal definition for the business model of 'born globals' in the literature, and different authors use different connotations (such as international new ventures, global start-ups, infant multinationals, micro multinationals, born international or innate exporters) when exploring the concept. This has consequences for data collection, comparability and relevance. Most definitions refer to enterprises which, immediately or quickly after their inception, strongly engage in international activities in multiple countries, either through exports, international sourcing or internationalisation of R&D activities. These main characteristics are translated by existing studies into a number of criteria. As regards the company's maximum age at the start of the international activity, values range between 2–3 (the most common values in the definitions) and 7–10 years. Most definitions establish a minimum 25 per cent of foreign sales as a portion of the overall sales of the company, but also focus on the company's activity in multiple (more than one) foreign markets. This is often complemented by additional characteristics, such as the global mindset of the management, the international orientation since the outset, the independency of the firm and, in some definitions, the relatively small size of the company, among others.

Eurofound (2012a) tried to conflate the different criteria included in the existing literature and to propose a first approach towards a European definition of born globals, whereby a born global enterprise has a number of minimum characteristics.

According to Eurofound's proposal for a European definition, a born global company:

- is an independent, individual company (in line with the respective criteria in the EU SME definition (European Commission, 2003);
- has been started, is a spin-off, or has been a business transfer (in terms of ownership and management) within the last five years;
- has an active, strategic intention to internationalise (which is, for example, mentioned in its business plan);
- has an export share of at least 25 per cent of total sales during at least two of these first five years;
- is active in at least two foreign countries, with 'close markets' (from a geographic, language or cultural perspective) also being considered as different markets (for instance, when all countries are within Europe);
- is active in any economic sector, but offers an innovative product or service with good market potential or uses a new technology or design.

The company size and the market share are not considered to be fundamental criteria for a company to be classified as a born global.

Extant literature explored additional characteristics that can help to distinguish born globals from other young and internationally active businesses. In most cases, these firms are SMEs in their growth phase. Being relatively small, young and new to foreign markets, they are subject to resource constraints and to different liabilities, such as newness and foreignness (Cavusgil and Knight, 2009). Their internationalisation process is often driven by founders and employees with higher educational and experience levels as compared to their peers in other young companies. This is combined with an international vision and ambition, reflected and supported by the born globals' (or their management and staff) involvement in successful cross-border relationships and in international networks and global value chains. There, they tend to fill existing gaps, by offering specialised and advanced products and processes, often characterised by high levels of technology, innovation – either in terms of innovation capacity or ability to serve clients in an innovative manner (Leonidou and Samiee, 2012) – and/or exclusive design. Most research on these kinds of companies focuses on the ones operating in niche markets, high technology or high value added sectors. Nonetheless, born globals can be found in any economic sector, including the more traditional ones, such as manufacturing and services (Spowart and Wickramasekera, 2012; Gabrielsson and Kirpalani, 2012).

Born globals do not necessarily define their internationalisation in function of the geographic and cultural distance. While traditional SMEs move to export markets organically, born globals are often driven by the attractiveness, potential growth rate and profit potential of export markets (Moen and Servais, 2002), where the market demand for the company's product or service plays a central role. Their market selection often has a reactive nature, whereby born globals initially enter the markets where they have identified a need for their products or services (they can serve multiple markets simultaneously from inception) using their existing network ties and previous experiences (Coviello, 2006; Leonidou and Samiee, 2012). Strongly customer-oriented, born globals usually set the features of their product offering and marketing strategies according to the characteristics of their target market and clients (Gabrielsson *et al.*, 2012).

Moreover, born globals do not follow successive stages in terms of entry modes, which can take any shape since the beginning (Leonidou and Samiee, 2012). Nonetheless, given their resource constraints, they are expected to adopt less resource-intensive entry modes (Cavusgil and Knight, 2009), such as using direct exports through international agents (Crick and Jones, 2000), or engaging in alternative collaborative governance structures (subcontracting, licensing, franchising or volunteering) to limit their costs and the related entry and exit risks (Leonidou and Samiee, 2012), or networking and sharing their knowledge with partners.

3.3 Economic and labour market contribution of born globals in Europe

Born globals, usually limited in size, can be assumed to face the challenges that SMEs in general encounter regarding high dependency on market developments and higher vulnerability caused by individual events. Furthermore, their potential can be hampered by challenges such as access to finance; the need for an advanced management capacity, specialised human resources and processes for product development; access to knowledge on the target market; and related marketing capacities. Their survival can depend on aspects such as their speed towards making a profit and their participation in high quality networks. Born globals are typically flexible and dynamic in product development and expansion, often more than larger, well-established firms.

The available literature on born globals provides only fragmented evidence on the economic and labour market contribution of this business model. Existing studies either follow a qualitative research approach or are based on small-scale surveys, hence quantitative information is scarce. Furthermore, the above-mentioned diversity of definitions puts strong limitations on the comparability of existing data. However, in order to provide some insight into the economic and labour market contribution of born globals across Europe, proxy data stemming from the Global Entrepreneurship Monitor (GEM) can be used. In its adult population survey (data from 2011[1]), it identifies companies of up to 3.5 years of age that have more than 25 per cent of their customers abroad. In the following, these are considered as 'born globals'.

According to the GEM, born globals represent 2.5 per cent of all SMEs and 12 per cent of young enterprises (Eurofound, 2016). Nonetheless, shares seem to vary greatly across countries and an inverse correlation seems to exist between the size of the country and the share of born globals among companies.

As regards the economic sector of activity, most European born globals operate in the service sectors. Given their export orientation, they are more likely to be active in manufacturing as compared to other young companies or SMEs, and less likely to be found in more domestically oriented sectors, such as community, social and personal services, agriculture and construction (see Figure 3.1).

Evidence on the economic benefits of born globals' activities is scattered. Financial data for French born globals show that on average they are more profitable than other companies, mainly thanks to the pioneering character and superiority of the products or services offered when compared to the ones of their competitors (Eurofound, 2012a). This could be related to the fact that these firms may be more forward-looking, motivated or forced to improve their products and services in order to remain competitive in foreign markets.

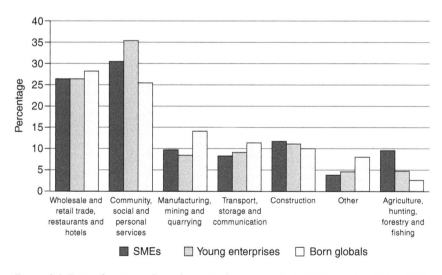

Figure 3.1 Type of company in each economic sector, selected EU Member States, 2011.
Source: Eurofound, 2016.

GEM data (see Figure 3.2) show that, when compared to young enterprises as a whole, born globals are more likely to have none or just a few competitors (45 per cent of European born globals versus 38 per cent of young enterprises and one-third of SMEs), to provide new or unfamiliar products to their customers (37 per cent versus 34 per cent for young enterprises and 26 per cent of SMEs) and to use new and innovative technology for their products (30 per cent for both born globals and young enterprises, versus 20 per cent for SMEs). See Figure 3.2.

Born globals' involvement in technological sectors and activities and the innovativeness of their portfolios and strategies represent relevant preconditions for economic sustainability and growth, being key factors for a company's competitiveness and creation of added value. The combination of internationalisation and innovation also seems to support sales growth, performance and productivity. Available evidence points to the potential for a virtuous circle, whereby innovation and exporting positively impact on growth, and the related acquisition of knowledge from export markets further enhances innovation and growth (Golovko and Valentini, 2011).

This allows born globals to develop key dynamic capabilities that enable a company to reorganise its resources to adapt to a changing environment, having an imprinting effect on their ability to grow and survive (Sapienza *et al.*, 2006). Despite the existence of both positive and negative employment effects deriving

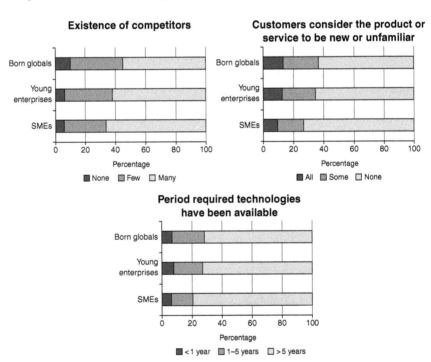

Figure 3.2 Type of company and degree of innovativeness, selected EU Member States, 2011.

Source: Eurofound, 2016.

from innovation, in the long terms the effects of innovation on productivity and job creation tend to be positive (Vivarelli, 2014).

Moreover, being young enterprises and in their growth phase, born globals are likely to need additional workforce to perform tasks such as product development and marketing in multiple international markets. This suggests that they are particularly dynamic in terms of job creation – although in relative terms, as they represent only a small share of European companies. Indeed, born globals' managers (Eurofound, 2016) identified the increased demand for the company products as a key cause for increased levels of labour demand. Demand for workers, in turn, represents the main driver for hiring additional workforce, and the availability of sufficient financial resources, good economic performance and a perceived long-term sustainability of these factors are key preconditions for hiring new staff (see Section 3.2 for more information on drivers and barriers).

The born globals' dynamism in job creation is also confirmed by GEM data which shows that, on average in European countries, born globals employ more staff than young enterprises or SMEs in general (9.6, 5.6 and 6.7 employees on average, respectively). Moreover, as Figure 3.3 shows, they report job creation plans more frequently than other companies (about 60 per cent compared with about 45 per cent of young companies and 30 per cent of SMEs).

Economic and employment effects generated by born globals can also go beyond these companies and positively affect other organisations and partners along their value chains and within their international networks. Partly, this is due to the common practice of born globals outsourcing activities beyond their core business portfolio, given their small size and high specialisation. Additionally, it can derive from the generation of social capital, the provision of benchmark orientation for

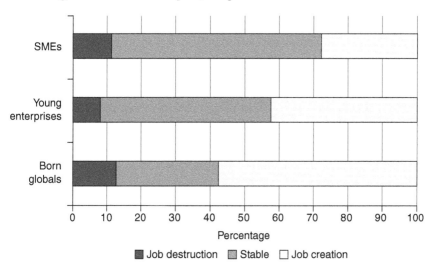

Figure 3.3 Employment values: change expected in five years by company type, selected EU Member States, 2011.

Source: Eurofound, 2016.

larger, well-established firms (Vapola *et al.*, 2008) and the creation of spill-over effects linked to knowledge and innovativeness. Knock-on effects in terms of job creation are observed both in foreign countries (Mettler and Williams, 2011) and in the country of origin (Legrain, 2010).

3.4 Drivers and constraints for job creation

As highlighted in Chapter 2, job creation in SMEs is influenced by a combination of internal and external elements which are often interrelated and act as drivers and/or barriers for this process (Eurofound, 2016). The impact of the single elements depends on the characteristics of each individual company and of the context in which it operates.

As far as the motivations for and barriers to job creation in born globals are concerned, research evidence is still scattered. Based on 17 case studies (Eurofound, 2016),[2] this section proposes some reflections on the main factors influencing job creation in these companies.

In the born globals analysed, the company's economic situation is the most important pre-condition for hiring staff. Only if the business performance and market demand are deemed satisfactory and at least sustainable (if not growing) in the future, will management consider recruiting employees. This highlights that the creation of new jobs is a direct reaction to an expanded business and market, and to the operational need for an increased workforce to cover the necessary tasks and higher workload. Born globals almost inevitably go through this enlargement phase quite soon after their inception, which is often characterised by a strong involvement of a small team, including the owners/managers, and important initial strategic and financial efforts. Furthermore, due to the multiple challenges born globals need to master during a short period of time (starting up, innovating, internationalising), they tend to have intensive HR needs immediately, rather than growing organically over time.

For the management team of the Austrian '**ecoduna**' born global, the job creation process is exclusively driven by company internal aspects, whereby the economic growth of the company is the main reason for recruiting additional staff. The expansion requires additional human resources with the same skills and expertise as already available in the company, but in a larger scale in order to cope with the increased workload.

In the Austrian '**Power Units**' born global, the need for additional staff is a result of the increase in work orders and the associated workload. As they produce very complex technical products, they clearly favour recruitment instead of outsourcing or relying on temporary work agency staff.

In the case of the Spanish '**Enigmedia**' born global, the main motivations for creating jobs are internal to the company and linked to the business strategy and the company performance, and the consequent need for additional workers. Since its inception, the firm has grown progressively and this development has entailed the creation of jobs. Positive economic development of the company, including sales growth, is a driver for job creation.

A key motivation for job creation and the expansion of the teams is the company management's ambition to grow and to improve its capacity and capability, being linked to the typical young age and small size of these firms. Related to that is the management's confidence towards future development and their limited fear of failure and risk. Born globals tend to have an attitude more open to taking (sound) risks which positively influences their business ambitions and hence growth plans – although in some occasions it can also be considered overoptimistic due to their limited previous experience. Moreover, managers' positive ambitions are often combined with clear intentions to continuously investigate new market potentials and to internationalise quickly. The aim of growing is often supported by/translated into the company's strategy reflecting the management thinking and mindset, it being an overall business strategy or a more specific plan related to human resources, international expansion or the enhancement of innovation. In most interviewed born globals, the company has a business plan stating its strategic and growth ambitions (Eurofound, 2016). Often drafted by the company founder or CEO, this plan is revised or updated on a regular basis.

The employment growth in the Austrian '**FRESNEX**' born global is strongly related to the company's innovation and internationalisation strategy. The CEO of the company argues that employment creation is a continuous process and virtuous circle of product development, attracting customers and hiring additional staff for further progress in the production field.

Similarly, in the case of the British '**BBOXX**' born global, the ambition to boost sales and the firm's growth act as internal drivers for the creation of new jobs. As BBOXX continues its global growth, the company plans to improve its capability and capacity. This involves expanding the product range, having innovative products and seeking more customers as well as extending its distribution network. Along this line, the company has increased its employment numbers, particularly for skilled engineers to undertake R&D and develop product innovations and systems.

To expand their team, born globals tend to look for highly skilled employees who can carry out (multiple) advanced tasks (such as supporting innovation, R&D, engineering and design, among others) and specific functions related to sales and customer services, product quality, marketing and distribution. The latter gain special relevance when it comes to accessing and developing international markets and dealing with international clients, distribution channels and the specificities of different national legislations and frameworks.

The CEO of the Swedish '**Zaplox**' born global aims to recruit only high skilled employees who can play an active role in a variety of functions within the company. A low-skilled employee with a specific function cannot participate as easily in complex tasks, which require understanding of the company's entire operation, as a high-skilled worker with profound knowledge of the product.

The need for such specialised staff can, however, pose a barrier to job creation in born globals. Due to their young age, these companies are often not highly visible on the labour market and are confronted with strong competition from other – more established – employers, for whom it is easier to attract skilled workforce. This is compounded by the small size of the born global, which limits career development pathways, and the scarce financial resources which limit income levels that can be offered to prospective staff.

For the Estonian '**Defendec**' born global, main barriers for job creation have changed over the course of the company's lifecycle. At the beginning, the founders had to prove the viability of their idea and did not have resources to recruit staff. For the first two years, the three founders did all the work themselves without any payment and used savings for living expenses. Thereafter, the first employee was hired. The founders knew him personally, as well as his abilities. At the same time, this employee knew the founders and believed in their idea and took the risk to work for them. According to the CEO, total strangers would not have dared to join their team as the future of the company was not yet certain. A year after hiring this first employee, the company started to hire additional employees.

At the same time, the specific characteristics of born globals can be attractive to a workforce looking for positions in which they can contribute to and influence the induction phase of a multinational company, with high levels of autonomy and flexibility or working in small, highly committed teams. Overall, born globals' managers acknowledge the relevance of team working and the need for a diverse, specialised and creative workforce; social capital, indeed, represents a richness and key source for market expansion and performance improvement. Through the staff, businesses can be strengthened in terms of access to new networks, partners, markets and opportunities, and the perspective to get involved in such activities can be a good incentive for workers to decide for a born global employer.

In the case of the Austrian '**Evercyte**' born global, the management have confidence in their personnel and offer them great autonomy in carrying out their work, as well as taking into account the timings of their working day. Interviewed employees appreciate this flexibility for different reasons, such as own preferences and family duties.

Similarly, interviewed employees of the Austrian '**FRESNEX**' born global stress their satisfaction as regards their jobs and enjoy working in a young company which is in its development phase. They appreciate the flexibility of the working day, the absence of hierarchies, and the strong emphasis on team work and informal work procedures. Furthermore, they appreciate the dynamism of the company, which challenges them with continuous change, giving them the opportunity to constantly learn something new and be involved in a broad spectrum of activities, rather than being limited to an individual task.

Strengthening the business and creating a solid and increasing customer base are conditions for the business expansion also in terms of workforce, and born globals, having experienced recent growth and a positive financial situation, are accordingly more likely to create new jobs. Next to internal company considerations, a positive business environment is crucial for a born global's development and growth. When commenting on the consequences of the global and financial crisis and the related contraction of resources, some European born globals stressed that their international character allowed them to operate in foreign markets that had not been so heavily affected by the recession, and that helped them to decrease production costs and attract customers, and to continue an expansion (or at least not suffer a reduction) of profits and jobs. In periods of economic downturn, being embedded in international networks can better support companies as compared to purely domestically oriented ones (Eurofound, 2012a).

> Referring to periods of downturn, the founder of the Spanish '**i-lanza**' born global reckons that the deep economic crisis period suffered by Spain since 2008 had a limited effect on the enterprise, precisely due to its strong international orientation. The severe effects of the crisis at national level drove i-lanza to go international, leading to increased success in winning projects abroad, in turn leading to better results and thus encouraging job creation.

From a policy perspective, the liabilities of smallness and limited resources stimulate born globals to look for additional financial means in order to allow for the company's growth. The availability of relevant support instruments, both in the public and in the banking sector, are seen as useful external factors by some of the born globals analysed, although only in some cases did they represent the main driver for the company's growth and job creation. The potential effects of these instruments are hindered in those contexts where the related information is limited and scattered, while centralised systems providing a unique access to information on the available measures are considered to effectively and efficiently support the company in its development phase.

> For the Swedish '**ProposalsFactory**' born global, the main barrier to employment growth encountered is access to capital, an obstacle shared by many Swedish start-ups and despite the well-developed Swedish venture capital market. For Proposals-Factory this issue seems to represent an impasse, as it prevents the company from getting more capital until their product attracts more interest on the market, while the product needs more capital in order to be able to attract more interest.

Often described as a time-consuming, complicated and burdensome process, the expansion of the company's workforce is intensive not only at the time of recruitment, but also in the previous strategic phase of assessment and anticipation of the expected additional staff needs, and in the following phase of (re)organising and setting up the human resource management structures and practices if the firm exceeds a size that requires such. In addition, hiring is not only difficult from a resource perspective: finding the right employees is a complicated task, both from an efficiency and an effectiveness viewpoint. Making sure that a selection process provides access to the best candidates and allows the recruitment of the employees with the most relevant profiles seems particularly complex for born globals, given the high levels of technical content and the complexity of their core portfolio, and the specialised competences needed to comply with the related tasks. Above all, the availability of skilled and specialised staff on the labour market is often seen as limited, and even more so if the desired candidate needs to have also an international profile/experience.

> In the case of the Spanish '**i-lanza**' born global, the most important barrier refers to the difficulties that the enterprise faces in hiring suitable blue-collar workers with a profile/personality adequate to its requirements, especially in relation to international skills. In particular, the CEO suggests that many blue-collar workers lack skills such as foreign languages or the ability to work with people from other cultures.
>
> For the Estonian '**Defendec**' born global, the main barrier for job creation is a lack of experienced software and hardware engineers in Estonia. This is caused by the annual small number of university graduates in these fields.
>
> Similarly, for the Swedish '**Zaplox**' born global, the primary barrier to expanding the workforce is the lack of skilled labour. Being a front-end tech company, their requirements for future employees are very high as they demand not only graduate level education but also seniority and expertise in specific fields. The CEO also stresses that personal characteristics are of great significance for Zaplox, and that an applicant with fewer qualifications might be a better option for the company if personal characteristics are a good match with the designated team.

Company internal practices that help to face and counterbalance these issues are: the use of flexible approaches in the recruitment processes to capture a higher number of potentially relevant profiles; the promotion of flexible working conditions (such as offering flexible working time or teleworking) to increase the attractiveness of the workplace; a boost to the company's public image and reputation (for instance by accessing relevant funds or winning company prizes) which enable the born global to stick out from competitors; and the use of alternative types of contracts, such as apprenticeships and traineeships, to attract young graduates who are eager to learn. These also contribute to an increase in the staff's commitment to the company – indeed, a crucial aspect for its success given the specificities and ambitious missions that characterise born globals, which require a specific dedication and mindset.

According to the Estonian '**Taxify**' born global CEO's perspective, hiring people is not difficult as the company's brand reputation is very good and it often finds echoes in the media. This makes finding the people with suitable skills simpler. For instance, an interviewed Taxify employee suggested that his main motivation to join the company was that it is a small start-up with very strong international orientation, and he knew the company very well already before applying for the job.

Meanwhile, the Spanish '**Enigmedia**' born global has received a significant number of prizes and awards, which have reinforced the public image of the company. This makes the company better known on the labour market, increases its access to more potential candidates, as well as extending the network of relevant contacts for the enterprise.

Access to relevant workers is also conditioned by the existing legislative frameworks in the home and, in some occasions, host countries. Migration law is perceived as a key obstacle in terms of access to relevant candidates: often strict, burdensome and time consuming, it limits the ability to recruit international talents from outside the European Union. In reaction, some owners/managers restrict their workforce recruitment scope to the European Union, where the principle of free movement of workers applies. Despite being a quick-fix solution in the short term, this approach is perceived as a limitation for a successful expansion of the born globals in the longer term. Companies which are global need a diverse, international workforce beyond Europeans in order to effectively operate in different markets and institutional contexts. Heterogeneity in terms of citizenship and origin among staff could indeed help to confront the cultural and institutional specificities in the multiple target markets and customers abroad.

The CEO of the Swedish '**SmartShake**' born global suggests that one prominent obstacle that prevents employment growth in the company is their limited ability to recruit international talent from outside the EU due to migration legislation. In his opinion, migration legislation and the management of migrant workers by the Swedish Migration Agency constitute very large obstacles both for the individual migrant and for the company wishing to hire international employees. This is especially true for non-EU citizens who need to obtain a permanent working visa to take up permanent employment in Sweden. For SmartShake, whose primary export markets are the US and China, this is highly problematic. Moreover, according to the CEO, the negative experience of hiring non-EU employees and dealing with the Migration Agency has made the company reluctant to recruit international personnel, despite their need for such employees.

Additional external barriers relate to other costly and restrictive legislative and administrative settings and requirements that can imply inefficiencies in terms of financial and time resources (such as considerable gaps between the company's search for new staff and the effective commencement of the post). Particularly relevant are rigid labour legislations and regulations for employees who are working abroad (for instance, as regards time management and working hours), high payroll taxes/costly social contributions, time consuming procedures for the provision of licenses, and differences between national procurement legislations and cultures. Some managers observe that these barriers increase as the company grows, while others stress that economies of scale and learning (for instance of the administrative procedures and practicalities) can help to reduce some of them over time.

> For the Austrian '**seamtec**' born global, the main challenge during the stays abroad of its personnel is to meet the legal time regulations. Moreover, the owner and manager observed that the legal framework often does not meet the needs of the employees either. He has a very young and well-motivated team, who often travel abroad to get work. In these cases, his employees would prefer to work long hours (even longer than the legal standards) in order to be able to return home as soon as possible. They would be interested in extending their working hours during their stays abroad if they could then make use of compensatory time-off when they return home.

3.5 Processes and characteristics of job creation

Research evidence on the characteristics of job creation processes in born globals is limited. Case studies collecting information on these issues (Eurofound, 2016) allow the identification of some key features for this specific type of company.

Recruitment decisions in born globals are mainly based on their business plan and on the estimation of workforce needs in carrying out the current and expected workload and production levels. Additional staff needs are, in most cases, identified in the continuous dialogue with the current employees, which is facilitated by the small size of the born globals and their team-based work organisation. They are subsequently followed-up by the management, by carrying out a thorough analysis of the available and expected levels of financial resources, demand and required workforce.

> The CEO of the Swedish '**ProposalsFactory**' born global is responsible for the entire recruitment process. As he manages everyday work, he pays great attention to the needs of the company and he identifies recruitment needs in dialogue with the CTO and the development team. Upon identification of a recruitment need, the process can be initiated immediately. The CEO estimates that the entire recruitment process, from the identification of the recruitment need to the hiring of an employee, takes approximately three to four months.

Since the inputs needed often relate to specific tasks and skills, managers tend to identify whether they are just contingent in nature or likely to last in the longer-term. In order to cover the momentary shortage of certain skills, specific tasks tend to be outsourced or assigned to temporary employment agencies staff. On the contrary, if the demand for additional work is relevant in terms of number of hours and sustainable in a longer-term perspective, and if managers assume they will be able to sustainably afford additional personnel costs, decisions tend to favour hiring new staff rather than outsourcing. This allows for the accumulation of knowledge and capital within the company and for the creation of specialised profiles that, after an induction period, can adapt to the business culture while responding and covering the complexity and specificity of the products or services offered. Maintaining and building the expertise in-house is a strategic approach that aims to increase the capabilities within the company, to strengthen the basis for future development and specialisation, and the capacity to carry out production with high technical contents – which would not be feasible without specific in-company training and learning.

The Austrian '**Evercyte**' born global considers outsourcing particularly in those fields that do not belong to the core competencies of the company. In detail, they outsource accounting, ICT-support and legal consultancy. Furthermore, they make use of outsourcing in cases where they need specific scientific input to a limited extent, that is where the workload would not justify the creation of a new full-time job and the position would not be sustainable.

Similarly, the Estonian '**Taxify**' born global does not recruit people to all positions and tasks. Some tasks which are not connected to their main activities, such as accounting and office cleaning, are outsourced. To conduct marketing activities, in addition to own employees, local marketing agencies have been used.

Regarding the types of recruitment approaches adopted, born globals do not tend to implement standardised procedures, but rather act on an ad hoc, case-by-case basis, and especially so at their inception and in the first recruitment processes. This means that different approaches can be used for different vacancies. However, eventually, the accumulation of experience and the related learning allow these companies to put more standardised recruitment and induction procedures in place, which still tend to follow a rather informal approach. The standardisation mainly refers to the selection of the most suitable approaches, tools and recruitment channels, the formulation of vacancy notices, or the identification of the most relevant selection criteria, among others. Nevertheless, the processes used by born globals in the end do not show great differences over time, as the human resources tasks, including recruitment, are mostly centralised in the figure of the owner/manager.

As the Swedish '**SmartShake**' born global has expanded, so has the necessity for a more structured way of identifying recruitment needs. Current recruitment needs are detected in dialogue with the employees, the management team and the CEO, who is ultimately responsible for the whole process and who makes the final recruitment decision. It is often the employees who make the initial identification, based on their experiences of the capacity of their respective function or role. If employees feel that they have too much work, they report this to the management who then may decide to either redistribute tasks or to recruit additional staff.

For the recruitment processes, born globals' managers prefer simple and low-cost tools, although this varies according to the degree of complexity of the post. As to the choice of the recruitment channels, the word of mouth and the use of personal and professional contacts and acquaintances are often considered to be an efficient and effective approach. In addition, and in contrast to a large share of other SMEs, social media are also used intensively, mainly to publish vacancy notices or search for candidates who have registered their profiles online. Managers appreciate this route, considered to be cost-efficient and easy to manage. Sometimes, vacancies are also published in local or national newspapers.

Within the Estonian '**Defendec**' born global, the recruitment process is not based on a specific plan and is usually implemented on a case-by-case basis. They select the routes for recruitment that are most relevant for each specific role. As they mostly look for highly qualified people, they usually prefer to find them directly via online means (such as Facebook, Twitter and LinkedIn). They also use (although less often) other routes such as (Estonian and international) recruitment portals, recruitment companies or other personal contacts. The final decision on which routes to use is usually made by the CEO and the COO in cooperation, and whether they are used at all depends on the results of the recruitment process – if the process fails using one route, then another is used, including moving from Estonian to international level.

On the other hand, relying on public or professional recruitment intermediaries or third parties (such as public employment services, recruitment agencies or head-hunters) or attending specialised recruitment fairs is not frequently used among born globals, probably due to the higher costs involved. Some exceptions exist, for instance in the use of public employment services for the identification of lower skilled profiles and the creation of a pool of relevant resources (especially in the case of blue-collars), the contact with universities or public organisations to attract skilled graduates, or the use of head-hunters for high managerial positions or very specialised profiles.

In recruiting new employees, the British '**BBOXX**' born global utilises head-hunters, university networks, start-up associations, business partners, friends and social media. According to the CEO, the most important and effective route is head-hunters, who are frequently used for key managerial and senior positions. Over 45 per cent of their engineering team were hired through this process, while 30 per cent were derived from existing acquaintances, and 25 per cent were attracted from university advertised internships. Even though it is quite costly, using head-hunters helps the company to find the right talent within a short time. This has helped BBOXX to quickly improve its performance.

The recruitment routes used imply that, from a geographic perspective, born globals often have a regional or national scope to recruit new staff – while being open to international candidates who proactively approach the company. On other occasions, and especially in cases of shortages of relevant profiles at a national level or need for local staff in premises abroad, the companies are more likely to recruit internationally and even to foresee forms of remote work.

In the case of the Spanish '**Enigmedia**' born global, business needs in strategic foreign markets (Brazil, Egypt, China and Russia) have acted as a driver for international job creation. These four countries are of particular interest for strategic reasons, given the type of product that Enigmedia sells. In 2014, they started to implement an 'experimental process' for hiring international interns, by which they tried to employ first-generation immigrants from these four countries, with the main idea being to adapt the Enigmedia software to the culture of these countries. They have hired an Egyptian and a Russian worker, but up to the time of interview had not been able to find workers from Brazil or China. Both the Egyptian and the Russian workers, who initially started as interns, were later employed on a contract.

The interviewed born globals' managers report that they have received between 10 and 40 applications in response to vacancy notices. Differences in the numbers are related to the level of specialisation of the profile, whereby lower skilled positions attract a higher number of candidates, against the limited number of applications for more specialised ones. When it comes to the screening of applications and selection of the candidates, the process is usually done in-house by applying criteria that often touch upon specific and technical skills for the post, but that also cover a number of transversal skills such as language knowledge, international profile and experience, passion, motivation, determination to work hard, personality traits and aspirations, the potential to learn and progress within the organisation, autonomy, initiative, flexibility and adaptability, problem solving and the capacity to work in teams. These are considered particularly relevant within born globals (and smaller companies in general, as compared to larger companies), as the feeling and perceptions on the candidate's relevance and suitability to the business are often crucial. This is justified by the specific business culture, nature, dynamism, small size and ambitions of the company, where the working environment and commitment to work are key elements for the success of the business. Here, profiles such as recent graduates or professionals with previous working experience in similar business models (SMEs rather than big corporations) are likely to be preferred against profiles coming from a completely different business culture, in order to ensure a better fit.

> As a small tech start-up, the Swedish '**Zaplox**' born global attracts the attention of many candidates from larger companies that are restructuring. The CEO suggests that candidates coming from large companies are often not aware of the challenges of working for a smaller company. The CEO highlights that working in a small, tightknit company such as Zaplox is very different because every person is virtually irreplaceable for the company to operate successfully. From the CEO's experiences, this level of responsibility is often challenging to candidates who have only worked in large companies, as they are used to a higher level of stability and security provided by a larger organisation, where there are multiple employees for each function. It is crucial for Zaplox to find candidates who are willing and able to work efficiently in the context of a small company.

In the born globals analysed, the manager/owner is involved directly in and is responsible for the selection process. Other experienced, senior staff and/or future colleagues of the candidate can also contribute to the assessment and selection, as it is deemed important that the new staff member fits into the existing team. Consequently, face-to-face interviews are the most important tool to explore the candidates' suitability. Several rounds of interviews are carried out and these are more important in assessing the applicants' actual knowledge and potential contribution to the company than the certified qualifications held. Born globals more rarely test the applicant's knowledge and technical skills – and when they do, it is mainly for specific roles or functions, such as engineers or sales persons.

> The recruitment process itself in the Estonian '**X**' born global usually consists of three stages – three face-to-face interviews carried out first by the head of the field/ department in the company, then by the COO and the head of the department, and third by the CEO. The aim of the first interview is to get basic information about the applicants, their competences and background. The second interview aims to test and find out about applicants' skills and knowledge. The idea of the third interview with the CEO is to look at applicants' suitability to the company, thus focusing mainly on the applicant's soft skills and values.

In general, it takes around two months from the decision to recruit to the selection of a specific candidate. Although time-consuming, this process is considered to be worthwhile to capture the best candidates, who will stay and grow within the company. Nonetheless, one of the biggest difficulties is reaching a satisfactory number of potential candidates who have relevant profiles.

When consulted on the outcomes of the job creation processes in their companies, born globals' managers stress the positive contribution of the new jobs created in terms of performance effects, increased financial turnover, and internationalisation. These range from the primary effect of better coverage of the customers' needs and demands, to a boost of the company's service quality, productivity and competitiveness thanks to the participation of relevant, motivated employees, which ultimately results in an increased reputation and strengthened public image for the company. Moreover, the involvement of additional skilled staff with innovation and internationalisation experience and orientation contributes to strengthening the company's sustainability, through access to new competences and ideas, and to new networks, business partners and markets.

The creation of new jobs has had positive effects on the business performance of the Austrian '**Evercyte**' born global. The employees are responsible for the good reputation of the company in the industry of biotechnology. This leads to further orders and enables the management to employ new personnel.

In the case of the Spanish '**Enigmedia**' born global, the created jobs have had positive effects for the company in terms of increased competitiveness, as well as in its capacity for innovation and internationalisation.

When it comes to the company structure, the expansion of the workforce (again, taking into account the young age of the firms and the related limited development of the organisational structure and processes) often requires some adjustments from an organisational viewpoint, in order to better manage the workflow. This can consist of the creation of new departments; a clearer division of responsibilities and assignment of more specialised functions; stronger coordination between roles; and the creation of new roles (such as regional managers) in cases of expansion abroad. Ensuring balanced growth across the business units is often deemed important in these organisational adaptations.

The increased number of staff has resulted in several changes in the management and organisation of the British '**BBOXX**' born global. They have created new departments and dynamic staff have received promotions and started managing their own teams. The rapid expansion of BBOXX has, however, been time consuming for the management and disruptive for the company. The company has had to change its management structure as well as to introduce new systems to handle the increased staff numbers and deal with the complications associated with different administrative and payroll requirements in various markets.

From a worker's perspective, the job creation effects of born globals have features that, in some occasions, show differences and specificities as compared to other SMEs and bigger companies. In contrast with other, smaller companies, which tend to employ mainly women (Eurofound, 2012b) and people who have previously been unemployed for more than one year (De Kok *et al.*, 2013), the born globals analysed (Eurofound, 2016) are more inclined to hire younger employees (between 20 and 40 years of age), and predominantly men (probably due to the male domination of some of the main economic sectors of activity of these companies).

> In 2015, the Austrian '**seamtec**' born global employed a young team of six persons aged between 20 and 32. The young age of the team members was deemed relevant to the internationalisation strategy of the company, entry in new foreign markets and innovations.

As opposed to the main literature observing that smaller companies are less likely to ensure job security and tenure, these values seem to be particularly high in the born globals analysed, which tend to ultimately offer permanent full-time contracts to their employees (generally, after a probation period). This may derive from the aim of the company to accumulate knowledge and create profiles that are often very specialised and aligned with the corporate culture. Despite their limited resources, especially at inception, and the fear of competition from bigger and more established companies as regards access to talented candidates, born globals in Europe are found to offer higher wages than other young companies, and in certain occasion they may even exceed the sector averages (Eurofound, 2012a). Evidence is heterogeneous in the case studies analysed, where some companies indicate wage levels above the sector average, while others report that they cannot afford generous wages due to resource constraints. Interestingly, several of them used financial employee participation schemes as a way to compensate for low wages, but also to increase the workers' motivation and commitment towards the company.

> The Austrian '**Evercyte**' born global pays good salaries. The management of the company is not only interested in their own success and profit; they also care about the conditions for their employees. For example, they think about the development of employee shareholding programmes. In 2014, the employees took a financial share of the awards the company won.
>
> By way of contrast, for the Spanish '**Enigmedia**' born global, an important barrier to job creation is its difficulties in offering high salaries, as it does not have sufficient resources to compete with large companies located in the area offering higher salaries. In order to break down this barrier and attract high-profile professionals, Enigmedia tries to offer advantageous working conditions, particularly concerning teleworking and flexible working time arrangements.
>
> Meanwhile, the British '**Plumis Ltd**' company provides share option schemes as a form of bonus to the staff members, enabling employees to have some ownership of the company, therefore raising their responsibilities and commitment to the firm.

The levels of intrinsic job quality in born globals are perceived to be particularly high by employees, as is also the case in other small enterprises (De Kok *et al.*, 2013), and act as an additional draw, and motivation, for workers. Moreover, the born global case studies confirm extant evidence showing higher job satisfaction levels for workers employed in smaller companies (Storey *et al.*, 2010; De Kok *et al.*, 2013), despite the typically high levels of dedication and workload. This is mainly related to the working climate offered, the informal, friendly and supportive atmosphere, the culture of trust, and the limited levels of hierarchy. These horizontal management settings are favoured as compared to rigid top-down approaches. Thanks to their high specialisation, workers tend to be provided with great autonomy and flexibility in terms of task implementation, time management and physical presence at the company's premises, while regular communication and meetings are maintained to ensure coordination. Respecting the committed deadlines and objectives is often deemed more important by managers than fulfilling a set working time schedule.

The Swedish '**Zaplox**' born global almost exclusively recruits high skilled employees, providing them with a great degree of autonomy in relation to their work. According to both the CEO and the interviewed employee, there is no strict hierarchy at Zaplox. While there is naturally a management structure with heads of units, managers and employees, the employees and the managers work together on projects in a flat hierarchy. There is a collegial atmosphere at the workplace. The open organisation of Zaplox is seen as beneficial as the staff from all divisions of the company interact daily, enabling a natural transfer of knowledge between the divisions, which helps the company provide a better product to the customer.

Moreover, born globals tend to ensure and encourage regular communication and exchanges between the staff and the management, and some of them follow an inclusive management approach, whereby staff are involved in the company's decision-making processes and encouraged to share ideas for the improvement and further development of the products or services offered. This contributes to create a learning environment, with informal training effects.

As a young team, the relationship between managers and employees at the British '**KwickScreen**' born global is based on trust with a friendly and informal communication system. Employees are given 'optimal' autonomy within their responsibilities and duties. They also keep regular contact with their line manager to ensure a smooth workflow.

Training can indeed represent an additional motivational factor for workers but, like other SMEs, born globals offer fewer formal training opportunities as compared to bigger companies. This is mainly due to the costly procedures, the limited management capacities and the scarcity of available time, but also to the limited perception of training needs given the often high levels of specialisation and skills of the workforce. Nonetheless, informal training approaches such as an intensive induction of the new employees and on-the-job training are likely to be used by born globals, especially to constantly maintain the internal skills. Some companies adopt internal training systems, whereby interns and new staff are monitored and trained by more senior colleagues.

Within the Spanish '**Enigmedia**' born global, technology applied and products developed are very complex. Therefore, training is of the utmost importance for the company, and induction processes are also highly important for new recruits, particularly for interns. The peculiarities of the technology developed in Enigmedia make it necessary for the company to train their new employees, as the required knowledge is practically non-existent in schools and universities. This is done through a well-arranged 'system of couples', by which an experienced professional works alongside a non-experienced worker. In addition, managers are strict with the evaluation of the probationary period, as they do not want to 'waste their time' training someone who will not be useful for the organisation.

Related to the improvement of the employees' profiles, career opportunities within the born globals can be limited by the relatively small size of these companies. Nonetheless, different born globals offer perspectives for professional development consisting of the acquisition of managerial responsibilities beyond purely technical functions, or the coverage of more specialised and complex tasks and senior roles with a higher degree of responsibility.

Career opportunities within the Estonian '**Defendec**' born global are limited as the company is quite small. A career is seen more as an opportunity to carry out more complicated tasks, rather than connected with managerial tasks. Career steps for engineers start from a junior position, followed by a further four or five steps, including senior, expert and lead engineer. The same progression is seen for employees on the business development side. The number of managerial positions is limited. But still, it is possible to join the management board if someone has the ambition and is ready to take on considerably more responsibilities.

Probably due to the flat hierarchical structures in place, these and other issues of interest for employees tend to be discussed directly between the employees and the employers in the born globals analysed, none of which has a work council of other forms of company representation.

Notes

1 GEM data in this chapter refer to data from the Adult Population Survey (APS) 2011, namely information regarding owners or managers of companies surveyed in European countries – Belgium, Croatia, Denmark, Finland, France, Germany, Greece, Hungary, Ireland, Italy, Latvia, the Netherlands, Romania, Slovenia, Spain, Sweden and the UK. The analysis is based on a total of 6,462 observations.
2 Eurofound (2016) carried out 17 case studies on companies from Austria (5 cases), Estonia (3 cases), Spain (3 cases), Sweden (3 cases) and United Kingdom (3 cases).

References

Cavusgil, S. T. and Knight, G. A. (2009), *Born global firms: A new international enterprise*, Business Expert Press, New York.

Coviello, N. E. (2006), 'The network dynamics of international new ventures', *Journal of International Business Studies*, Vol. 37, No. 5, pp. 713–731.

Crick, D. and Jones, M. V. (2000), 'Small high-technology firms and international high-technology markets', *Journal of International Marketing*, Vol. 8, No. 2, pp. 63–85.

De Kok, J. M. P., Liebregts, W., Som, O. and Neuhaeusler, P. (2013), *The impact of the economic crisis on European SMEs: Does a country's innovativeness affect the reaction of enterprises to a major economic crisis?*, Zoetermeer, the Netherlands.

Eurofound (2012a), *Born global: The potential of job creation in new international businesses*, Publications Office of the European Union, Luxembourg.

Eurofound (2012b), *Fifth European Working Conditions Survey*, Publications Office of the European Union, Luxembourg.

Eurofound (2016), *ERM annual report 2015: Job creation in SMEs*, Publications Office of the European Union, Luxembourg.

European Commission (2003), *Commission recommendation of 6 May 2003 concerning the definition of micro, small and medium-sized enterprises*, 2003/361/EC, Brussels.

Gabrielsson, M. and Kirpalani, V. H. M. (2012), 'Overview, background and historical origin of born globals: Development of theoretical and empirical research', in Gabrielsson, M. and Kirpalani, V. H. M. (eds), *Handbook of research on born globals*, Edward Elgar, Cheltenham, pp. 3–15.

Gabrielsson, P., Gabrielsson, M. and Seppälä, T. (2012), 'Marketing strategies for foreign expansion of companies originating in small and open economies: The consequences of strategic fit and performance', *Journal of International Marketing*, Vol. 20, No. 2, pp. 25–48.

GEM (Global Entrepreneurship Monitor) (n.d.), *Adult Population Survey (APS)*. Available at www.gemconsortium.org/data/key-aps.

Golovko, E. and Valentini, G. (2011), 'Exploring the complementarity between innovation and export for SMEs growth', *Journal of International Business Studies*, Vol. 42, No. 3, pp. 362–380.

Johanson, J. A. and Vahlne, J. E. (1977), 'The internationalization process of the firm: A model of knowledge development and increasing foreign market commitments', *Journal of International Business Studies*, Vol. 8, No. 1, pp. 23–32.

Johanson, J. A. and Vahlne, J. E. (1990), 'The mechanism of internationalization', *International Marketing Review*, Vol. 7, No. 4, pp. 11–24.

Legrain, P. (2010), *Aftershock: Reshaping the world economy after the crisis*, Little, Brown, New York.

Leonidou, L. C. and Samiee, S. (2012), 'Born global or simply rapidly internationalising? Review, critique, and future prospects', in Gabrielsson, M. and Kirpalani, V. H. M. (eds), *Handbook of research on born globals*, Edward Elgar, Cheltenham, pp. 16–35.

Madsen, T. K. (2013), 'Early and rapidly internationalizing ventures: Similarities and differences between classifications based on the original international new venture and born global literatures', *Journal of International Entrepreneurship*, Vol. 11, No. 1, pp. 65–79.

Mettler, A. and Williams, A. D. (2011), *The rise of the micro-multinational: How freelancers and techonology-savvy start-ups are driving growth, jobs and innovation*, Lisbon Council Policy Brief, Vol. 5, No. 3, Lisbon Council, Brussels.

Moen, O. and Servais, P. (2002), 'Born global or gradual global? Examining the export behavior of small and medium-sized enterprises', *Journal of International Marketing*, Vol. 10, No. 3, pp. 49–72.

Oviatt, B. and McDougall, P. (2005), 'Defining international entrepreneurship and modeling the speed of internationalization', *Entrepreneurship: Theory and Practice*, Vol. 29, No. 5, pp. 537–553.

Rennie, M. (1993), 'Born global', *McKinsey Quarterly*, No. 4, pp. 45–52.

Sapienza, H. J., Autio, E., George, G., and Zahra, S. A. (2006), 'A capabilities perspective on the effects of early internationalisation on firm survival and growth', *Academy of Management Review*, Vol. 31, No. 4, pp. 914–933.

Spowart, M. and Wickramasekera, R. (2012), 'Explaining internationalization of small to medium sized enterprises within the Queensland food and beverage industry', *International Journal of Business and Management*, Vol. 7, No. 6, pp. 68–80.

Storey, D. J., Saridakis, G., Sukanya, S., Edwards, P. and Blackburn, R. A. (2010), 'Linking HR formality with employee job quality: The role of firm and workplace size', *Human Resource Management*, Vol. 49, No. 2, pp. 305–329.

Vapola, T. J., Tossavainen, P. and Gabrielsson, M. (2008), 'The battleship strategy: The complementing role of born globals in MNC's new opportunity creation', *Journal of International Entrepreneurship*, Vol. 6, No. 1, pp. 1–20.

Vivarelli, M. (2014), 'Innovation, employment and skills in advanced and developing countries: A survey of economic literature', *Journal of Economic Studies*, Vol. 48, No. 1, pp. 123–154.

4 Job creation in Swedish born globals

Svante Andersson

4.1 Introduction

This chapter deals with how Swedish born globals have contributed to economic growth and job creation in Sweden. The chapter starts with an overview of the Swedish economy and international trade. Thereafter follows a description of born globals in Sweden, including information on their sector, number of employees, and willingness and expectation to grow. This is illustrated by two examples of Swedish born globals that have experienced a continued international growth and have created jobs in Sweden. These examples are from the manufacturing and med-tech sectors, which are over-represented when it comes to born globals. After that, the creative sector is presented as a new growing sector in Sweden. The creative sector has been identified as one of the key sectors, with many born global firms, which can help Europe remain competitive in the changing global market driving economic growth and job creation (Collins *et al.*, 2014). Subsequently, this chapter discusses how born globals in Sweden have influenced economic growth and job creation in different sectors and finishes with reflections on implications for policy and managers.

4.2 Sweden's economy and international trade

Sweden is a Scandinavian country in Northern Europe. At a size of 450,295 km², it is the third-largest country in the European Union by area, with a total population of over 10 million (Statistics Sweden, 2017). Sweden joined the European Union in 1995, but it is not part of the Euro area and has the Krona as currency.

The Swedish business economy (excluding financial services) amounted to over 1 million companies and employed 2.7 million persons (measured in full-time equivalents) in 2014 (Ekonmifakta[1], 2017). These companies had together a turnover of SEK 7,331 billion (€772 billion) and created value added equal to SEK 2,165 billion (€228 billion) (Ekonomifakta, 2017). Their total assets amounted to SEK 16,675 billion (€1,755 billion) (Ekonomifakta, 2017). Sweden has an export-oriented economy. In 2013, it exported 44 per cent of its GDP; 31.4 per cent were products and 12.6 per cent services (Ekonomifakta, 2017). Approximately one-quarter of the GDP is exported to other EU Member States and around one million employees, or approximately one-fifth of the total labour force in Sweden, work in firms that export to the EU. Sweden's largest export partners are Norway (10 per cent), Germany (10 per cent), the US (8 per cent), the UK (7 per cent), Denmark (7 per cent) and Finland (7 per cent) (Statistics Sweden, 2017).

The dominant export sector is machinery and transport equipment (45 per cent, including machinery at 16 per cent, electronics/telecom at 12 per cent and vehicles at 12 per cent) followed by chemicals (14 per cent, including pharmaceuticals at 6 per cent) and forestry (12 per cent, including papers at 6 per cent) (Statistics Sweden, 2017).

The business economy consists largely of small and medium sized enterprises (SMEs). A very large proportion (97 per cent) of these are micro enterprises with fewer than 10 employees. In 2014, the micro enterprises accounted for less than one-quarter of the value added created in the business economy. Large companies with 250 or more employees made up less than 0.1 per cent of the total enterprise population, but contributed a total of 39 per cent to the value added (see Table 4.1).

The three largest industries in Sweden by share of employment are manufacturing (21 per cent), wholesale and retail trade (18 per cent), and construction (11 per cent) (Statistics Sweden, 2017). Well-known large Swedish manufacturing companies include Volvo, Scania, Saab and Ericsson, while IKEA and H&M are famous Swedish retail companies. Although the large manufacturing companies are still very important for the Swedish economy, and some of them are still growing, they are no longer contributing to employment growth in Sweden.

Previous research has documented the importance of SMEs for employment growth and wealth generation in domestic and global economies (Etemad, 2004; OECD, 1997). In relatively small markets, such as Sweden, internationalisation is often necessary for a company to grow. However, smaller and younger firms are not as international as larger and older firms in Sweden. Small firms have fewer resources than larger firms due to liabilities of smallness, and new firms have less experience than older firms due to liabilities of newness. Foreign markets have different institutional and cultural contexts than the home market. To be able to compete in foreign markets it is necessary to have knowledge

Table 4.1 Distribution of enterprises and employment in the non-financial business economy by size of enterprise, 2012

Size of enterprise, by persons employed	Enterprises (%)	Jobs (%)
0–9	96.6	23.8
10–49	2.8	22.4
50–249	0.5	18.3
250+	0.1	35.6
Total	100	100

Source: Structural business statistics, Statistics Sweden, 2012.

about the different contexts. This knowledge can be acquired through market experience or by hiring local staff. As small firms seldom have local representation or personnel with extensive international experience, many small firms with competitive products do not grasp international opportunities, although advances in terms of lower trade barriers, better communication technologies and low transportation costs have made internationalisation easier for smaller firms as globalisation increased. The globalisation has affected firms in Sweden and all over the world (Andersson and Florén, 2011).

4.3 Born globals in Sweden

Although most Swedish SMEs are not focusing on international growth strategies, there are some Swedish new ventures that, from inception, regard the world as their market. Swedish research on born global firms has followed the most well-known international definitions of this type of company (Oviatt and McDougall, 1994; Knight, 1997): 'The born global is defined as a company which, from or near its founding seeks to derive a substantial proportion of its revenue from the sale of its products in international markets' (Knight, 1997).

However, one of the first studies on born globals which was done in Sweden (Andersson and Wictor, 2003) concluded that even if Sweden's large firms were very international (e.g. Electrolux, Volvo, Saab, Scania), most Swedish SMEs focused on the home market. Many Swedish SMEs were suppliers to the large Swedish firms and did not actively market themselves internationally (Andersson *et al.*, 2004).

The born globals are limited in number in Sweden; for instance, Halldin (2012b) found that just 3 per cent of new firms (started 1998–2003) in the manufacturing sector were born globals. On the other hand, they are over-represented in high-tech industries (Halldin, 2012b) and some successful firms that have been able to use new technology and business models, such as Spotify[2] and Skype,[3] are Swedish born globals. In this sense, born globals have proved important for the Swedish economy as they are innovative, offering new solutions to customer demands and needs to the market, and bringing in new ideas to traditional industries, such as manufacturing.

Born globals are built on a new and highly internationalised business model, that seems to be a natural choice in an increasingly globalised world, and they have increasingly gained attention in both academia and among policy and governmental institutions in Sweden. Business Sweden (a joint venture between the Swedish state and an organisation owned by private companies, supporting Swedish companies to grow internationally and foreign actors to invest in Sweden) is using the concept of born globals and is offering specialised programmes for these firms.[4]

Born globals have also shown a positive contribution to job creation in Sweden. Halldin (2012a) found that five years after their foundation, born global firms had higher growth in employment and sales per employee compared with other young firms, but no such effect is found when performance is measured by profitability or labour productivity. This shows that born globals are of special interest when it comes to employment.

Overall, born globals show stronger willingness and expectations to grow when compared to young enterprises and SMEs. This is shown by Halldin (2012a) to be the case for Sweden. This study indicates that born global firms compared to other young firms perform better in terms of average number of employees. Compared to their prevalence in the economy overall, their share in the manufacturing and information and communication sectors is large (Halldin 2011, 2012a).

Oxford Research used a survey carried out in 2014 in Sweden to analyse the importance of born globals for the Swedish economy (Eurofound, 2016).[5] The survey, called 'Enterprises' conditions and realities' ('Företagens villkor och verklighet'), was carried out among Swedish-controlled enterprises with an annual turnover of at least SEK 200,000 (€21,757 as at 6 March 2017) and between 0 and 249 employees, that operate in the industries included in Table 4.2. The survey included responses from about 120 born global enterprises, defined as enterprises formed in 2008 or later that had at least 26 per cent of exports in 2013 (that is, that achieved 26 per cent or more of exports in at least one of the first five years).[6]

The results from the survey show that approximately 1 per cent of SMEs, and approximately 3.7 per cent of young enterprises are born global firms. These results are in line with the results by Halldin (2012a), showing that the proportion of born globals out of new firms within the industries studied (manufacturing and knowledge intensive business services) was around 3 per cent.[7]

The sector with the highest share of born globals is the information and communication industry, where born global enterprises represent approximately 3 per cent of SMEs. This is considerably above the average share of born globals in any other sector and in the economy overall (see Figure 4.1). Nevertheless, the information and communication sector is a relatively small sector representing around 6 per cent of the enterprises in the sampling frame. It includes activities such as publishing, programming and data processing – in other words it is heavily based on new and high technology-related services. This is in line with earlier findings in research about born globals showing that those firms are over-represented in sectors built on high-tech and modern IT technology (Andersson *et al.*, 2014).

The data also show that born global enterprises are relatively prevalent in extraction and manufacturing (2.5 per cent), as well as electricity, gas and water (2.1 per cent). Manufacturing is the strongest export sector in Sweden (45 per cent) and even if competition has grown strong from emerging economies, such as China, automatisation and digitalisation have rendered some specialised manufacturing still competitive in Sweden.

Furthermore, the results show that born global enterprises are almost non-existent within construction (0.1 per cent), accommodation and food service (0.1 per cent), education, and health and social work sectors (0.05 per cent). These sectors are largely domestically oriented in Sweden. This can be explained by

Table 4.2 Industries included in the 'enterprises' conditions and realities' survey

Code	Detailed code (SNI 2007)	Industry	Sampled number of enterprises	Sample	Response rate (%)
BC	05–33	Mining and quarrying (B); Manufacturing (C)	2,978	1,610	54.1
DE	35–39	Electricity, gas, steam and air conditioning supply (D); Water supply; Sewerage, waste management and remediation activities (E)	805	501	62.2
F	41–43	Construction	3,015	1,425	47.3
G	45–47	Wholesale and retail trade; Repair of motor vehicles and motorcycles	3,524	1,705	48.4
H	49–53	Transportation and storage	2,478	1,263	51.0
I	55–56	Accommodation and food service activities	2,865	1,170	40.8
J	58–63	Information and communication	1,997	1,040	52.1
M	69–75	Professional, scientific and technical activities	3,193	1,913	59.9
N	77–82	Administrative and support service activities	2,578	1,340	52.0
P	85	Education	2,222	1,251	56.3
Q	86–88	Human health and social work activities	2,482	1,481	59.7
RS	90–96	Arts, entertainment and recreation (R); Other service activities (S)	2,477	1,120	45.2
		Total	30,614	15,819	51.7

Source: Statistics Sweden on behalf of the Swedish Agency for Economic and Regional Growth, 2014.

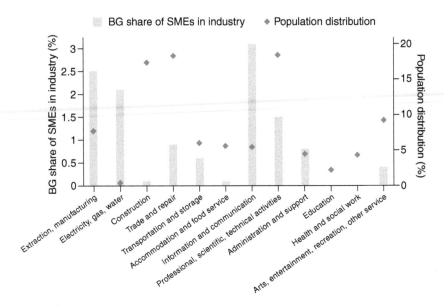

Figure 4.1 Born global enterprises' share of SMEs by industry, 2014.

Source: Oxford Research for Eurofound (2016), based on survey results from Swedish Agency for Economic and Regional Growth (2014).

the fact that health service and education in Sweden is financed through taxes and owned by the state and municipalities. In these sectors there are few new actors and few Swedish actors with an intention to grow internationally. The sectors with few born globals are dominated by traditional services that need local personnel to deliver their offers. That makes it difficult for new and small firms to grow internationally, as it demands resources to employ personnel abroad (Andersson, 2006).

The share of born global enterprises out of young enterprises by industry is presented in Figure 4.2. Interestingly, the distribution is somewhat different from the overall share of born globals within the sectors. Born globals represent over 14 per cent of the young enterprises in extraction and manufacturing, and over 8 per cent of young enterprises in the information and communication industry. Considering the industry where the share of young enterprises is the largest, namely accommodation and food services where 39 per cent of SMEs in the survey are young enterprises, born global enterprises – unsurprisingly – represent less than half a per cent of these young enterprises (see Figure 4.2).

4.4 Number of employees in born global enterprises

The number of employees in born global enterprises is small: in 2014, born globals employ 0.7 per cent of employees in SMEs. 16.1 per cent of employees

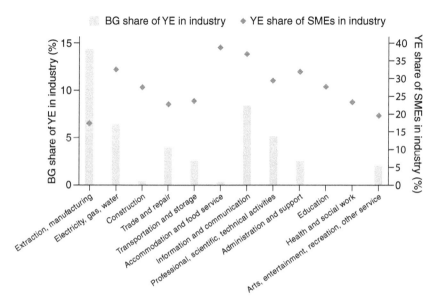

Figure 4.2 Born global enterprises' share of young enterprises (YE) by industry, 2014.

Source: Oxford Research for Eurofound (2016), based on survey results from Swedish Agency for Economic and Regional Growth (2014).

work in young enterprises, and 4.4 per cent of employees in young enterprises work in born globals (Eurofound, 2016). Consistent with their young age, both born global enterprises and young enterprises represent a larger share of SMEs (1.0 per cent and 26.5 per cent) than they do of employees (0.7 per cent and 16.1 per cent). Indeed, born globals are on average smaller than SMEs, employing on average 2.6 individuals compared to 3.6 for SMEs. They are, however, on average somewhat larger than young enterprises overall, which employ 2.2 individuals on average. Results from the survey are in line with Halldin's findings (2011), indicating that born global firms compared to other young firms perform better in terms of average number of employees.

4.5 Willingness and expectation to grow

Swedish Born globals display a higher willingness to grow in terms of number of employees than other types of SMEs. When asked an open question (Eurofound, 2016) about whether they would like to grow if there was opportunity to do so, 60 per cent of born global enterprises responded that they would like to grow in terms of turnover and number of employees, and 21 per cent responded that they would like to grow in terms of turnover only (see Figure 4.3). For SMEs (young enterprises), 38 per cent (48 per cent) would like to grow in terms of employees and turnover and 32 per cent (31 per cent) would like to grow in terms of only turnover

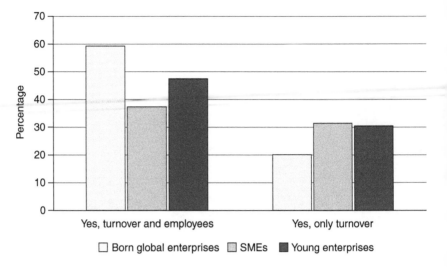

Figure 4.3 Willingness to grow (turnover and employees) among SMEs, young enterprises and born globals, 2014.

Source: Oxford Research for Eurofound (2016), based on survey results from Swedish Agency for
Economic and Regional Growth (2014).

(see Figure 4.3). This shows that, for born globals, growth involves increasing both
headcount and turnover. The survey also shows that 30 per cent of SMEs and 21
per cent of young enterprises do not want to grow if there was opportunity to do
so, compared to 19 per cent of born global enterprises.

When asked about their expected company development in the next three
years (Eurofound, 2016), born globals are generally more positive than other
enterprises when it comes to increasing the number of employees. In particular,
44 per cent of born globals think that their number of employees will increase,
compared to 23 per cent of SMEs and 32 per cent of young enterprises.

A similar pattern arises for turnover: 66 per cent of born global enterprises
think that their turnover will increase in the next three years, compared to 58 per
cent of young enterprises and 43 per cent of SMEs. The same order does not
apply to profitability: 53 per cent of born global enterprises expect that profitability will increase in the next three years compared to 55 per cent for young
enterprises and 41 per cent for SMEs. This implies that born globals are in
general more positive about their turnover than their profitability development.
One explanation for this could be that born global enterprises expect a higher
cost base – as, for example, they are also more positive when it comes to increasing the number of employees, which implies higher wage costs. However, it
could also indicate the inconsistencies that can arise in these questions that
concern subjectively predicting future development. See Table 4.3.

Data from the survey made by the Swedish Agency for Economic and
Regional Growth do not allow a conclusion on absolute job growth, including on

Table 4.3 Expected company development in the next three years, 2014

	Decreased (%)	Unchanged (%)	Increased (%)
Turnover			
Born global enterprises	12	22	66
SMEs	16	41	43
Young enterprises	11	31	58
Number of employees			
Born global enterprises	9	48	44
SMEs	11	66	23
Young enterprises	7	61	32
Profitability			
Born global enterprises	10	37	53
SMEs	16	43	41
Young enterprises	10	34	55

Source: Survey results from the Swedish Agency for Economic and Regional Growth, 2014.

whether born global enterprises are likely to create more jobs than other types of enterprises. However, Halldin (2012a) found that born globals have a better performance than other young firms, when this is measured by employment and sales per employee. Performance measured by profitability and labour productivity is not found to be greater for born globals compared with other young firms. The results from both Halldin (2012a) and the Swedish Agency for Economic and Regional Growth survey show that born globals are small in number and consequently employ a small share of individuals in Sweden. This is unlikely to change in the immediate future. However, as the born globals show a greater growth in employment compared with other SMEs, it is likely that some of them will evolve into new large multinational companies.

The distinguishing feature of born globals is their international behaviour at birth and soon thereafter. The firms' behaviour is initiated by the entrepreneurs' and management's global mindset and the commitment of resources leading to international growth (Andersson, 2000; Knight and Cavusgil, 2004). Born globals are, by definition, a born global firm 'forever'; that is, even if they grow older they could be considered as born globals as they started off as this business model and are influenced by their early years. As mentioned above, Halldin (2012a) showed that born globals were few in Sweden, but they showed greater growth in employment than other firms. Thus, it is relevant to consider what happens in born globals after their early years in order to get insight into whether they continue to grow and create jobs. The experiences from the early years make these firms a special type, ones that will influence their further international development. A key distinguishing feature of born globals is that they lack the deeply rooted administrative heritage that is created in firms that grow older with a focus on domestic markets (Miller and Friesen, 1984). Firms with a long-term focus on the domestic market must unlearn routines rooted in the domestic context before new, internationally oriented routines can be learned (see Chapter 8). An early entrance into international markets forces born globals to adapt to new contexts and create new knowledge that leads to new routines and creates a culture allowing the firms to adapt to new international opportunities (Andersson and Evers, 2015; Autio *et al.*, 2000; Knight and Cavusgil, 2004). Few studies have captured the long-term behaviour and growth of born globals (Gabrielsson and Gabrielsson, 2013; Melén Hånell *et al.*, 2014). A question that has been very little addressed is what happens to born global firms when they grow up (Cavusgil and Knight, 2015). As employment growth was the characteristic that distinguished Swedish born globals (Halldin, 2012b), the sections below will focus on examples of born globals that have succeeded in surviving, maturing and growing (see, for instance, Hagen and Zuchella, 2014, on maturing born global firms).

4.6 Examples of Swedish born globals

To illustrate how born globals can continue to grow and create jobs in Sweden and abroad, examples of some successful firms in different industries are considered. The cases chosen illustrate how born global firms have continued to grow after their first year and continued to create jobs (Hagen and Zuchella, 2014). Axelent operates in the traditional manufacturing sector, and has succeeded in growing internationally but kept all production in Sweden. Camp Scandinavia is active in the med-tech sector. The firm was originally a wholesaler for medical products but has started own product development and production, and large parts of those activities are in Sweden. This is then illustrated by an example from the creative sector in Sweden. This sector is highly internationalised as over 50 per cent of the total turnover from creative industries are exports.[8] Many firms in this sector are born globals firms.

4.6.1 Axelent

History and strategy

Axelent develops, manufactures and sells machine guarding, warehouse partitioning, and anti-collapse and property protection. The company was founded in 1990 and immediately from inception it aimed at international markets. As early as 1990, a subsidiary was established in the Netherlands. In 1991, subsidiaries were established in France and the UK, and Axelent's products were sold in Iceland, Denmark, Finland and Norway. In 1992, new subsidiaries were established in Germany and Spain. The international growth has continued and in 2015 the Axelent group had a turnover of €50 million and the company had 200 employees. The objective is to reach 10 per cent organic turnover growth per year. This has led to continued job creation in the company. Axelent's head office is located in Sweden, from where they also serve the Nordic markets. They also have own subsidiaries/associated companies in Benelux, UK, France, Germany, the Netherlands, Spain, Japan, Australia, Brazil and the USA. Axelent has about 20,000 customers in 50 countries. Its strategy is to have a small niche, which the firm can serve very well. The company gives the customer a computer programme (for free) that can calculate which ones, and how much, of Axelent products are needed in accordance with the EU Machinery Directive.[9] The firm's innovative solutions have to do with offering a bundle of benefits, examples being quality products, after sales services, quick delivery, and safe and reliable processes. This strategy has resulted in the firm having a high sustainable profitability and growth over time. Axelent always has a large over-capacity of products and a large warehouse to store the products, plus over-capacity, even of own their personnel. All this helps the firm to meet its growth objective and to respond quickly to orders and other demands. The above strategies have led to Axelent taking over many customers from their competitors. In Germany, for example, Axelent wins about 25 new customers every month.

According to the CEO of Axelent, the company's success, which is based on the company's niche market, its quality, quick delivery and after-sales services, is to be attributed to a joint effort by the firm's network partners, namely, customers, suppliers, and own personnel.

Job creation in Axelent

Axelent is located in a small municipality, Gnosjö, which had 9,615 inhabitants in 2016 (Statistics Sweden, 2017). The area is known for its entrepreneurial spirit and has many SMEs. In 2015, the company had 200 employees. The growth in employment and turnover is presented in Table 4.4. The majority of their sales growth is outside Sweden and, in 2015, 77 per cent of the turnover was outside Sweden. In Axelent, job creation is closely connected to sales growth. To create sales Axelent has developed a competitive offer that fulfils customer needs. The customer needs Axelent's products when it is buying new machinery. Machinery is placed in a building with other equipment and walls that make each installation unique. When the machine is installed it is important that safety equipment is set quickly and in accordance with regulations so the machine can start working. Axelent helps the customer with designing and delivering this protection. Axelent has all production in Sweden and is also mostly using local suppliers, meaning that it does not only create jobs within its own company, but also among local suppliers. This also happens in different international markets, where Axelent has its own representatives and hires local employees and managers. Working with own personnel, who are highly motivated,

Table 4.4 Employees and turnover for Axelent

Axelent holding	2006	2007	2008	2009	2010	2011	2012	2013	2014	2015
Employees (number)	109	113	126	129	131	143	150	160	170	200
Turnover (thousand €)	25,577	31,729	32,487	26,126	29,393	32,680	35,557	39,711	44,508	50,962

Source: www.allabolag.se.

flexible, and skilful, contributes greatly to the firm's ability to meet its object-ives. According to the CEO, the personnel are skilled at marketing, product development and engineering. Working with network partners such as robot manufacturers, warehouse designers (those who will need Axelent's protective products around robots and machines), agents (those distributing the firms' prod-ucts in various markets), and own personnel (to provide needed services for the installed robots and machines) needs to be carefully managed and coordinated. Here, the firm has invested, in cooperation with a small IT firm in Helsingborg (Sweden), in a software programme, called 'snapper-works', which aids the firm's quick logistical delivery solutions all over the world. The firm has also used acquisition strategies in expanding its business.

Through this example, it is shown that it is possible for a born global to con-tinue to grow, with production and product development located in Sweden, and also to use the local context as a competitive advantage. A high level of automa-tisation and a close cooperation with local suppliers are an important part in the business model that is the base for the company's successful growth strategy, which has created jobs in Axelent as well as jobs for the suppliers.

4.6.2 Camp Scandinavia

History and strategy

Camp Scandinavia was established in 1996 as a spin-off from an established medical equipment company through a management buyout (MBO). Before the MBO, the company distributed products that were developed and produced by other companies. Product development resided at the core of the new company, with a focus on the orthopaedic rehabilitation market. It led to a series of unique patented products. The most important product of the company is an orthosis, an orthopaedic apparatus that helps correct deformities or improve function of movable body parts. After the MBO, the company started with own product development and an international growth strategy, with the majority of sales outside Sweden. In Scandinavia, the company operates under the name 'Camp Scandinavia', while 'Allard International' is used in other markets. From 1996 to 2001, the turnover increased by 70 per cent, mainly through sales outside Sweden. The combination of own product development and an international growth strategy has led to continued job creation in the company, as detailed below.

Camp Scandinavia is committed to the development of products in response to patients' needs. This commitment has been the foundation for the develop-ment and ownership of innovative products to provide people with disabilities with an opportunity to function better and improve their quality of life. The first product that was developed was the unique Foot Drop orthosis produced of com-posite materials which was given the name ToeOFF. This product has been very successful. Growth has been achieved by increasing in export volume to various markets. The company has own subsidiaries in Scandinavia, the UK, Ireland and the USA and works through distributors in Germany, Benelux, Austria and Switzerland. Other strategies for achieving growth are to invest in own product development and also finding 'right partners' (in-house or external ones) to help in that effort, which for the most part has been successful.

Camp manufacture an orthopaedic product, which is a raw material reworked to be a product ready to try out on a patient. Their most important customers are the orthopaedic departments at hospitals, where their orthopaedic facilities are tested out. The persons testing the products are medical engineers. Medical engineers are important, together with physiotherapists and medical doctors, as opinion builders influencing potential clients choosing the company's products. Many users are also influenced by social media and the internet. The products are sold via distributors, who are often found via the CEO's networks and trade fairs.

The company has an overall goal of international growth. However, detailed planning has not been characteristic for the growth. The most crucial approach for the company's international growth has been to grasp opportunities when they turn up. The most important part in the establishment of the international subsidiaries was to find local employees in key positions who could be trusted and who could deal with unexpected incidents. The second subsidiary was set up in the UK. However, here it was at first hard to find a suitable subsidiary manager. An opportunity turned up to buy an Irish company. The UK market was served via the Irish subsidiary and this has proven to be a successful solution. Another important and large market is Germany, but this is still served via a distributor. The distributor is a good friend of the CEO who sees no need to start a subsidiary as the market is well served via the distributor.

Job creation in Camp Scandinavia

In 2015, the company had 186 employees – the growth in employment and turnover is presented in Table 4.5. Job creation is closely connected to sales growth. According to the CEO, the firm strives for a controlled organic turnover and employment growth. The sales growth is predominantly from outside Sweden, however employment growth is predominantly in Sweden. Employees are hired

Table 4.5 Employees and turnover for Camp Scandinavia

Allard support for better life (Camp Scandinavia)	2006	2007	2008	2009	2010	2011	2012	2013	2014	2015
Employees (number)	59	73	80	92	124	147	161	167	180	186
Turnover (thousand €)	12,147	14,194	16,607	21,702	23,325	24,122	25,738	25,643	26,922	30,128

Source: www.allabolag.se.

Note
'Allard support for better life' is the name of the holding company, including both Swedish and international activities.

for functions such as sales, marketing and production, among others. The crucial event for the successful growth in Camp Scandinavia was the development of ToeOFF; this patented product was the base for successful international sales. The decision to invest in own production and sell the products in own sales subsidiaries and via distributors has been a successful growth strategy that has created new jobs over time. In the USA, for example, the firm increased its revenue from $4 (€3.8) million in 2006 to $13.5 (€12.1) million in 2011. The trend today is to produce more in Sweden because of the threat of designs being copied. This has led to more employees being needed for production. The CEO in Camp Scandinavia underlines the relative importance of finding the 'right personnel', and he sees finding the 'right personnel' for key positions (such as subsidiary managers) as one of the most important parts of his job. However, he has no recipe for how to find them; he says it is a 'feeling'. With the 'right personnel' working for the firm, the CEO maintains that their firm is performing well in markets such as the USA, Ireland and UK. The company has highly motivated personnel, and the leadership of the firm strongly contributes to the trustful and hardworking atmosphere in the firm. Besides their own personnel, Camp Scandinavia works with independent actors such as consultants, inventors (the firm's main products are developed in cooperation with such actors), distributors, and suppliers. The firm has also invested in an acquisition strategy, to have better control over production (acquisition of production facilities) and distribution and marketing (acquisition of sales subsidiaries) which has been part of the growth in turnover and employees.

4.6.3 Creative industries sector

Culture and creativity have been recognised as high value growth areas, with an increasing number of employees, and economic contributors for knowledge-based economies built upon creation and innovation (Florida, 2006). The EU has also begun to quantify and measure the creative industries in a green paper entitled: 'Unlocking the potential of cultural and creative industries' (European Commission, 2010). This report identified the creative industries as one of the key sectors in helping Europe remain competitive in the changing global market driving economic growth and job creation, due to their ability to imagine, create and innovate. This sector is highly internationalised and has shown a large number of born globals in Sweden (Kraetiv sektor, 2015).

Creative industries can be defined as 'those industries which have their origin in individual creativity, skill and talent and which have a potential for wealth and job creation through the generation and exploitation of intellectual property (Department for Culture, Media and Sport – UK, 2015). Examples of industries in this sector are film, music, fashion and game industries. The green paper highlighted the dual role of cultural and creative industries in leveraging and developing local resources, and of knowledge and creative talent to spur innovation for regional development. Hence, it has become officially recognised by industry and policy that creative industries create jobs, enhance the competitiveness of countries, cities, regions and businesses, as well as contributing to personal and social development. Furthermore, enabled by rapid advancements in digital technologies, creative industries have become highly internationalised with the result that companies become not only a national export driver, but also, highly dependent on global consumers and resources for revenue and firm growth. In terms of global export and import growth, the last decade has seen an average annual turnover rise for creative goods of over 10 per cent, while creative services have seen a global annual rise of over 13 per cent for the 10 years up to 2011 (Collins *et al.*, 2014). These trends reflect an obvious pattern of increased trade, production and demand. In the then 27 economies across the EU, creative sectors had generated 6.1 million jobs and represented 2.7 per cent of GDP in 2010 (Collins *et al.*, 2014). In Sweden over 50 per cent of the total turnover in the creative sector is export (Kraetiv sektor, 2015). Some key export growth sectors within the Swedish creative economy are fashion, music and gaming. In global terms, the fashion industry in Sweden in 2015 had a total merchandise export over five times that of 1990 figures (Statistics Sweden, 2017).

In 2014, the Swedish music industry's revenues amounted to SEK 8.2 billion (€0.8 billion) and export represented 18 per cent of the Swedish music industry's total sales. This was the highest music-export percentage value recorded since 2009, representing a 5 per cent increase compared to the previous year. Revenues from music export alone amounted to more than SEK 1.5 billion (€0.14 billion), which is an increase of 29 per cent over the previous year. The export of copyrighted music in 2014 was worth SEK 734 million (€69.7 million) and represented an increase of approximately SEK 132 million (€12.5 million) over the previous year. In the five years from 2009 to 2014, the Swedish music industry's revenues increased by nearly 25 per cent to SEK 1.6 billion (€0.15 billion), of which revenues from export were responsible for more than SEK 0.5 (€0.05 billion) The job creation is growing in this sector and, in 2013, 9,699 persons were employed in the Swedish music industry, which is 900 individuals more than in 2011 (Musiksverige, 2015). Sweden has many artists and groups that have been successful internationally, such as ABBA, Roxette, Avicci etc. However, producers and song-writers (e.g. Max Martin) have also been successful.

Finally, the Swedish gaming sector is export driven and is Sweden's most important cultural export, with 99 per cent of the gaming sales derived from abroad (Swedish Games Industry, 2015). The growth in companies, employees and turnover in the Swedish Game Industry is shown in Table 4.6.

Table 4.6 Number of companies, employees and turnover in the Swedish Games Industry

Swedish Games Industry	2011	2012	2013	2014	2015
Companies (number)	117	145	170	213	236
Employees (number)	1,512	1,967	2,534	3,117	3,709
Turnover (M€)	161	199	272	299	355

Source: Spelutvecklarindex, 2016. Available at: www.dataspelsbranschen.se/rapporter.aspx.

With Swedish game export earnings of €930 million in 2014 and a compound annual growth rate (CAGR) of 39 per cent between 2006 and 2013, Sweden is ranked one of top global computer game exporters (Swedish Games Industry, 2015). Over 70 per cent of the Swedish gaming products are completely digitalised, compared with 52 per cent in the USA. Between 2012 and 2014, turnover increased by 800 per cent (Swedish Games Industry, 2015). Rising global internet usage has led to the global trend of games being sold digitally. Swedish companies have been quick at adapting to this new digital distribution channel. According to the Swedish Games Industry (2016), Swedish companies are well positioned to grow globally. As shown in Table 4.6, the job creation is quite substantial, with 3,709 employees in 2015. A main reason for the growth in the industry is an increasing international demand. Another reason for the growth in Sweden is a mix between large and small companies and education (such as university education) focusing on game development (Swedish Games Industry, 2015). Some of the world's most played, sold and cherished games such as *Minecraft* are developed in Sweden. *Minecraft* was developed by the Swedish company Mojang in 2010. Mojang was founded in 2009, their products are distributed digitally and, from inception, the majority of sales were outside Sweden. Mojang grew to a size of 12 employees within a year and continued developing new computer games such as *Scrolls*. In 2013 the company had 28 employees. In March 2012, the company had accumulated revenues of over $80 million (€76 million). Microsoft acquired Mojang in 2014 for of $2.5 billion (€2.4billion). Compared with the enormous development in shareholder value and revenues, the industry does not create jobs at the same rate.

4.7 Discussion

The number of born globals in Sweden is limited, and those companies only employ 0.75 per cent of the overall number of employees working in Swedish SMEs. Still, born globals are important for the Swedish economy. They show higher willingness to grow and a greater employment growth than other companies (Andersson and Florén, 2011). Born globals are found in all sectors but are over-represented in high-tech sectors (Halldin, 2012a). Growth is dependent on many external and internal factors.

A very important internal factor is the growth intention of the decision makers in the firm (Andersson, 2003). Born global entrepreneurs have the capacity to find and create international opportunities. They also create firms with competitive capabilities that perform better than their counterparts who remain focused on the home market. The born globals' competitive advantage is created through networking with and learning from international partners. Knowledge and networks from different markets, information technology, inexpensive communication, and decreasing trade regulations, allow born global entrepreneurs to design, produce and distribute customised products to target narrow, cross-national market niches (Cavusgil and Knight, 2015).

Industry factors also influence firms' ability to grow abroad. International growth in industrial product industries is less complicated than in other marketing contexts, which can partly explain why 45 per cent of Swedish exports come from the manufacturing sector. It is possible to manufacture a product in one place and send it to another country while services are consumed and produced simultaneously. Digitalisation has made some services easier to distribute internationally. However, most services are still not digitally distributed. The barriers are fewer in industrial product industries than in other industries: firms do not have to grow to a large size, or have extensive external capital to be able to expand abroad. Marketing is predominantly done by personal selling and born globals are more often found in this industry. Marketing and selling is often done through personal selling and important customers are few when compared with consumer goods industries. The cost for a salesperson in the south of Sweden to visit Germany and Denmark is lower than to go north in Sweden (Andersson and Wictor, 2003; Andersson *et al.*, 2014).

Firms in consumer goods industries internationalise later than firms in industrial goods industries. It takes longer to saturate the home market as there are many consumers and, as opposed to the manufacturing sector, firms need more resources to enter a foreign market. It is not possible to start with one consumer and grow incrementally, as with industrial products. To be successful, firms need resources to build a position with enough customers to make the market entry profitable. Consumer goods are also more influenced by the local culture, which makes entry into new countries more expensive as products need to be adapted. Marketing to enter a new market is costly and often includes investments in brand building (e.g. through TV advertisements). Digitalisation has created new opportunities for firms to create new products and also new ways to distribute products. The game industry in Sweden is an example that shows how offerings built on new technologies can be distributed digitally. In the Swedish game industry, 99 per cent of the turnover is realised abroad while creating job opportunities in Sweden. More research is needed to explore how digitalisation is influencing internationalisation in different industrial contexts.

For firms producing industrial services, the individual relationships with customers are more important than national cultures and broad promotion campaigns aimed at many end-consumers. As the relationships are few compared with consumer marketing, it is possible to handle them individually. However, as services are personnel- and resource- intensive, it is not possible to internationalise as fast as in the industrial product industry.

Firms in the consumer service industry take the longest time to internationalise and need the most resources. These firms have a lot of customers at home who are easier to reach than international consumers (Andersson, 2006).

4.8 Managerial and policy implications

The discussion above shows that born global firms are a positive for job creation. Born globals have higher growth aspirations than other SMEs, and they also show a greater employment growth. Following on from that, born globals are influenced by entrepreneurs with special characteristics and a global mindset, but there are also lessons that can be learned from successful, growing born globals about a firm's strategy and organisation that can facilitate those with early and rapid internationalisation. To create new jobs, policies promoting the creation, prospering and continued international growth of born globals are useful,

Research has shown that managers in born global firms behave differently, have a different activity pattern and uphold different roles within their firms compared to managers in firms focused on domestic markets: born global mangers are less oriented towards operative work and are more proactive in using their networks. Born global managers' behaviour is often intended and planned to achieve the aim of international growth. In contrast to managers in non-international firms, the ones in international firms have made a strategic decision to grow internationally and to implement an international strategy; they have devoted time that favoured international expansion. They also often implement a decentralised organisation that could deal with operative matters, while the managers focus on building relationships with international strategic partners (Andersson and Florén, 2011). Born global entrepreneurs can work proactively with networks and stakeholders both inside and outside the focal firms to develop marketing capabilities to create international growth (Evers *et al.*, 2012).

Extant research has shown that an entrepreneurs' global mindset is positively related to the creation of born global firms (Nummela *et al.*, 2004; Andersson, 2000; Andersson and Evers, 2015). Entrepreneurs' mindset develops from birth and thus affects people's business behaviour later in life (Ghannad and Andersson, 2012). Equally, entrepreneurs can develop the needed capabilities and skills sets required for internationalisation out of various situations, as well as by necessity. Thus, education is a key area where policy makers could intervene to influence individuals' global mindset and enhance the possibility of the creation of born globals. For instance, they could promote the inclusion of international activities in different stages of education programmes. An example could be in international activities, such as exchange programmes between schools in different countries for pupils at primary and secondary levels of education. Similarly, at college and university level, this could consist of the inclusion of international elements in business and entrepreneurship courses to develop students' international business mindsets.

Many publicly financed programmes aim to develop firm capabilities for international growth, but these initiatives have received a mixed assessment among firms taking part in the programmes (some are very satisfied, while others have not experienced any added value from these programmes). Much of the criticism is that they are too general and not adapted to firms in different contexts and situations (Evers and O'Gorman, 2011; Leonidou, *et al.*, 2007). Managers and firms have different needs and motivations for taking part in these programmes. Some managers have already extensive experience and knowledge about internationalisation, but might need specific help in, for instance, entering emerging markets with different institutional contexts, while others have very little experience and need more basic support through education. In line with the discussion above, it would be fruitful for policy makers to target different types of participants for programmes that promote firms' internationalisation. For example, it could be useful to target managers with an international mindset in internationalisation programmes for firms that already have internationalisation experience. These programmes could include activities that improve both managerial human and social capital, e.g. support for taking part in trade fairs (Evers and Knight, 2008). Other types of programmes could target managers who have not started internationalisation yet. These programmes can provide basic information, but also present positive examples of internationalisation to motivate managers to implement proactive internationalisation strategies.

Moreover, different industries face different challenges from other industries when it comes to internationalisation. Along these lines, the organisation for the creative industries in Sweden argues that their industry is facing specific challenges related to dealing with digital distribution, new business models and intellectual property (Kraetiv sektor, 2015). More research and specific policy programmes targeted towards this sector are recommended.

Notes

1 Ekonomifakta is run by the Confederation of Swedish Enterprise, the Swedish private employers' central organisation. It uses both official Swedish sources of statistical information and international sources.
2 www.spotify.com.
3 www.skype.com.
4 www.business-sweden.se/Export/tjanster/born-globals.
5 In the context of the research project 'Job creation in SMEs' by the European Foundation for the Improvement of Living and Working Conditions, focusing on employment creation in born globals.
6 The Swedish Agency for Economic and Regional Growth has conducted this survey every third year since 2002. The 2014 wave of the survey was targeted towards a representative sample of SMEs in order to gain a better understanding of their view of growth opportunities, innovation and internationalisation. The data was collected by Statistics Sweden between November 2013 and March 2014. The sample was stratified according to firm size, industry, region and gender of business leader. Approximately 16,000 out of an asked 31,000 firms responded to the survey (52 per cent), including 118 born global enterprises. Weighting was applied to the analysis in this fact sheet to calculate population estimates. The results of the survey are representative for over 320,000 firms, once firms in the sampling frame but outside the target population are excluded.
7 Halldin (2011, 2012a) used three different definitions of born globals, which differ slightly to the one used for analysing the survey by the Swedish Agency for Economic and Regional Growth. However the results are very similar, showing the small number of born globals in Sweden and an overrepresentation in high-tech sectors.
8 Innehållsinnovation och internationell tillväxt i kreativa näringar, en rapport från kreativ sektor (2015).
9 http://ec.europa.eu/growth/sectors/mechanical-engineering/machinery_en. The aim of the Machinery Directive is to improve safety when using machines, removing technical

obstacles to trade and creating similar regulations within the EEA area. The 98/37/EC Directive came into force on 1 January 1995 and applies to machines manufactured after this date. Machines manufactured before 1995 must meet the minimum requirements.

References

Andersson, S. (2000), 'Internationalization of the firm from an entrepreneurial perspective', *International Studies of Management and Organization*, Vol. 30, No. 1, pp. 63–92.

Andersson, S. (2003), 'High-growth firms in the Swedish ERP industry', *Journal of Small Business and Enterprise Development*, Vol. 10, No. 2, pp. 180–193.

Andersson, S. (2006), 'International growth strategies in consumer and business-to-business markets in manufacturing and service sectors', *Journal of Euromarketing*, Vol. 15, No. 4, pp. 35–56.

Andersson, S. and Evers, N. (2015), 'International opportunity recognition in international new ventures: A dynamic managerial capabilities perspective', *Journal of International Entrepreneurship*, Vol. 13, No. 3, pp. 260–276.

Andersson, S., Evers, N. and Kuivalainen, O. (2014), 'International new ventures: rapid internationalization across different industry contexts', *European Business Review*, Vol. 26, No. 5, pp. 390–405.

Andersson, S. and Florén, H. (2011), 'Differences in managerial behavior between small international and non-international firms', *Journal of International Entrepreneurship*, Vol 9, No. 3, pp. 233–258.

Andersson, S., Gabrielsson, J. and Wictor, I. (2004), 'International activities in small firms: examining factors influencing the internationalization and export growth of small firms', *Canadian Journal of Administrative Sciences*, Vol. 21, No. 1, pp. 22–34.

Andersson, S. and Wictor, I. (2003), 'Innovative internationalisation in new firms: born globals – the Swedish case', *Journal of International Entrepreneurship*, Vol. 1, No. 3, pp. 249–276.

Autio, E., Sapienza, H. J. and Almeida, J. G. (2000), 'Effects of age at entry, knowledge intensity, and imitability on international growth', *Academy of Management Journal*, Vol. 43, No. 5, pp. 909–924.

Cavusgil, S. T. and Knight, G. A. (2015), 'The born global firm: an entrepreneurial and capabilities perspective on early and rapid internationalization', *Journal of International Business Studies*, Vol. 46, No. 1, pp. 3–16.

Collins, P. Cunningham, J. Murtagh, A. and Dagg, J. (2014), *From growth to sustainability: Supporting the development of creative economy in Europe's northern periphery. The creative edge policy toolkit*, Whitaker institute, National University of Ireland, Galway, Ireland.

Department for Culture, Media and Sport – UK (2015), *Creative industries economic estimates January 2015: statistical release*. Available at: www.gov.uk/government/statistics/creative-industries-economic-estimates-january-2015.

Ekonomifakta (2017), 'Export och import över tid' ['Exports and imports through time']. Available (in Swedish) at: www.ekonomifakta.se/sv/Fakta/Ekonomi/Utrikeshandel/Export-och-import-over-tid/.

Etemad, H. (2004), 'Internationalization of small and medium-sized enterprises: A grounded theoretical framework and an overview', *Canadian Journal of Administrative Sciences*, Vol. 21, No. 1, pp. 1–21.

Eurofound (2016), *ERM annual report 2015: Job creation in SMEs*, Publications Office of the European Union, Luxembourg.

European Commission (2010), 'Green paper: Unlocking the potential of cultural and creative industries', *EUR-Lex*, COM(2010) 183 final, Brussels. Available at: http://eurlex.europa.eu/legal-content/EN/TXT/?uri=CELEX:52010DC0183.

Evers, N., Andersson, S. and Hannibal, M. (2012), 'Stakeholders and marketing capabilities in international new ventures: Evidence from Ireland, Sweden and Denmark', *Journal of International Marketing*, Vol. 20, No. 4, pp. 46–71.

Evers, N. and Knight, K. (2008), 'Role of international trade shows in small firm internationalization: A network perspective', *International Marketing Review*, Vol. 25, No. 5, pp. 544–562.

Evers, N. and O'Gorman, C. (2011), 'Improvised internationalization in new ventures: The role of prior knowledge and networks', *Entrepreneurship and Regional Development*, Vol. 23, No. 7–8, pp. 549–574.

Florida, R. (2006), *The flight of the creative class: New global competition for talent*, HarperBusiness, New York.

Gabrielsson, P. and Gabrielsson, M. (2013), 'A dynamic model of growth phases and survival in international business-to-business new ventures: The moderating effect of decision-making logic', *Industrial Marketing Management*, Vol. 42, No. 8, pp. 1357–1373.

Ghannad, N., and Andersson, S. (2012), 'The influence of the entrepreneur's background on the behaviour and development of born globals' internationalisation processes', *International Journal of Entrepreneurship and Small Business*, Vol. 15, No. 2, pp. 136–153.

Hagen, B. and Zucchella, A. (2014), 'Born global or born to run? The long-term growth of born global firms', *Management International Review*, Vol. 54, No. 4, pp. 497–525.

Halldin, T. (2011), 'Born global firms in knowledge intensive business services (KIBS): What do we know of their performance?' *Cesis Working Paper*, Royal Institute of Technology, Stockholm.

Halldin, T. (2012a), 'Born global firms: Do they perform differently?' *Cesis Working Paper*, Royal Institute of Technology, Stockholm.

Halldin, T. (2012b), *Born globals*, Globaliseringsforum Rapport #3, Entreprenörskaps forum, Stockholm.

Knight, G. A. (1997), *Emerging paradigm for international marketing: The born global firm*, PhD Dissertation, Michigan State University. Department of Marketing and Supply Chain Management.

Knight, G. A. and Cavusgil, S. T. (2004), 'Innovation, organizational capabilities, and the born global firm', *Journal of International Business Studies*, Vol. 35, No. 2, pp. 124–141.

Kraetiv sektor (2015), *Innehållsinnovation och internationell tillväxt i kreativa näringar*. Available at: http://kreativsektor.se/.

Leonidou, L. C., Katsikeas, C. S., Palihawadana, D. and Spyropoulou, S. (2007), 'An analytical review of the factors stimulating smaller firms to export: implications for policy-makers', *International Marketing Review*, Vol. 24, No. 6, pp. 735–770.

Melén Hånell, S., Rovira Nordman, E. and Sharma, D. D. (2014), 'The continued internationalisation of an international new venture', *European Business Review*, Vol. 26, No. 5, pp. 471–490.

Miller, D. and Friesen, P. H. (1984), *Organizations: A quantum view*, Prentice Hall: Englewood Cliffs, NJ.

Musiksverige (2015), *The Music Industry in Numbers*. Available at: www.musiksverige.org/.

Nummela, N., Saarenketo, S. and Puumalainen, K. (2004), 'Global mindset: A prerequisite for successful internationalisation?' *Canadian Journal of Administrative Sciences*, Vol. 21, No. 1, pp. 51–64.

OECD (1997), *Globalization and small and medium enterprises (SMEs)*, OECD publishing, Paris.

Oviatt, B. M. and McDougall, P. P. (1994), 'Toward a theory of international new ventures', *Journal of International Business Studies*, Vol. 25, No. 1, pp. 45–64.

Statistics Sweden (2017), *Företagens ekonomi* [Structural Business Statistics]. Available (in Swedish) at: www.scb.se/sv_/Hitta-statistik/Statistik-efter-amne/Naringsverksamhet/Naringslivets-struktur/Foretagens-ekonomi/.

Swedish Games Industry (2015), *Game Developer Index 2015*, Stockholm.

Swedish Games Industry (2016), *Game Developer Index 2016*, Stockholm.

5 Employment and job creation in born global enterprises in Austria

Thomas Oberholzner and Andrea Dorr

5.1 Introduction

In times of low or negative employment growth, high unemployment, and the bulk of the general business population experiencing stagnation or even job reductions, economic policy and research become increasingly interested in specific segments of enterprises with high growth potential. One such particular group are so-called born globals, i.e. young – often innovation-driven – companies which strongly engage in international activities and markets from their foundation. Previous research (for example Eurofound, 2016; Eurofound, 2012) have pointed to various positive labour market impacts of this company type, including not only job creation in quantitative terms, but also relatively high job quality, sustainability of jobs and wage levels.

In Austria, several studies have also underlined that early international orientation and extending business to foreign markets are important for young firms and start-ups to achieve high growth and a significant employment impact, and well targeted policy support for internationalisation activities of start-ups has been called for (Pöchhacker-Tröscher and Lefenda, 2013; Kemler *et al.*, 2016; Hölzl *et al.*, 2010; Bachinger *et al.*, 2016). Indeed, in their strategy document 'Land der Gründer' (Country of Founders), the Austrian Federal Ministry of Science, Research and Economy have included a dedicated chapter on 'Going Global' of young and newly founded enterprises and have proposed a broad set of measures to create and support born globals (Bundesministerium für Wissenschaft, Forschung und Wirtschaft, 2015). Increased public and policy attention to born globals in Austria is furthermore reflected, for example, in the award (and corresponding brochure) 'Austria's Born Global Champions' which was introduced by the Austrian Federal Economic Chamber in 2015 (Austrian Federal Economic Chamber, 2016).

In spite of the recent policy attention they received, little is actually known about the size, structure and behaviour of born globals in Austria, while related phenomena such as 'start-ups' and 'gazelles' have already been the subject of studies and empirical analyses. Against this backdrop, this chapter intends to fill some of the evidence gap and in particular contribute to the following research questions:

- What is the size and structural characteristics of the born globals segment in Austria?
- What is their entrepreneurial behaviour and strategic orientation?
- What types of jobs do they create? What type of workers do they need? What barriers do they face in relation to job creation and recruitment?
- What recruitment and general human resources (HR) management procedures do they use?
- How could they be supported with recruitment and job creation?

This chapter uses two sources of data to investigate the above-mentioned questions. First, it draws upon a general online survey of SMEs – i.e. enterprises with fewer than 250 persons employed – conducted by the Austrian Institute for SME Research on behalf of the Austrian Federal Economic Chamber in May 2013. While that survey was not specifically designed to examine born globals, it still aids the identification of young firms that are highly internationalised. The survey covered all important market-oriented sectors and industries[1] but excluded others such as education, health, arts and entertainment, and some personal services. The sample of businesses was drawn randomly from the Chamber's register[2] and the final dataset encompasses a total of 2,492 observations (SMEs). To improve representativeness, the data have been weighted using the combined size and industry structure of the enterprise population according to the 'Structural Business Statistics' of the Austrian Statistical Office. Second, this chapter analyses five detailed company case studies of born globals in Austria, which have been carried out in 2015 in the context of a Eurofound project on 'Job Creation in SMEs' (2016). Table 5.1 gives a brief overview of these case studies. Further information on the companies is provided in the Annex.

The remainder of this chapter is organised as follows: section 5.2 discusses the size and some structural characteristics of the group of born globals in Austria, based on the survey data mentioned above. Section 5.3 looks at the strategies in terms of business goals and at the key factors determining the performance of born globals. Section 5.4 discusses what types of jobs are created and what personnel are needed by born globals, while section 5.5 scrutinises in detail the specific recruitment procedures applied by born globals. Section 5.6 focuses on what is hampering the creation of jobs and recruitment of workers in those companies. Actual and potential (external) support for recruiting is dealt with in Section 5.7. Finally, in Section 5.8 key results of this chapter and relevant policy pointers are discussed.

5.2 Mapping and characterising born globals in Austria

A born global is understood as a firm with high activity in international markets from or shortly after its foundation. However, at a more operational level, there is no generally agreed and concerted definition of born globals, e.g. in terms of the extent of international activity or the age when that activity begins. In their project on born globals, Eurofound have proposed *inter alia* the following criteria:

Table 5.1 Overview of company case studies

Company name	Start-up date	Industry, products	Headcount at time of interview (2015)	International activity at time of interview (2015)
ecoduna AG	2010	Industrial-scale production of biomass (algae-culture)	30	Pilot projects in Germany and Denmark
Evercyte GmbH	2011	Licensing of single cell lines for research and screening procedures	12	Export ratio > 90%
FRESNEX GmbH	2012	Mirror module using concentrated solar power (CSP) technology in small-scale applications	6	Starting off
Power Units GmbH	2008	Three-phase electronic lamp power supplies	3	Export ratio = 100%
seamtec GmbH	2009	Turbine control systems for hydro-electric power plants	6	Project-based; export ratio 75%–90%

the company should not be older than five years[3]; it should have an export share of at least 25 per cent of total sales during at least two of these first five years; and it should be active in at least two foreign countries (Eurofound, 2012).[4] However, the Austrian SME survey data from 2013 do not allow full compliance with that definition. In the dataset, born globals have been specified as follows:

1   SMEs that have been founded in 2007 or later (which implies that some firms may be a little older than five years), and
2   had an export share of at least 25 per cent in 2012 (whether that threshold was also exceeded in another year and whether there were exports to at least two countries cannot be confirmed by the available data).

Those SMEs that fulfil only the first criterion (date of founding) will be referred to as 'young enterprises'. In the analysis, this group is used for the purpose of comparison when relevant.

5.2.1 The number and share of born globals

Table 5.2 shows the number of born globals and their percentage share in the survey's total sample of SMEs as well as an extrapolation to the overall SME population. Approximately 4.8 per cent of all Austrian SMEs qualify as born globals and almost 30 per cent qualify as young enterprises according to the above definitions. This also means that approximately 16 per cent of all young enterprises constitute born globals. In order to estimate their numbers in the actual total population, the total number of SMEs according to the official Structural Business Statistics has been used as a reference basis. This would result in about 15,000 born globals in Austria in 2013.

5.2.2 Prevalence of born globals by sector

Because of the limited size of the sub-sample of born globals in the survey data (120 observations) any results disaggregated by sectors are of relatively low

Table 5.2 Number and share of born globals in Austria in 2013

	Number of enterprises in sample	Share of enterprises in total sample (%)	Estimated number of enterprises in overall SME population
SMEs	2,492	100.0	313,500
Young enterprises	732	29.4	92,200
Born globals	120	4.8	15,000

Source: Survey of Austrian Institute for SME Research on behalf of the Austrian Federal Economic Chamber, 2013.

Table 5.3 Share of born globals by sector in Austria in 2013

	Share of young enterprises among the sector's SMEs (%)	Share of born globals among the sector's SMEs (%)
Mining, quarrying, manufacturing, utilities (NACE B–E)	21.7	4.0
Construction (NACE F)	19.6	0.3
Wholesale and retail trade (NACE G)	26.5	5.7
Transportation; financial and insurance services; real estate (NACE H, K, L)	34.5	5.1
Accommodation and food service activities (NACE I)	23.7	0.5
Information and communication, professional, scientific and technical activities (NACE J, M)	42.1	9.7

Source: Survey of Austrian Institute for SME Research on behalf of the Austrian Federal Economic Chamber, 2013.

reliability and of only tentative nature. Nevertheless, Table 5.3 presents the relative prevalence of born globals by very broad sectors.

From the Table it is apparent that the incidence of born globals differs markedly between sectors. The by far highest share of young enterprises as well as born globals can be found in information and communication, professional, scientific and technical activities (NACE J, M). Almost 10 per cent of SMEs qualify as born globals in this group of industries. Second ranked is wholesale and retail trade (NACE G) with a born global incidence of almost 6 per cent. Presumably wholesale in particular is certainly often internationally oriented. The group of industries consisting of transportation, financial and insurance services, and real estate (NACE H, K, L) also includes sectors with a significant propensity to international business, notably the transportation sector. The manufacturing sector (NACE B–E) shows a medium incidence of born globals of around 4 per cent. In construction (NACE F), and accommodation and food service activities (NACE I) born globals are quite rare. In general, the variance of the born global incidence over sectors is mainly due to differences in internationalisation propensity and, to a lesser extent, to differences in the age structure.

5.2.3 Size and workforce of born globals

With respect to the size – in terms of employment – of Austrian born globals the analysis of the SME survey data reveals that born globals are on average smaller than the overall SME population. Table 5.4 shows that the mean number of persons employed in born globals is 3.9 compared to 6.2 in the entire SME

Table 5.4 Percentage distribution of enterprises over size categories and average enterprise size in 2013, Austria

	Born globals	Young enterprises	All SMEs
1 person employed	57.9%	55.4%	36.4%
2–9 persons employed	35.2%	40.5%	51.3%
10–49 persons employed	6.1%	4.0%	10.6%
50–249 persons employed	0.8%	0.2%	1.8%
All size categories	100.0%	100.0%	100.0%
Mean number of persons employed	3.9	3.1	6.2

Source: Survey of Austrian Institute for SME Research on behalf of the Austrian Federal Economic Chamber, 2013.

sector. This is also reflected by the distribution patterns over size categories presented in the Table. A very large part (57.9 per cent) of born globals consists of one-person enterprises. One reason for their very small size is, of course, that they (by definition) are very young. Another reason is their strong prevalence in sectors such as ICT, where even solo-entrepreneurs can in fact operate on international markets. However, comparing born globals with young enterprises in general, and therefore controlling for enterprise age, shows that the probability of growing into a small or medium-sized firm (more than 10 persons employed) within the first five years of existence is somewhat higher for born globals than for nationally oriented starters.

When measuring size by turnover it can be observed that born globals have a significant edge over other young enterprises. For instance, while 37 per cent of born globals reported an annual turnover above €250,000 this is true for only 21 per cent of young enterprises overall. Again a sector effect might play a role as born globals are over-proportionally prevalent in wholesale where high sales volumes can go along with relatively low input of labour.

5.2.4 Innovation activity of born globals

The literature on born globals suggests born globals to be more innovative than SMEs on average. Based on the survey data of Austrian SMEs, Figure 5.1 depicts the share of enterprises having introduced innovations, distinguishing between born globals, young enterprises and SMEs overall. Indeed, born globals appear to be slightly more innovative than SMEs and young enterprises in general. However, significant differences can be found mainly for process and product innovations, where the share of born globals implementing such novelties is 10 percentage points higher than for the other two groups of enterprises. With a view to organisational and service innovations there is no significant difference in innovation activity between company types.

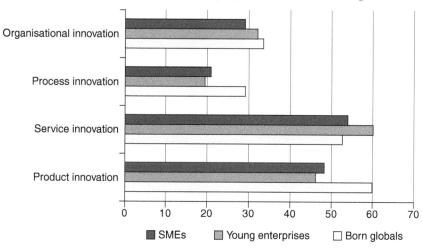

Figure 5.1 Share of enterprises having introduced innovations in 2010–2012, by type of innovation, Austria.

Source: Survey of Austrian Institute for SME Research on behalf of the Austrian Federal Economic Chamber, 2013.

5.2.5 Owners and managers of born globals

Table 5.5 looks at the owners/managers of born globals in Austria.[5] With regard to gender, the share of female entrepreneurs is around one-fifth and seems to be slightly lower in born globals as compared to SMEs or young enterprises in general. This may be due to a sector effect, i.e. the high concentration of born globals in the ICT, transportation and manufacturing sectors which are traditionally male-dominated industries. The average age of the born global entrepreneurs is 46 years and there are no significant differences compared to the general SME population in this respect. More striking however are the differences in educational backgrounds: around half of the born global entrepreneurs have completed tertiary education while this is the case for only approximately 20 per cent of entrepreneurs in the overall SME population and 30 per cent of entrepreneurs in young enterprises in general. Conversely, while dual vocational education is the most frequent educational background of SME entrepreneurs in general (almost 40 per cent), this can hardly be found among born global entrepreneurs (frequency of less than 10 per cent).

5.2.6 Growth performance of born globals

The SME survey of 2013 also looked into the enterprises' development between 2010 and 2012.[6] In accordance with the classical business life-cycle model one would expect that (surviving) young enterprises – including born globals – perform better than the average SME population, which includes many mature

Table 5.5 Key features of owners and managers by type of enterprise in 2013, Austria

	Born globals	Young enterprises	All SMEs
Woman-led enterprises	21.2%	25.5%	25.3%
Mean age of owner/manager	46 years	43 years	47 years
Owner/manager with dual vocational education (apprenticeship)	9.2%	34.6%	38.3%
Owner/manager with higher secondary vocational education	30.4%	17.6%	19.8%
Owner/manager with tertiary education	52.5%	29.2%	21.1%

Source: Survey of Austrian Institute for SME Research on behalf of the Austrian Federal Economic Chamber, 2013.

companies (Eurofound, 2016). In terms of turnover growth, this is confirmed in Figure 5.2: the share of growing enterprises is higher within the group of young firms than in the overall SME population, and the opposite is true for the share of shrinking firms. However, born globals performed even better than nationally oriented young enterprises. More specifically, Figure 5.2 shows that the main difference is the share of firms reporting a strong increase of turnover from 2010 to 2012. That share was around 50 per cent for born globals, but only about 35 per cent for young enterprises in general. This seems to confirm the above observation that the probability of significant growth within the first five years of existence is higher for born globals than for nationally oriented starters.

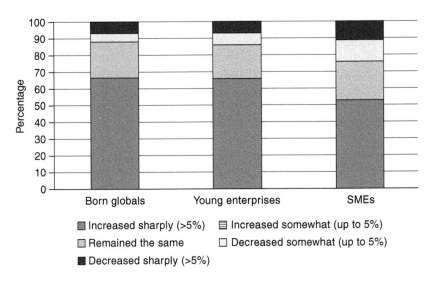

Figure 5.2 Development of turnover between 2010 and 2012 (share of enterprises by growth categories), Austria.

Source: Survey of Austrian Institute for SME Research on behalf of the Austrian Federal Economic Chamber, 2013.

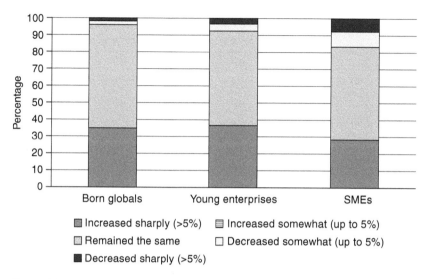

Figure 5.3 Development of staff headcount between 2010 and 2012 (share of enterprises by growth categories), Austria.

Source: Survey of Austrian Institute for SME Research on behalf of the Austrian Federal Economic Chamber, 2013.

In terms of staff headcount, growth patterns are much more modest (see Figure 5.3). The clear majority of companies in all groups (SMEs overall, young enterprises, and born globals) reported stable employment numbers, even though increases were somewhat more frequent among the younger ones, including born globals. It is again born globals where *significant* employment growth happens most often (27 per cent). However, when comparing turnover growth and employment growth it is apparent that even strong increases in sales are not necessarily immediately associated with the creation of new jobs. There may possibly be a lagged effect on employment, which could not be captured by the relatively short period of observation (two years) of the survey.

5.3 Strategic orientation of born globals

The previous section mainly looked into various structural characteristics of born globals in Austria. This section will shed some light on the strategic orientation and behaviour of born globals. The SME survey of 2013 provides information on the attitudes and goals of the surveyed owners and managers using a scale from one to six where one and six represent two opposite poles or extremes (see Table 5.6). Born globals differ from the general population of SMEs or young enterprises in three ways: first of all, they feature a higher inclination to *innovation and change*, i.e. they focus more on developing new areas of business (average grade = 3.84), act more often as pioneers or at least perceive themselves

Table 5.6 Average position (mean) of business owners/managers for the stated strategic
orientations on a scale from 1 to 6, Austria

	Born globals	Young enterprises	All SMEs
Focus on maintaining existing areas of business (1) vs. developing new areas of business (6)	3.84	3.33	3.02
Focus on continuing with established practices (1) vs. readiness for change (6)	4.69	4.20	3.85
Relying on externals (1) vs. relying on own capacities (6) to develop business	4.34	4.37	4.41
Focus on low-risk projects (1) vs. high-risk/yield projects (6)	2.81	2.44	2.21
Rarely pioneer (1) vs. often pioneer (6) with introducing new products and services	4.47	3.86	3.73
Aiming at growth and expansion (1) vs. stability (6)	3.13	3.55	3.88
Business strategy is very informal (1) vs. very formal (6)	2.88	3.01	3.16
Great latitude (1) vs. little latitude (6) given to individuals and teams	2.16	2.34	2.42

Source: Survey of Austrian Institute for SME Research on behalf of the Austrian Federal Economic
Chamber, 2013.

so (4.47), and are more open to change (4.69). This is in line with the higher
incidence of implemented innovations reported in the preceding section. Second,
born globals or their entrepreneurs are more oriented towards *growth and expansion* (3.13) than SMEs in general. Finally, they have a higher readiness to pursue
more risky projects (2.81). However their score in that category is still rather on
the low-risk side of the scale, so that one could speak about a somewhat *lower
risk aversion* rather than about pronounced risk-friendliness.

With a view to their staff, born globals attach great importance to the quality
of their human resources. This is regarded as a most crucial factor of competitiveness by approximately 45 per cent of born globals (see Figure 5.4). Among
the overall SME population this view is shared by only 35 per cent. However,
considering the high proportion of one-person enterprises among born globals
(see Section 5.1) the difference between these percentages becomes even more
remarkable and strongly underlines the importance of staff for born globals.

5.4 Types of jobs created and personnel needed by born globals

Even though not all born globals experience strong growth and many of them
actually may remain very small, the previous sections have flagged that for this

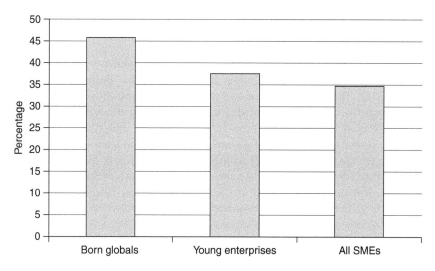

Figure 5.4 Share of enterprises stating that quality of human resources is very important for the firm's competitiveness, Austria.

Source: Survey of Austrian Institute for SME Research on behalf of the Austrian Federal Economic Chamber, 2013.

type of enterprise the likelihood of significant (employment) growth is higher than for other groups of businesses. It was also shown that born globals may have higher requirements with respect to human resources, e.g. in terms of workers' competencies and capabilities. This may be because of, amongst others, their inclination to innovation and change. Both, potential quantitative growth and personnel requirements, imply a risk for born globals to face in bottlenecks when creating jobs and recruiting people. This section looks more closely at five exemplary born global enterprises[7] from Austria to better understand the jobs and labour needs of this type of firms.

ecoduna, a producer of algae-culture, employed a team of 30 in 2015. Because of the company's growth, the headcount has doubled since 2013, which also means that the company has continuously been engaged in recruiting and restructuring work organisation and processes. Five employees (with university education) come from foreign countries. The majority of employees are highly educated construction and facility engineers as well as biologists.

Evercyte, offering cell-based products, had nine employees in 2015 (mainly women, about 30 years old and of Austrian nationality). Two of them are working in the office as a secretary and as administrative staff. Another one is active in the field of business development concentrating on new markets and clients, and six scientists are employed in the laboratory (all of them are university graduates). In addition there are three owner-managers, two male and one female. A very good knowledge of the English language is mandatory for

Evercyte's employees. Working arrangements for the employees are highly flexible and they are closely involved in strategic decision-making. Because of the company's growth, work organisation, task allocation and work flows need to be continuously adjusted.

FRESNEX, active in the solar power business, employed four staff members (two men and two women) to work alongside the two owner-managers in summer 2015. The first job created was that of an administrative assistant (part-time). Next, two employees were employed to work in the field of technical product development. Both of them have a university education. The fourth employee works on experimental set-ups (part-time). The team is quite young: the managers and one of the staff members are in their early forties, the other three staff members are around 30 years old. One of them is Spanish and also works on developing the Spanish market; the others are Austrian, but one of them has English as a native language and was raised in the US. FRESNEX consciously focuses on diversity in their recruitments: they have a female technical production specialist (although women are rare in this kind of occupation) and a foreign origin is generally seen as an asset for job candidates. The FRESNEX management underlines that recruitment is very much related to the company's strategy to innovate and internationalise. Work organisation is characterised by high working time flexibility, great autonomy and informality, and continuous change.

Power Units, producing innovative lamp power supplies, had two technical production workers (one man and one woman) with completed apprenticeship education as well as one female apprentice in 2015. In addition to that, the three owner-managers, all male, are also involved in the day-to-day business. The apprentice is trained as an office assistant and provides administrative support, including communication in English. Employees were being hired from 2010 when the company started serial production. In the prior product development phase it was not possible to employ workers because of financial reasons. The development work was exclusively done by the owner-managers without any significant remuneration.

seamtec, which produces turbine control systems for hydro-electric power plants, increased their number of employees from one in 2012 to six in 2015 (five men and one woman) as a result of growing demand for their products. The employees are aged between 20 and 32 years and of Austrian nationality. While the woman is working as an office assistant, all the men have a technical education background (apprenticeship or higher secondary vocational school) and perform production tasks including electrical planning, product development and assembling. Their young age is considered to facilitate creating innovations on a continuous basis. Some of the employees (especially the technicians and assembly workers) need to work at the construction sites of power plants in different countries. There, a highly competent team is seen to be essential to gain acceptance on the market. All employees need to be able to speak English.

In a synopsis of the five cases, the labour needs of born globals can be summarised as follows:

- The companies are usually founded by one to three individuals, who engage heavily in the development and commercialisation of an innovative product which can take several years. When product development and commercialisation are successful, the company finds its market, starts growing, and the work tasks change. This triggers a need for personnel in two ways:

  - In the first place, there is usually a need for additional technicians and scientists to be able to produce at a larger scale. Often tertiary education levels are required as the products are complex. However, depending on the product, there is also a need for technicians with apprenticeship or vocational school education.
  - Second, the born globals also require, to some extent, administrative support staff to disburden the owner-managers of administrative tasks as they need to change their focus of work as the company grows.

- Some born globals explicitly value having workers from foreign countries, i.e. with a migration background, in the team. This is partly because of their language capabilities and their ties to target markets, but more generally because diversity is seen to be conducive to a climate of innovation.
- For the same reason, some born globals seem to prefer relatively young people in their teams. Young people may be regarded as more adaptable to an environment of constant change (e.g. adjustments of work organisation, high flexibility). In turn, most born globals grant high flexibility and autonomy to their employees. This is also in line with the survey results shown in Section 5.3, Table 5.6, indicating that born globals give slightly more scope in discretion to their employees in terms of how to organise work or achieve results.
- Depending on the nature of the business, the worker's willingness to travel and work abroad – either on projects or to visit trade fairs and customers – is a condition for some born globals. In most of the born globals a good knowledge of English is important.

5.5 Recruitment practices used

Section 5.5 deals with the specific management practices applied by born globals in the context of recruitment. A key question is to which extent born globals use formalised and standardised procedures or more informal, ad-hoc and situational approaches. In general one would expect that the smaller the company the more informal their HR management practices will be (Eurofound, 2016).

At **ecoduna**, the assessment of HR needs is done by the CEO by estimating the current and future workload based on projects to be delivered. The CEO is in touch with his staff on a day-to-day basis and is therefore up-to-date at any time with regard to their workload. In addition there are regular unit meetings where not only workload but also skills required for each project are discussed. In case there are capacity gaps the CEO first of all scrutinises whether the workload could be coped with by changing work organisation and procedures. If not, short term gaps may be temporarily filled with the help of partner organisations, while medium to long term gaps will be filled by new employees. Job profiles and vacancy notes are then drafted by the CEO and published on large internet platforms. For young graduates they also approach relevant institutes of universities (e.g. for biologists). International job platforms or platforms in foreign countries are not used by ecoduna, i.e. they do not actively look for staff outside Austria. The number of applications depends on the profile; there may be only very few for very specific profiles. The first round of screening of CVs is done by the CEO's assistant based on clear minimum requirements (e.g. education). The best candidates are then invited for a personal interview with the CEO and possibly the Chief Technology Officer (CTO). Interestingly, the interviewed candidates are then asked to again confirm their interest within a few days. The CEO will then hold a second round of interviews with the top three candidates. Based on this, the CEO will take the final decision. No written tests are used. On average recruitment processes take approximately two months from kick-off to decision.

At **Evercyte**, job profiles for recruitments are discussed among all staff and on the basis of the business plan. Most recruitment refers to scientific and research staff and for publishing these job postings they primarily make use of the free online platform of the Austrian Association of Molecular Life Sciences and Biotechnology. The platform of the Public Employment Service is seen as less useful for highly qualified personnel. Also, they do not use HR consultants. So far recruiting had a regional/national focus but this may change in the future. A small 'committee' is formed, consisting of the management and selected employees, to establish a ranking of candidates based on the CVs and other documents. Around five candidates are then invited for the first round of interviews, which are conducted by two employees of Evercyte. Written tests are not used. Three candidates then get to the second round of interviews, which are conducted by other employees not involved in the first round. A separate interview is done by the CEO who focusses on the personality rather than on technical knowledge. After the interviews all employees involved in the selection process hold a meeting to agree on a final decision in a democratic way. A recruitment process usually takes two months altogether. For the first three months new employees have a temporary contract. In that period Evercyte are able to check the skills of the newcomer at work and to observe their integration into the team.

At **FRESNEX**, personnel needs are identified by the two managers. It is them who draw up a job description and a vacancy note. They try to recruit as much as possible through their professional and personal networks and via universities in particular. They also use the platforms of the Public Employment Service (for administrative staff) and of student networks (e.g. IAESTE) as well as social media. For technical occupations it is difficult for FRESNEX to attract a reasonable number of applications. A first screening of applications is carried out by the CEO. Three to five candidates are then invited for a personal interview with the two managers. The interview focusses on the personality of the candidates. After the first round, the two managers agree on the most promising applicant and invite him/her for a second interview. The second interview serves the purpose of verifying their first impression of the candidate. It also covers practical issues such as the salary and other contractual aspects. The recruitment process from start to decision usually takes three months.

At **Power Units**, personnel needs are assessed by the owner-manager on the basis of work orders and the associated workload. Vacancies are published in newspapers as well as on internet platforms. Power Units also uses the Public Employment Services, including a pre-selection service. Geographically they focus on the regional level including the German and Swiss border regions. In terms of qualifications, most of the recruitments require completed apprenticeship education in electronics, and here the number of applications is usually limited. About five candidates are usually invited for an interview by the owner-manager. In the interview the focus is on the candidate's personality, motivation, behaviour and how he or she will fit into the team. Prior work experience is also high on the interview agenda. One to three candidates are then invited for a second interview with all three managers of the company. Subsequently a final decision is taken. In general, new employees need a training period of six months to become fully acquainted with the production process.

At **seamtec**, the owner-manager is responsible for the whole recruitment process and the identification of any personnel need. He is regularly in touch with his employees with regard to their workload and the possible need for additional staff. The first step in a recruitment process is making use of the personal networks to find candidates. Furthermore, seamtec uses the services of the Public Employment Service. On one occasion, they have also used a temporary work agency. Geographically the focus is on the regional level. Next to the above-mentioned channels, job advertisements are placed in regional newspapers and on internet platforms. After the screening of applications with a focus on education and work experience, the owner-manager conducts interviews with up to five candidates. The interviews concentrate on the candidate's personality and ability to learn as well as on their prior work experience. The candidates' (non-verbal) behaviour during the interview also influences the decision. Often other seamtec employees participate in the interviews to assess whether the candidate would fit into the team. In addition to the interview, the applicants also have to complete various tests related to technical questions and problem solving. Some may even be asked to produce a specimen piece.

Table 5.7 provides an overview of the recruitment practices of the five exemplary born globals. Overall, the recruitment processes are very much driven by and centred on the owner-managers of the enterprises. Only in one of the companies is there a strong involvement and participation of other employees in defining the job profiles, screening and ranking the CVs, and decision making. In two companies, employees participate in job interviews. The need for additional personnel is usually identified by the owner-managers on the basis of the order situation, their close involvement in day-to-day business, and regular exchange with their staff. In terms of dissemination channels for vacancies, a broad variety is being used, but somewhat surprisingly, there is hardly any search activity outside Austria, although the firms obviously value a workforce

Table 5.7 Overview of recruitment practices

	ecodama	Evercyte	FRESNEX	P.U.	seamtec
Identifying need of personnel	Owners/managers	Owners/managers	Owners/managers	Owners/managers	Owners/managers
Defining job profile	Owners/managers	All staff	Owners/managers	Owners/managers	Owners/managers
Dissemination	Online platforms	Personal networks			
Relevant university departments	Profession-specific online platform				
Students platforms					
Social media	Online platforms				
Newspapers	Personal networks				
Online platforms					
Newspapers					
International dissemination	No	Planned	No	No	No
Use of Public Employment Service	No	Rarely	Yes (admin staff)	Yes	Yes
Use of HR consultants	No	No	No	No	No
CV screening	Assistant	Committee including staff	Owners/managers	Owners/managers	Owners/managers
First round interviews	Owners/managers	Selected employees	Owners/managers	Owners/managers	Owners/managers
Selected employees					
Second round interviews	Owners/managers	Owners/managers, selected employees	Owners/managers	Owners/managers	–
Focus of interviews	–	Various	Personality	Personality	
Motivation					
Behaviour					
Work experience	Personality				
Ability to learn					
Work experience					
Tests	No	No	No	No	Yes
Final decision	Owners/managers	Owners/managers, selected employees	Owners/managers	Owners/managers	Owners/managers
Duration of process	2 months	2 months	3 months	–	–

Source: compiled by the author.

of diverse nationalities (see above) and some experience difficulties in attracting an appropriate number of applicants. The services of the Public Employment Service are used mainly in the case of administrative jobs and/or lower education levels, but not when searching for highly qualified people (tertiary education). None of the born globals uses HR consultants. Written tests are used by only one of the companies.

5.6 Barriers to job creation and recruiting

Successful and growing born globals may have significant and specific labour needs as was shown in previous sections. This section investigates, on the basis of the five case studies of born globals, the major bottlenecks these companies face in meeting these needs and therefore in creating jobs.

ecoduna has been investing heavily in technology and product development and therefore needs pre-financing of its activities. This is also a condition for recruiting the employees needed. In this respect, ecoduna experienced a lack of support from the banking sector. Loan conditions are seen to have recently become more restrictive, for example in regard to high collateral requirements that cannot be met by an innovative start-up. Banks are seen to be increasingly reluctant to support investments which are deemed risky, making it difficult for young and innovative companies lacking significant tangible assets and proven track record to access funds.

FRESNEX has experienced two major challenges and difficulties in hiring employees and creating jobs: first, due to limited financial means in the start-up phase, they could initially only offer part-time jobs. However, it was difficult to find highly qualified experts willing to work on a part-time basis. Another challenge is that employing additional workers also means expanding the premises. A flexible solution would be ideal for the company, where one hires a small location in the beginning with the possibility of later extension to accommodate a larger number of employees in the same building. This would help to avoid searching for alternative premises and moving in each growth phase. This is particularly burdensome because getting new facilities approved by authorities is very time-consuming for the managers, may impede the company's development, or can even halt operations causing adverse financial effects.

seamtec also faced various difficulties with recruitment and job creation. One challenge referred to the time and efforts needed for the induction of new employees. Especially in the case of his first employee, the owner had to keep the daily business going and train the new employee in parallel. A second barrier is the increasing administrative burden, including payroll accounting and the need to implement a clock system. In particular, complying with the Austrian Working Time Act and the special regulations for employees who are working abroad is challenging. There is often a conflict between the maximum hours per day permitted and the desire of employees to complete their work and return home as quickly as possible.

Evercyte pointed to the high incidental wage costs in Austria as the most important barrier to creating new jobs. **Power Units** did not report any significant barriers in finding suitable employees.

So, from the case studies, the barriers to job creation and recruiting faced by born globals may be pinpointed as follows:

- Innovative and technology-oriented born globals often start with relatively long phases of technology and product development with no cash flow from sales coming in. In these phases it is difficult to raise the funds needed to pay employees, especially highly qualified experts and/or full-time workers. Employee participation models have been suggested as an alternative way to attract and retain such experts (Bachinger *et al.*, 2016).
- Another challenge specific to high-growth born globals is related to workspace. New or additional workspace has to be made available for each additional worker. However, adaptations of or changing premises is often difficult and burdensome in terms of administrative procedures. This could limit the creation of new jobs or make born globals reluctant to do so.
- Employing workers also increases red tape and regulations which must be complied with. Labour regulations are even more demanding for employees sent to work abroad temporarily, which is often required in born globals.

5.7 Support for recruitment and job creation

Finally, this section looks at the use of (public) support by born globals in the context of creating jobs and recruitment. Born globals are an innovative type of business and often invest significantly in technology development, which is also true for many of the case examples presented in this chapter. They often receive public financial support for their development and research projects, which makes it possible to engage employees and create jobs. However, here the intended focus is on support which is more directly related to (the process of) employing workers.

For some of the born globals investigated here it is important to use matching services and search platforms which are free of charge. Some (e.g. FRESNEX and Power Units) have used the free matching and pre-selection services of the Public Employment Service with good results. However, as far as highly qualified engineers and scientists are concerned, the Public Employment Service – which focuses on unemployed people – can hardly offer suitable candidates. For example, both ecoduna and Evercyte sought the support of the Public Employment Service with a view to getting candidates for their vacancies. In both instances the Public Employment Service could not come up with candidates meeting the companies' requirements. Thus, the usefulness of their support services seems to be somewhat limited for born globals with a need for highly qualified personnel.

One of the born globals made use of a subsidy for non-wage labour costs for their very first employee. The amount, however, was regarded as too small to really make a difference. Another company used a quite significant subsidy for employing long-term unemployed offered by the Public Employment Service. Although the subsidy cannot compensate for any skills deficits, it may tip the scales in favour of the unemployed if there are two equally qualified candidates.

In terms of information and advice, one company uses the support of the Chamber of Commerce. They have provided detailed and helpful advice on registration of employees, social insurance of employees, flexible working hours, and assisted with designing employment contracts. Another born global would appreciate the offer (by the Chamber or other organisations) of short seminars on recruitment, covering issues such as phrasing job postings, effective dissemination channels or employer branding.

5.8 Key results and policy pointers

Born globals, young companies which strongly engage in international markets early on, have recently received increasing policy attention as a potential source of growth and employment creation. Based on an enterprise survey conducted in 2013 and using a definition suggested by Eurofound (Eurofound, 2012) it is estimated that born globals account for almost 5 per cent of total SMEs or 16 per cent of all young enterprises in Austria. Born globals can be found in various sectors and industries, but their incidence is particularly high in the ICT sector and in scientific and technical services. Just as for other young enterprises, the vast majority of born globals are micro enterprises with fewer than 10 persons employed; however, the probability of significant growth and developing into a small or medium-sized firm within is higher for born globals than for nationally oriented young firms. While an average young enterprise has created approximately three jobs in its first five years, born globals have created approximately four jobs on average.

Born globals are more inclined towards innovation than SMEs or young enterprises in general. This applies to both levels: strategic orientation and attitude as well as actual product and process innovations developed and implemented. Furthermore, they are focussing relatively more on growth and expansion and their risk aversion is lower compared to the average SME population.

Compared to other SMEs, born globals attach great importance to the quality of their human resources (competencies and capabilities) and to a higher extent regard their personnel as a key factor of competitiveness. Together with the need, prompted by growth, to find and recruit many new employees in a short time, this can put born globals in a challenging situation on the labour market. The largest need is for technicians, engineers and scientists from apprenticeship to tertiary education levels. There is also a need for administrative support staff and people working on business development as the company grows. Austrian born globals obviously value a diverse workforce in terms of ethnic origin and nationality, although in practice they hardly actively recruit outside Austria. Born globals also seem to prefer younger workers as they are regarded as more flexible and open to constant change, and the companies in turn usually offer high flexibility and autonomy in the workplace. Many jobs in born globals also require willingness to travel and good foreign language skills (English in particular).

There are different barriers to job creation over the lifecycle of a born global. In the product or technology development phase, which can be quite extensive, as well as there not yet being cash flow from sales, born globals often face difficulties with financing highly qualified employees. In the growth phase following successful commercialisation of the product or technology, the main challenges are associated with aspects such as attracting a sufficient number of applicants; making available the required workspace for additional employees and extending (or changing) the premises; changing work organisation and task allocation in a growing team; and facing increasing red tape and compliance issues.

Against this background, born globals in Austria could be supported in several ways to better unlock and realise their job creation potential:

- (Financial) Support in hiring highly qualified experts in the phase of technology development.
- Facilitating and encouraging *international* recruiting by born globals.[8]
- Assistance with employer branding to make small companies more visible and attractive for the highly qualified.
- Disseminating and promoting employee participation models for highly qualified experts.
- Offering specific competence development and training in 'business development in foreign markets'.
- Providing quality information and advice to enterprises on recruitment, employment issues, and especially on posting workers abroad.

Annex: further information on company case studies

The following information refers to the situation of the companies at the time the case studies were conducted (2015).

ecoduna AG offers a unique process for industrial-scale production of biomass (algae culture) which was globally patented. The technology is applied by industrial users, for example in the field of cosmetics, chemistry, pharmaceuticals, drugs, food, animal feed, agriculture, or in the energy sector. After five years of research and development, the company launched in 2010. Since its inception, ecoduna has been awarded several national and international awards, such as innovation awards from the regional government of Lower Austria and the regional Economic Chamber in 2010 as well as the 'Energy Globe Award' in 2013 and 2014. ecoduna is located in Bruck an der Leitha, about 40 km from Vienna. The public limited company is funded by equity capital from private investors and European development funds. In 2012, the company established its demonstration and research facilities in Austria as well as two parallel pilot projects in Germany and Denmark. As of February 2015, ecoduna employs a team of 30, which is twice as many as two years ago. The employees are mainly construction and facility engineers as well as biologists. Their website can be found at: www.ecoduna.at.

Evercyte GmbH was founded in February 2011 by a management consultant and two associate professors at the University of Natural Resources and Life Sciences (Universität für Bodenkultur) in Vienna. Their intention was to offer innovative tools and services for the pharmaceutical industry. At the university they developed standardised immortalised human cells which were very useful for their own scientific research, and then explored the need for such cell lines among potential customers. Evercyte is providing cell based products for target discovery, drug discovery, drug development and batch release testing as well as for testing of toxicity of pharmaceutical, cosmetic, and chemical products or of environmental toxins. The business concept is to license single cell lines, cell panels (different cell lines from different tissues, donors) for basic research and different screening procedures. Evercyte offers these products and services to academic and non-profit-organisations. Evercyte is active on the international market because in Austria the number of potential customers for their cell based products is too small. Therefore, their export quota is more than 90 per cent. Next to the three co-founders Evercyte has nine employees. Their website can be found at: www.evercyte.com.

FRESNEX GmbH, located in Wiener Neudorf close to Vienna, was established in 2012. The company offers a mirror module allowing for the first time the implementation of the technology of concentrated solar power (CSP) in small-scale applications (such as the solar cooling of buildings) at reasonable costs. As of 2015, they have a tested and certified prototype available (funded by the founders' savings, supported by public grants and investments from business angels) and are in negotiations with potential customers, notably industries with a need for thermal energy (for example, food, paper, chemical industry) or the cooling of large buildings. The nature of their product favours target markets where there is a lot of sunshine, such as Spain, Italy or Greece. In Greece, first negotiations with potential customers have already taken place. Nevertheless, their first customer is located in Austria, not least because it is easier for the company staff to install and fine-tune their product in the client's premises. Including the two managers, by the summer of 2015 FRESNEX employed four staff members. Their website address is: www.fresnex.com.

Power Units GmbH was founded in 2008. The company is located in Millennium Park, a technology cluster in Lustenau in the Austrian region Vorarlberg. Power Units focuses on the development and manufacturing of highly efficient three-phase electronic lamp power supplies for the UV-industry. The main focus of their developmental activities is set on electronic ballast units for UV-applications. Power Units developed the 'efficient switch', which enables the efficient production of first-class, compact electronic control gears and endorses the realisation of high performance power supply units. Furthermore, Power Units offers special inductive components like planar transformers or planar chokes, DC-link chokes or storage chokes. The company won the Austrian Regional Prize for Innovation in 2012 for the most innovative company located in Vorarlberg. Power Units was also nominated for the Econovius 2013, a special award of the Austrian State Prize for Innovation. Power Units has 3000+ electronic power supplies sales per year. The company's export quota is 100 per cent. They export their products to countries ranging from Canada/ America to India, China and Korea, but they are also active in Europe. Their customers are mainly large international companies, but also some small plant manufacturers integrating their electronic power supplies to their machinery. As well as three owner-managers who are involved in the day to day business of the company, the company also has two additional members of staff as well as one apprentice. Their website can be found at: www.powerunits.at.

seamtec GmbH, which stands for sustainable energy automation measurement technologies, was founded in October 2009. At that time, the founder together with the long-established company 'WWS Wasserkraft' identified a market demand for automation solutions for local thermal plants and hydroelectric power plants. This market opportunity was the motivation for founding seamtec, which is operating at the same location as its cooperating partner WWS Wasserkraft in Upper Austria close to the German border. The main product of seamtec is the Turbine Control SCADA system which is one of the most modern turbine control systems for hydro-electric power plants and offers solutions for all turbine types. The Turbine Control SCADA system is the result of an in-house development and constitutes a Cloud-Server-based control technology. It is possible to monitor and control the power plant over any internet connection. At the beginning, going international was driven by the cooperation partner. Their first projects at international level were water power plants in Romania and Turkey. Now they deliver turbine control systems and automation systems for plants to a variety of countries. seamtec is focusing on the international market because the supply rate of hydro-electric power in Austria is already very high. In 2015, seamtec employed six persons. Their website is at: www.seamtec.at.

Notes

1 Sections B to N as well as S95 according to the NACE classification.
2 Because of mandatory membership the register includes all active enterprises in Austria apart from some professions such as lawyers, architects, and tax advisors.
3 This means being a born global is a temporary phenomenon; it would become a non-born global when it survives for more than five years.
4 For their 2016 award 'Austria's Born Global Champions', the Austrian Federal Economic Chamber uses the following definition: (1) foundation of the company in 2010 or later; (2) the company has an 'international focus'; (3) the company offers an innovative product; (4) international growth is a main priority of the company (Austrian Federal Economic Chamber, 2016).
5 The data refer to the person completing the survey. However, usually the owner and manager is the same person.
6 Of course only surviving firms have been observed, which should be borne in mind when interpreting the data.

7 For an overview of the case studies refer to section 5.1 and the Annex.
8 The Horizon 2020 SME Innovation Associate launched in 2016 is an example of a support instrument combining targeted international recruiting and financial support for salaries for one year: https://ec.europa.eu/easme/en/h2020-sme-innovation-associate.

References

Austrian Federal Economic Chamber (2016), 'Austria's Born Global Champions II', *FRESH VIEW*, Special edition, WKO, Vienna.

Bachinger, K., Heckl, E. and Gavac, K. (2016), *Startup-Report Österreich*, Austrian Federal Economic Chamber, Vienna. Available at: www.startupreport.at/.

Bundesministerium für Wissenschaft, Forschung und Wirtschaft (2015), *Land der Gründer – Auf dem Weg zum gründerfreundlichsten Land Europas*, Bundesministerium für Wissenschaft, Forschung und Wirtschaft, Vienna.

Dömötör, R. and Spannocchi, B. (2016), *European Startup Monitor 2016: Country Report Austria*, WU Gründungszentrum, Vienna.

Eurofound (2012), *Born global: The potential of job creation in new international businesses*, Publications Office of the European Union, Luxembourg.

Eurofound (2016), *ERM annual report 2015: Job creation in SMEs*, Publications Office of the European Union, Luxembourg.

Hölzl, W., Böheim, M. and Friesenbichler, K. S. (2010), *Expertise zum ERP-Jahresprogramm mit Schwerpunkt 'innovative Gazellen'*, Österreichisches Institut für Wirtschaftsforschung, Vienna.

Kemler, R., Csendes, O., Kainz, J., Preveden, V. and Womser, T. (2016), *Startup-Hub Wien: Zukunftschancen gezielt nutzen*, Roland Berger GmbH, Vienna.

Pöchhacker-Tröscher, G. and Lefenda, J. (2013), *Gazellen: Schnell wachsende industrie-orientierte Unternehmen in Oberösterreich*, Industriellenvereinigung Oberösterreich, Linz.

6 Estonian born globals' job creation

Tiia Vissak and Jaan Masso*

6.1 Introduction

Internationalisation processes have received substantial research attention since the 1970s but, during the first two decades, researchers mainly focused on slow/ incremental ('Uppsala model style') internationalisers (Bilkey, 1978; Johanson and Vahlne, 1977, 1990). Since the 1990s, several scholars have started paying attention to born globals, international new ventures and other fast internationalisers (Coviello, 2015; Madsen and Servais, 1997; Rialp *et al.*, 2005) as these young and small firms have benefitted considerably from better access to information, especially via the internet, but also from lower transportation costs; moreover, their access to foreign markets has improved as a result of economic integration (Cieślik, 2017).

Despite considerable research on born globals and other fast internationalisers, longitudinal studies on their activities are still scarce (Hagen and Zucchella, 2014; Knight, 2015; Prashantham and Young, 2011; Rialp *et al.*, 2015; Romanello and Chiarvesio, 2016; Welch and Paavilainen-Mäntymäki, 2014). This is a serious research gap as in all dynamic capitalist economies some firms enter new markets and otherwise thrive and grow, while others are declining and sometimes exiting some or all of their markets (Haltiwanger, 2012; Kuhn *et al.*, 2016). Moreover, although many authors have stressed the importance of international trade for countries in general (Kletzer, 2002), 'little is known so far about the relevance of these firms for the economy and the labour market' (Eurofound, 2012).

It is important to find out how born globals contribute to job creation[1] as several authors have stated that young, innovative and fast-growing firms – and many born globals could be regarded as such – create more jobs than other firms (Acs and Audretsch 1989; Anyadike-Danes *et al.*, 2015; Birch, 1981; Brown and Mawson, 2016; Decker *et al.*, 2014; Mettler and Williams, 2011; Stangler and Litan, 2009). Moreover, born globals' growth is not limited by their own home market's smallness. Thus, in small countries like Estonia (its population is only 1.3 million), born globals and other firms with good access to export markets could have a substantial a role in job creation (Cieślik, 2017; Masso *et al.*, 2005).

This chapter aims to find out whether in Estonia born globals differ from other firms in terms of their job creation. It is based on a database from the Estonian Business Registry encompassing all Estonian firms' business activities from 1995–2014. This database has been merged with detailed firm- and country-level foreign trade data from Statistics Estonia.

The chapter starts with a review of the existing literature on job creation by different firm types and, thereafter, focuses on born globals and their role as potential job creators. After the data and method section, the chapter gives an overview of the results and discusses them. Finally, it draws some policy and research implications.

6.2 Literature review

6.2.1 The literature on job creation

Several authors (see, for instance, Acs *et al.*, 2008; Anyadike-Danes *et al.*, 2015; Cieślik, 2017 and Landström, 2005) have emphasised the importance of the contribution of Birch (1979) as he was the first scholar to find that contrary to the common belief, small firms were actually creating more jobs in the US than large corporations. Since the publication of that work, several authors have found evidence in support of Birch, but several others have also come to different conclusions. Below, a short overview of some studies will be given.

Various scholars have found that small firms have created more jobs than large firms. For instance, Birch (1981) stated that, in the US, two-thirds of jobs were created by firms with 20 or fewer employees; moreover, a limited number of these firms grew especially rapidly during their early years and created many jobs during their growth. Acs and Audretsch (1989) agreed that 'small firms are the major generators of new jobs in the USA'. Moreover, according to Stangler and Litan (2009), young (1–5 years old) small- and medium-sized firms were mainly responsible for net job creation in the US in 2007. Anyadike-Danes *et al.* (2015) found that in the UK, a small number of mostly small firms created a significant number of new jobs in 1998–2013 while Jurajda and Terrell (2008) concluded, based on Estonian and Czech data from the 1990s, that 'small firms apparently create and sustain most jobs during transition'.

On the other hand, some authors do not fully agree with the above statements. For example, Haltiwanger *et al.* (2013) concluded, based on data from the USA: 'once we control for firm age, there is no systematic relationship between firm size and growth' while according to Davis *et al.* (1996), large firms were responsible for most newly created jobs in the US manufacturing sector. Acs *et al.* (2008) found that in the US, the average high-impact (high-growth) firm was about 25 years old. Moreover, according to de Morais Sarmento and Nunes (2015), in Portugal, large (with more than 250 employees) high-growth firms formed only 7 per cent of all high-growth firms but created 95 per cent of all jobs in this category.

Different authors have found that, although small firms create many jobs, they also destroy many. For instance, Masso *et al.* (2005) stated that, in Estonia,

SMEs' share of the total job creation and job destruction was 79 per cent and 75 per cent, respectively.[2] Similarly, Davis *et al.* (1996), de Morais Sarmento and Nunes (2015), Huber *et al.* (2017) and Wagner (1995), based on US, Portuguese, Austrian and German data respectively, concluded that smaller and/or younger firms had the highest failure rates, and they both created and destroyed more jobs. Moreover, according to the OECD (2009): 'firm entry and exit – and the associated creation and destruction of jobs – are highly concentrated among small businesses, which is reflected in a negative relationship between job turnover (job creation and destruction) and firm size'. Finally, Anyadike-Danes *et al.* (2015) found that in the UK, about 90 per cent of new-born firms had 1–4 employees; and about 70–80 per cent of them were usually closed down during the first 10 years from their inception.

In addition to finding out which firms create more jobs, various authors have also studied which external or internal factors affect job creation. According to Kletzer (2002), due to trade liberalisation, jobs move from import-competing to exporting industries. Banerjee and Jesenko (2014) found that growth in trading partner countries leads to increased demand and, through that, job creation in exporting industries. In addition, higher job creation has been associated with foreign ownership (Masso *et al.*, 2005) and investing abroad (Brown and Mawson 2016), increasing domestic sales and demand (Kletzer, 2002), firms' higher skill-intensity (Bentivogli and Pagano, 1999) and productivity (Decker *et al.*, 2014), better access to financing (Yazdanfar and Öhman, 2015), managerial capabilities, experience and aspirations (de Morais Sarmento and Nunes, 2015; Dencker *et al.*, 2009) but also their products' innovativeness, although the latter is not always guaranteed due to additional uncertainties (Audretsch and Elston, 2006). Finally, some authors have stressed that industry characteristics – for instance, export orientation (Banerjee and Jesenko, 2014) and the possibility to gain from economies of scale (Masso *et al.*, 2005) but also the level of foreign competition, technological and wage differences (Kletzer, 2002) – also affect job creation.

Based on the above, it is possible to support the conclusion of Cieślik (2017) that 'the results of several decades of intensive research on the contribution of different types of businesses to the creation of new jobs have not provided conclusive findings'. Some authors have agreed with Birch (1979, 1981) that small firms are the most active in job creation while some others have proved the opposite, and some have stressed the importance of studying fluctuations in terms of the number of jobs. Moreover, several authors have identified other factors in addition to size that can affect job creation and destruction.

The following section will give a short overview of specific characteristics of born globals. Thereafter, their potential role in terms of job creation will be discussed.

6.2.2 The literature on born globals

For born globals, the whole world is their 'market': they do not limit their activities to a few close countries (McDougall *et al.*, 2003; Moen and Servais, 2002).

Some of them start their business activities by exporting: they do not even try to sell anything locally (Chetty and Campbell-Hunt, 2004; Mets, 2016).

Born globals have emerged due to the increasing importance of specialised and customised (niche) products, shortened product life cycles, increased local competition, technological advances and advantages related to SMEs: for example, flexibility, adaptability and quicker response times (Coviello and Munro, 1995; Knight and Cavusgil, 1996; Rennie, 1993). In addition, some other factors – for instance, firm characteristics like reputation, unique resources and capabilities, network relationships (Vissak, 2007; Zahra and George, 2002), innovativeness (Knight, 2015) and top management's desire for and commitment to exporting (McKinsey and Company, 1993; Moen and Servais, 2002; Vissak, 2007) – have also influenced the emergence of these firms. Moreover, in Estonia, the small domestic market has made the emergence of born globals almost inevitable (Mets, 2016; Vissak, 2007).

On the other hand, although several authors have identified born globals' advantages compared to other internationalisers, these companies can also face challenges related to entering first foreign markets immediately or very soon after establishment: for instance, they usually lack considerable financial or other tangible resources (Knight and Cavusgil, 2004; Moen and Servais, 2002), sufficient foreign market experience or knowledge (Casillas and Moreno-Menéndez, 2014; Hohenthal *et al.*, 2014; Oviatt and McDougall, 1994) but also long-time network relationships with foreign suppliers or customers (Zhao and Hsu, 2007). Moreover, certain born globals exit some foreign markets or even go bankrupt because of overexpansion (Morgan-Thomas and Jones, 2009), due to entering their foreign markets too early or having to compete against larger and more experienced firms (Rialp *et al.*, 2015).

Similarly, different authors' results regarding born globals' employment effects have been dissimilar. They will be summarised in the next section.

6.2.3 The literature on born globals as potential job creators

According to Eurofound (2012), born globals are characterised 'by, on average, higher employment numbers (which is expected to continue) than domestically oriented firms. Moreover, the jobs they create are, in general, high quality, well paid ones and are assumed to be comparatively stable and sustainable'. According to a later publication (Eurofound, 2016), the above average job creation rate of born globals can be explained by their higher innovativeness, somewhat larger size and more ambitious future plans. Moreover, it was concluded that hiring additional staff can improve born globals' innovation and internationalisation capacities as this can enhance their access to knowledge, ideas and networks.

Other authors have not paid much attention to born globals as job creators. Still, certain scholars have added some additional insights. For instance, Cieślik (2017) stated that born globals – in his conception, ambitious start-ups oriented at achieving growth on a global scale – can grow faster if they expand on international markets, as then their growth is not limited by the domestic market's smallness and/or strong local competition. Foreign expansion can help them to increase the scale of their operations which, in turn, can positively affect their employment numbers and also increase their innovative capacity. Moreover, according to Romanello and Chiarvesio (2016) a maturing born global needs to invest in its human resources and hire people with international experience in the foreign markets that it has not yet entered, and people who have the necessary knowledge for expanding the firm's production line. Glaister *et al.* (2014) also agreed that in emerging economies larger and more export-oriented born globals need more skilled employees.

Born globals are, in general, regarded as high-growth firms.[3] As 'high-growth firms are known to be more likely than other firms to export their products and services' (de Morais Sarmento and Nunes, 2015), a short overview of some studies on such firms will follow.

High-growth firms create a disproportionate share of new jobs each year (Anyadike-Danes *et al.*, 2015; Henrekson and Johansson, 2010; Mason *et al.*, 2015; Stangler, 2010; Tracy, 2011). For instance, according to Decker *et al.* (2014), in the US 'high-growth businesses (which are disproportionately young) account for almost 50 percent of gross job creation'. Such firms are more innovative (Acs *et al.*, 2008) and more productive (Tracy, 2011) than other firms. Moreover, they need employees with diverse skills and capabilities (Bogas and Barbosa, 2015).

It was already mentioned in the previous section that innovativeness, higher productivity and the need for skilled employees also characterise born globals. Thus, taking into account Eurofound's (2012) study, but also studies on born globals and high-growth firms, it can be proposed that born globals are more active in creating jobs than other firms.

There is still no consensus on whether born globals are, in general, more successful than other firms in terms of survival (and, through that, their net job creation) in the long term. For instance, Sleuwaegen and Onkelinx (2014) found that fast internationalisers failed more frequently than slow ones and de Morais Sarmento and Nunes (2015) stated that fast (employment) growth does not guarantee survival. On the other hand, according to Mudambi and Zahra (2007), fast and slow internationalisers had similar survival rates.

Eurofound (2012) concluded that 'due to their limited size, born globals can be assumed to face the same challenge as all small enterprises in terms of high dependency on market developments and higher vulnerability caused by individual events'. Taking into account these statements but also some literature on born globals' disadvantages that were reviewed in the previous section, it can be proposed that born globals are also responsible for job destruction.

In the results section, it is analysed whether Estonian born globals create more jobs than they destroy. Also, it is studied which differences exist between Estonian born globals, other exporters and non-exporters in terms of size, survival and wage costs.

6.3 Data and method

This chapter is based on a database from the Estonian Business Registry encompassing the business activities of all Estonian firms – irrespective of their size, age or sector – in 1995–2014. It has been merged with detailed firm- and country-level foreign trade data from Statistics Estonia. The database contains the data of about 20,000–50,000 firms every year. The number varies as each year many firms exit the market while many new ones are established. Moreover, it has to be noted that about 20–30 per cent of firms do not report their employment numbers every year.

Consensus regarding definitions of born globals is still missing. For the purposes of the current study, two definitions were used[4]:

*   Classical born globals (CBGs): these firms enter at least three foreign countries (of which at least one is located outside their home continent (in the Estonian case, outside Europe) and achieve an export share of at least 25 per cent during any of the first three years since foundation. This follows the authors' earlier definition (Vissak and Masso, 2015) but with one exception: firms are classified as born globals also if they, after achieving the required criteria, exited any or even all foreign markets completely and/or partially.
*   Eurofound's born globals (EBGs): these firms have had an export share of at least 25 per cent for at least two years during a five-year period since their establishment. They have exported to at least two foreign countries, on any continent. This definition is based on Eurofound (2012) but it is somewhat less strict as it was not possible to check other criteria forming the definition, namely how innovative these firms' products were and whether they had a strategic intention to internationalise from the beginning.

In terms of classification, every firm was regarded as belonging only to one group: thus, for instance, if it was established in 1997 but became a born global in 1999, it was also regarded as a born global in 1997 and 1998. Following this principle, 6-year-old or older firms were not removed from the group of EBGs (although Eurofound, 2012 suggested it) as moving some firms from the group of EBGs to the group of other exporters would have reduced the comparability of the results. Regarding the other firms, two subgroups were identified: other exporters – firms that had exported during at least one year of their activities to at least one foreign country (including also those firms that had already exited any or even all their foreign markets completely and/or partially) and firms that had never exported (non-exporters).

In addition to the lack of consensus regarding definitions of born globals and other internationalisers, there is also no agreement on how exactly to measure (high-growth) firms' contribution to job creation (Anyadike-Danes *et al.*, 2015). The following relatively popular indicators were used in extant research (Banerjee and Jesenko, 2014; Davis and Haltiwanger, 1992; de Morais Sarmento and Nunes, 2015; Haltiwanger, 2012):

- Job creation rate: the sum of all employment gains of firms that started their operations or expanded during a specific period as a percentage of average total employment. Thus, if firms had 60 employees at the beginning of 2013 and 100 at the beginning of 2014, then the rate is $(100-60)/(0.5 \times (100+60))$ $=40/80=0.5$.
- Job destruction rate: the sum of all employment losses of firms that shut down or reduced their operations (exited) during a specific period as a percentage of average total employment. It is calculated similarly to the job creation rate. Thus, if firms had 60 employees at the beginning of 2013 and 40 at the beginning of 2014, then the rate is $(40-60)/(0.5 \times (40+60))=-20/50=-0.4$.
- Net job reallocation rate: the sum of gross job creation rate and gross job destruction rate. For instance, if the job creation rate is 0.5 and the job destruction rate is –0.4, then the net job reallocation rate is $0.5-0.4=0.1$. A positive net job reallocation rate indicates that job creation was larger than job destruction during a certain period while a negative rate means the opposite.
- Gross job reallocation rate: the sum of the absolute values of job creation rate and job destruction rate (in principle, the difference between the values of these rates). If the job creation rate is 0.5 and the job destruction rate is –0.4, then the gross rate is $0.5+0.4=0.9$. The larger the rate, the more jobs were created and destroyed during a certain period.
- Excess job reallocation rate: the difference between the gross job reallocation rate and the absolute value of the net job reallocation rate. With the above numbers, the excess job reallocation rate is $0.9-0.1=0.8$. According to Haltiwanger (2012), this rate 'captures the 'excess' reallocation over and above that needed to accommodate net employment growth'.

In the following section, the above-mentioned rates will be calculated for both types of born globals, but also for other firms. In addition, all firm types' dynamics of employment numbers, firms' overall survival and export survival rates, but also wage costs will be calculated, as these should give additional insights into the job creation performance of born globals.

6.4 Results

The rates of job creation and job destruction were calculated (see Table 6.1) and, based on those, it can be agreed with Masso *et al.* (2005) that 'job creation and destruction rates in Estonia are very high'. According to Table 6.1, EBGs have the highest job creation rate over all years (0.28), but non-exporters have a similar rate (0.27). CBGs' rate is lower (0.23) while other exporters have the lowest rate (0.15). So, Eurofound's (2012) conclusion that born globals create more jobs than fully domestic-market-oriented firms is not fully evident based on these numbers.

On the other hand, according to the same table, non-exporters destroyed more jobs (their job destruction rate was –0.21) than other exporters (–0.13), CBGs

Table 6.1 Estonian firms' job creation, destruction and reallocation rates in 1996–2013

Classical born globals

Year	Number of		Rates of				
	Active firms	Employees	Job creation	Job destruction	Net job reallocation	Gross job reallocation	Excess job reallocation
1996	52	1,635	0.77	-0.27	0.50	1.04	0.53
1997	77	2,303	0.28	-0.23	0.05	0.51	0.46
1998	103	2,161	0.45	-0.18	0.27	0.63	0.36
1999	126	2,909	0.42	-0.11	0.31	0.52	0.22
2000	137	3,755	0.27	-0.03	0.24	0.30	0.06
2001	150	4,168	0.19	-0.07	0.13	0.26	0.13
2002	168	4,938	0.21	-0.08	0.13	0.28	0.15
2003	170	4,846	0.19	-0.11	0.09	0.30	0.21
2004	186	5,781	0.15	-0.05	0.09	0.20	0.11
2005	196	6,192	0.13	-0.08	0.05	0.21	0.16
2006	213	7,311	0.21	-0.06	0.15	0.26	0.11
2007	215	7,513	0.11	-0.07	0.04	0.18	0.14
2008	217	7,894	0.14	-0.08	0.06	0.22	0.17
2009	233	7,736	0.15	-0.14	0.01	0.29	0.28
2010	253	9,223	0.21	-0.06	0.15	0.27	0.12
2011	276	10,032	0.10	-0.02	0.08	0.12	0.05
2012	296	10,189	0.10	-0.07	0.04	0.17	0.13
2013	296	10,500	0.09	-0.06	0.03	0.15	0.13

Eurofound's born globals

Year	Number of		Rates of				
	Active firms	Employees	Job creation	Job destruction	Net job reallocation	Gross job reallocation	Excess job reallocation
1996	29	355	1.00	0.00	1.00	1.00	0.00
1997	72	958	0.71	-0.03	0.68	0.74	0.06
1998	106	1,875	0.51	-0.03	0.48	0.54	0.06
1999	143	2,770	0.36	-0.03	0.32	0.39	0.06
2000	171	4,025	0.34	-0.03	0.30	0.37	0.06
2001	212	4,987	0.25	-0.02	0.23	0.27	0.04
2002	240	6,158	0.22	-0.05	0.17	0.27	0.10
2003	255	6,530	0.22	-0.09	0.13	0.32	0.19
2004	270	7,730	0.15	-0.04	0.10	0.19	0.09
2005	289	8,287	0.13	-0.07	0.06	0.20	0.14
2006	313	8,567	0.12	-0.07	0.05	0.20	0.15
2007	334	8,896	0.13	-0.07	0.06	0.19	0.13
2008	350	9,468	0.18	-0.10	0.07	0.28	0.21
2009	379	8,997	0.13	-0.16	-0.03	0.28	0.25
2010	437	10,374	0.16	-0.04	0.12	0.21	0.08
2011	482	11,841	0.15	-0.03	0.13	0.18	0.05
2012	524	12,266	0.12	-0.08	0.03	0.20	0.17
2013	530	12,775	0.11	-0.07	0.04	0.18	0.14

Other exporters

Year	Number of		Rates of				
	Active firms	Employees	Job creation	Job destruction	Net job reallocation	Gross job reallocation	Excess job reallocation
1996	2,188	56,675	0.39	-0.29	0.10	0.68	0.58
1997	2,679	65,685	0.37	-0.19	0.18	0.55	0.38
1998	3,035	68,154	0.21	-0.21	0.00	0.41	0.41
1999	3,200	66,831	0.20	-0.12	0.08	0.33	0.24
2000	3,271	73,547	0.20	-0.09	0.11	0.28	0.17
2001	3,429	74,478	0.11	-0.11	0.01	0.22	0.21
2002	3,577	81,637	0.18	-0.08	0.10	0.27	0.17
2003	3,628	83,130	0.10	-0.08	0.02	0.18	0.16
2004	3,674	84,847	0.11	-0.07	0.03	0.18	0.15
2005	3,815	88,015	0.12	-0.07	0.05	0.19	0.14
2006	3,929	87,250	0.09	-0.10	-0.01	0.19	0.19
2007	3,989	91,398	0.12	-0.13	-0.01	0.25	0.24
2008	3,936	81,969	0.07	-0.11	-0.04	0.19	0.14
2009	4,043	77,909	0.13	-0.20	-0.06	0.33	0.27
2010	4,164	75,150	0.09	-0.23	-0.14	0.32	0.18
2011	4,285	77,547	0.08	-0.05	0.03	0.13	0.10
2012	4,524	79,587	0.12	-0.10	0.02	0.22	0.20
2013	4,451	80,488	0.07	-0.09	-0.02	0.17	0.14

Non-exporters

Year	Number of		Rates of				
	Active firms	Employees	Job creation	Job destruction	Net job reallocation	Gross job reallocation	Excess job reallocation
1996	5,267	47,707	0.49	-0.44	0.06	0.93	0.87
1997	6,530	53,934	0.51	-0.27	0.24	0.78	0.54
1998	7,635	60,668	0.33	-0.22	0.11	0.55	0.44
1999	7,802	58,890	0.23	-0.23	0.01	0.46	0.45
2000	7,770	66,232	0.27	-0.19	0.09	0.46	0.37
2001	8,256	65,300	0.19	-0.16	0.03	0.36	0.32
2002	9,048	68,721	0.20	-0.18	0.02	0.37	0.36
2003	9,573	67,704	0.17	-0.15	0.03	0.32	0.30
2004	11,104	74,868	0.22	-0.13	0.10	0.35	0.26
2005	13,221	82,645	0.23	-0.12	0.11	0.35	0.24
2006	15,825	95,350	0.24	-0.13	0.11	0.37	0.25
2007	18,155	103,024	0.20	-0.17	0.03	0.37	0.34
2008	19,004	97,311	0.15	-0.21	-0.06	0.36	0.30
2009	25,342	94,400	0.31	-0.40	-0.09	0.71	0.61
2010	25,706	83,863	0.20	-0.25	-0.04	0.45	0.41
2011	30,582	92,157	0.20	-0.11	0.09	0.31	0.22
2012	42,245	123,517	0.37	-0.14	0.22	0.51	0.29
2013	46,025	140,403	0.26	-0.25	0.01	0.51	0.50

Note
All definitions are provided in section 6.3. The table is based on the data from Estonian Business Registry and foreign trade data from Statistics Estonia.

(–0.10) or EBGs (–0.06). Thus, as a result, in terms of net rates, EBGs contributed more to job creation (their net job reallocation rate was 0.22) than CBGs (0.13), non-exporters (0.06) or other exporters (0.02). Consequently, in terms of their net job creation, both types of born globals were more active than other firms – in other words, their jobs were more stable/sustainable (Eurofound, 2012) – while the nature of other firms' jobs was less permanent.

Gross and excess job reallocation rates were also calculated (see Table 6.1). The former was the highest in case of non-exporters (0.47), followed by both types of born globals (0.33 for both EBGs and CBGs), and the lowest in case of other exporters (0.28). The excess reallocation rate was also the highest in case of non-exporters (0.39), but the next were other exporters (0.23), followed by CBGs (0.20) and EBGs (0.11). According to Faggio and Konings (2003), a high excess job reallocation rate can be a sign of restructuring, especially in the context of transition economies. Thus, it is not surprising that these rates were higher in the 1990s but also during the economic crisis in 2009 (see also Meriküll, 2016).

In addition, it was studied how the number of employees changed with firm age (see Table 6.2). In both their first and eighteenth year of operations, both types of born globals were larger than other exporters and, especially, non-exporters. According to calculations based on all 19 years, CBGs had on average 40 employees, followed by EBGs (24), other exporters (14) and non-exporters (4). Thus, it can be agreed with Eurofound (2012) that born globals' employment numbers are, on average, higher. Moreover, a larger number of employees during born globals' early years can indicate that in Estonia, compared to other exporters, they have more resources (Zahra and George, 2002) and/or better access to financing (Yazdanfar and Öhman, 2015). In other words, they do not necessarily suffer from the lack of financial or other tangible resources (Knight and Cavusgil, 2004; Moen and Servais, 2002).

Comparing the increases in the number of employees between the first and nineteenth year (see Table 6.2), shows that born globals' staff numbers increased somewhat more in absolute terms than other firms' numbers: by 21.57 in the group of CBGs, 14.40 in case of EBGs and 11.63 in case of other exporters, while only by 3.45 in the group of non-exporters. Differences between firm types were already visible in their second year. Still, when taking into account growth in relative (percentage) terms, it can be seen that, compared to other firm types, non-exporters' number of employees grew the most between the first and nineteenth year while EBGs' number of employees did so between the first and second year of activities. Thus, there was only some support for Cieślik's (2017) observation that expanding on international markets allows firms to grow faster as internationalised firms' growth is not limited by the domestic market's smallness. On the other hand, a large relative employment growth rate of non-exporters is not surprising as their initial number of employees is very small: 2.16 on their first year. Thus, even hiring one to two more employees will substantially increase the rate. Moreover, as Estonian non-exporters are usually very small, especially during the first years

Table 6.2 Number of employees in Estonian firms by firm age (during the first 19 years since establishment, the period 1996–2014)

	Average number of employees by firm age					Total number of active firms				
Age	All	CBG	EBG	Other exporters	Non-exporters	CBG	EBG	Other exporters	Non-exporters	All
1	2.95	27.16	12.70	7.97	2.16	1,206	1,764	16,151	128,423	146,988
2	3.30	29.32	16.11	8.47	2.31	1,164	1,751	13,837	98,328	114,528
3	3.79	30.73	18.14	8.94	2.64	1,094	1,715	12,622	80,463	95,350
4	4.11	34.14	19.23	10.59	2.71	983	1,590	11,499	71,134	84,701
5	4.53	41.64	22.02	11.81	2.83	877	1,441	10,558	61,317	73,731
6	5.04	67.30	22.60	12.03	2.95	773	1,261	9,657	52,696	63,988
7	5.39	40.55	24.42	12.85	3.18	685	1,096	8,771	39,062	49,265
8	5.76	41.66	24.57	13.83	3.22	630	986	8,095	33,374	42,764
9	6.22	34.95	24.79	14.04	3.59	576	882	7,404	27,920	36,491
10	6.50	33.75	24.43	14.05	3.68	524	792	6,781	23,004	30,839
11	7.47	36.43	24.21	16.07	4.08	477	692	6,190	19,142	26,277
12	7.11	35.65	24.15	14.35	3.82	437	625	5,523	15,802	22,183
13	8.90	35.23	23.71	16.84	5.28	383	542	4,922	13,181	18,856
14	7.88	41.17	28.48	16.04	3.76	328	457	4,342	10,750	15,735
15	8.56	39.51	26.64	17.79	3.85	276	362	3,760	8,717	12,999
16	8.20	44.83	30.27	15.22	3.84	232	296	3,111	6,797	10,342
17	9.03	47.79	33.29	16.41	4.14	172	204	2,539	5,018	7,867
18	10.30	54.51	31.45	18.48	4.53	121	139	1,771	3,230	5,220
19	12.16	48.73	27.10	19.60	5.61	67	63	774	1,236	2,120

Note
All definitions and abbreviations are provided in section 6.3. The table is based on the data from Estonian Business Registry and foreign trade data from Statistics Estonia.

of their operation, the domestic market's smallness is not a considerable impediment for their initial growth.

It was also studied how many firms, in general, survived, and how many managed to continue exporting over the years (see Table 6.3). It was found that both types of born globals were more likely to survive until their eighteenth year than other exporters or non-exporters. While 43 per cent of EBGs and 34 per cent of CBGs survived, this rate was only 30 per cent among other exporters and 24 per cent among non-exporters. Still, there was support for de Morais Sarmento and Nunes (2015) that even fast (employment) growth does not guarantee survival as most born globals did not manage to survive to their eighteenth year either, although their overall survival rates were higher.

Differences between born globals' and other firms' survival rates were already visible in the second year of activities: while 94 per cent of EBGs and 97 per cent of CBGs survived, only 84 per cent of other exporters and 79 per cent of non-exporters managed to continue. Thus, this chapter's findings do not support the conclusion of Sleuwaegen and Onkelinx (2014) that born globals tend to fail more frequently than slow internationalisers. Again, this could indicate that Estonian born globals have more resources than other internationalisers or that they benefit more from some firm-specific characteristics/advantages (Knight, 2015; McKinsey and Co, 1993; Moen and Servais, 2002; Vissak, 2007; Zahra and George, 2002; Yazdanfar and Öhman, 2015) than other firms.

Based on Table 6.3, it can be also concluded that born globals were much more likely to continue exporting until their eighteenth year than other exporters: 15.2 per cent of EBGs, 7.5 per cent of CBGs and 1.5 per cent of other exporters belonged to this group. Again, differences were already visible in the second year of exporting: then, the shares of firms that continued exporting were 93.2 per cent, 87.4 per cent, and 35.9 per cent in case of EBGs, CBGs and other exporters, respectively. Also, there was support to a previous finding (Vissak and Masso, 2015) that in Estonia, export survival was, on average, much lower than overall survival. This difference was especially evident in the case of other exporters. This can indicate that, for other exporters, exporting is rather a result of an experiment (for instance, occurring due to an unsolicited export order) than a deliberate strategy, while born globals are more export-oriented from the beginning of their activities (Chetty and Campbell-Hunt, 2004; McDougall *et al.*, 2003; Moen and Servais, 2002). Taking into account that other exporters are, on average, smaller than born globals, this is not surprising: other authors have also stated that small firms' exporting is often unsystematic (see, for instance, Ellis and Pecotich, 2001 and Francioni *et al.*, 2017).

In addition to studying job creation dynamics and survival, in general, similarities and differences between born globals and other firms in terms of size and wage categories were also identified. In terms of size (see Table 6.4), in all categories, the largest number of firms was in the group 1–9 (micro firms), but born globals' share was somewhat lower: while 43.1 per cent of CBGs and 48.4 per cent of EBGs belonged to this group, the share of other exporters was 56.4 per cent and non-exporters 49.0 per cent. Moreover, while the share of firms with at

Table 6.3 Estonian firms' overall survival and export survival rates (during the first 18 years since establishment, the period 1996–2013)

	Overall survival					Export survival			
Year	All firms	CBGs	EBGs	Other exporters	Non-exporters	All firms	CBGs	EBGs	Other exporters
1	1.000	1.000	1.000	1.000	1.000	1.000	1.000	1.000	1.000
2	0.798	0.937	0.972	0.839	0.790	0.405	0.874	0.932	0.359
3	0.683	0.874	0.953	0.741	0.670	0.251	0.745	0.866	0.198
4	0.598	0.800	0.905	0.667	0.581	0.182	0.627	0.776	0.132
5	0.532	0.741	0.852	0.607	0.513	0.142	0.541	0.677	0.097
6	0.497	0.678	0.787	0.565	0.476	0.117	0.459	0.578	0.078
7	0.455	0.631	0.724	0.525	0.433	0.098	0.398	0.496	0.063
8	0.422	0.584	0.670	0.491	0.398	0.083	0.354	0.442	0.050
9	0.395	0.546	0.623	0.458	0.371	0.072	0.324	0.394	0.041
10	0.371	0.526	0.588	0.429	0.347	0.060	0.279	0.342	0.032
11	0.347	0.495	0.543	0.403	0.322	0.054	0.260	0.304	0.028
12	0.325	0.483	0.535	0.383	0.298	0.052	0.242	0.289	0.027
13	0.309	0.458	0.494	0.365	0.282	0.049	0.230	0.263	0.025
14	0.295	0.422	0.478	0.354	0.267	0.046	0.208	0.259	0.023
15	0.284	0.414	0.466	0.336	0.256	0.043	0.194	0.252	0.022
16	0.278	0.381	0.442	0.337	0.249	0.038	0.165	0.229	0.020
17	0.274	0.358	0.450	0.327	0.244	0.037	0.155	0.235	0.018
18	0.265	0.341	0.434	0.304	0.236	0.027	0.075	0.152	0.015

Note
All definitions and abbreviations are provided in section 6.3. The table is based on the data from Estonian Business Registry and foreign trade data from Statistics Estonia.

least 250 employees was 2.9 per cent among CBGs and 1.3 per cent among EBGs, it was only 0.7 per cent among other exporters and 0.03 per cent among non-exporters. As it was concluded based on Table 6.2 that born globals were, on average, larger, and as in case of CBGs, firms with 250 or more employees employed 47.3 per cent of this firm group's employees, this can indicate, similarly to several previous studies (Acs and Audretsch, 1989; Anyadike-Danes *et al.*, 2015; Birch, 1981; Brown and Mawson, 2016; Decker *et al.*, 2014; Mettler and Williams, 2011; Stangler and Litan, 2009) that some higher-growth firms create many more new jobs than others.

In terms of wage costs (see Table 6.4), most firms were in the category of more than €10,000 per employee a year (only non-exporters spent less) but the share of born globals was higher than the share of other firms: while 72.1 per cent of CBGs and 63.0 per cent of EBGs belonged to this group, the share of other exporters was 51.7 per cent and non-exporters 24.6 per cent (while 30.3 per cent of the latter firm type spent only €4,000–€7,000). Also, while in the 1990s born globals did not spend more per employee in every year than other exporters, in all years after that, their wage costs have been higher. Thus, there was support for Eurofound (2012) that born globals are more active in creating well-paid jobs. Still, it has to be noted that a large share of firms did not report their wage costs, so it is not possible to estimate if such firms had lower or higher wages than the studied firms.

6.5 Conclusion and implications

This chapter showed that in terms of their net job creation, Estonian born globals were more active than other exporters and non-exporters in 1995–2014. Also, they had, on average, more employees and they were more likely to survive and continue exporting than other firms. Moreover, they had higher wage costs per employee.

Based on the findings, some policy suggestions can be made. Still, it has to be taken into account that, due to the impossibility of foreseeing future industry conditions and to study firms that will start their activities in the future, there is no scientifically perfect way to use current evidence for designing the best future policy (de Morais Sarmento and Nunes, 2015). Thus, it is only possible to review the suggestions of other authors and select some that could be applicable in the Estonian or wider context.

It can be agreed with Cieślik (2017), and Mettler and Williams (2011), that born globals and other more globally-focused firms can create many jobs, thus these firms may need policy-makers' attention. On the other hand, it has to be stressed similarly to Eurofound (2012) that (especially in the case of larger countries) not every new firm should be pushed to internationalise, as international success also depends on several firm-, product- and market-specific factors. Moreover, policy-makers should not only focus on firms' size, but also pay attention to their age as this can affect firms' ability to create jobs (Haltiwanger *et al.*, 2013). Policy-makers should also understand that improving entrepreneurship education (Mets, 2016) and removing entry, growth and exit barriers can be

Table 6.4 Number of Estonian firms by size (number of employees), wage costs and average wage costs per employee, 1995–2013

	All firms	CBGs	EBGs	Other exporters	Non-exporters
Number of firms by their number of employees					
0	44,048	71	141	1,581	42,290
1–9	50,045	267	493	5,421	43,997
10–49	5,464	186	270	1,991	3,119
50–249	970	77	101	552	276
250 or more	122	18	13	71	29
Missing data	681	65	60	468	115
Number of employees in size groups					
1–9	116,690	963	1,701	18,233	96,288
10–49	106,267	4,369	6,361	41,953	56,013
50–249	95,631	7,661	10,058	55,658	25,686
250 or more employees	83,643	11,671	4,639	47,080	23,582
Number of firms by annual wage costs per employee, EUR in 2013					
0–2,000	6,298	11	18	274	6,000
2,000–4,000	6,764	15	28	398	6,329
4,000–7,000	14,009	42	116	1,531	12,344
7,000–10,000	7,439	65	126	1,303	5,979
More than 10,000	14,436	344	491	3,753	10,022
Missing data	38,795	234	349	3,193	35,135
Average wage costs per employee, EUR in 1995–2013					
1995	1,610	2,670	3,706	2,330	1,251
1996	2,105	2,729	2,097	2,854	1,654
1997	2,822	3,777	2,459	3,655	2,214
1998	3,115	5,203	3,269	4,094	2,426
1999	3,216	5,086	3,607	4,233	2,511
2000	3,389	5,732	4,199	4,489	2,653
2001	3,703	6,457	4,770	4,837	2,971
2002	4,094	7,147	5,297	5,393	3,308
2003	4,645	7,840	6,130	6,220	3,749
2004	5,062	8,753	6,990	6,603	4,227
2005	5,727	9,114	7,724	7,322	4,962
2006	6,659	10,565	9,249	8,609	5,855
2007	7,950	12,483	10,853	10,228	7,111
2008	8,810	14,167	12,789	11,462	7,861
2009	7,992	13,694	12,065	10,706	7,173
2010	7,647	12,635	11,612	10,253	6,817
2011	8,165	13,717	12,244	10,993	7,326
2012	8,634	15,025	13,579	11,827	7,779
2013	8,699	16,125	14,528	12,736	7,823

Note
All definitions and abbreviations are provided in section 6.3. The table is based on the data from Estonian Business Registry and foreign trade data from Statistics Estonia.

sometimes even more important than offering direct financial support (de Morais Sarmento and Nunes, 2015; Henrekson and Johansson, 2010; Huber *et al.*, 2017; Stangler, 2010) and that focusing only on a few target industries that are currently growing well could be dangerous as some others could start growing more in the future (Acs *et al.*, 2008). Finally, they should also take into account that not all firms create high-quality jobs (Davis *et al.*, 1996; Kuhn *et al.*, 2016), that some high-growth firms prefer to create jobs mostly outside their home country (Brown and Mawson 2016; Decker *et al.* 2016; Mason *et al.* 2015) and that due to considerable failure rates, it is hard to predict, especially in case of young and small firms, which of them would manage to grow faster and create more jobs in the future. Thus, such firms should be monitored more during their support periods to be certain that they will achieve the expected targets (de Morais Sarmento and Nunes, 2015).

In future research, it would be useful to distinguish between job flows based on full-time equivalent employment and those based on head-count employment,[5] but also worker flows versus job flows (Banerjee and Jesenko, 2014; Davis and Haltiwanger, 1992; Meriküll, 2016) and low- versus high-quality jobs (Davis *et al.*, 1996; Glaister *et al.*, 2014; Kuhn *et al.*, 2016). Moreover, to find out if survived firms differ from others, it would be interesting to study the differences between firms that have remained operating and those that already closed down all local and foreign operations (Cieślik, 2017). In addition, it would be useful to find out whether job creation and job destruction rates differed by firm age and size, as this would help to understand better whether small firms created more jobs than large firms (Acs and Audretsch, 1989; Anyadike-Danes *et al.*, 2015; Birch, 1979, 1981; Stangler and Litan, 2009) or vice versa (Acs *et al.*, 2008; Davis *et al.*, 1996; de Morais Sarmento and Nunes, 2015). Finally, it would be important to study how foreign ownership (Masso *et al.*, 2005) and making foreign investments (Brown and Mawson, 2016; Mason *et al.*, 2015), other changes in firm structure like (local) divestitures, acquisitions and mergers (Haltiwanger *et al.*, 2013) and industry characteristics (Banerjee and Jesenko, 2014; Masso *et al.*, 2005; Kletzer, 2002) have affected job flows. This would also allow developing somewhat more detailed policy implications although, again, it is not possible to foresee all changes that could happen in the future.

Notes

* This work was supported by the Institutional Research Funding IUT20–49 of the Estonian Ministry of Education and Research and, in the case of Tiia Vissak, also by the Estonian Research Council's grant PUT 1003. Jaan Masso is also grateful to Oxford Research, for involving him in the project 'Job creation in SMEs' by the European Foundation for the Improvement of Living and Working Conditions, focusing on employment creation in born globals; that involvement also contributed to him becoming interested in the subject area of this book.

1 According to Birch (1981), jobs are created 'whenever a new firm starts up, an existing firm expands, or a firm located elsewhere moves in. Jobs are lost whenever an establishment closes its doors, lays off people, or moves out'.

2 Still, this has not always been so: for instance, Haltiwanger and Vodopivec (2002) explained that especially in the first half of the 1990s, larger Estonian firms had higher job destruction rates due to the economic restructuring.

3 Some authors have also used terms such as high-impact firms, fast growing firms and gazelles. Their definitions have differed but an overview of these definitions will not be given here as the focus of this chapter is elsewhere.
4 Two types of born globals were identified to improve the comparability of the results. Still, it has to be noted that due to some similarities between some of the criteria used for defining these firms, some firms belonged to both categories.
5 Although in Estonia, the part-time employment rate has mostly been below 10 per cent (Krillo and Masso, 2010).

References

Acs, Z. J. and Audretsch, D. B. (1989), 'Job creation and firm size in the U.S. and West Germany', *International Small Business Journal*, Vol. 7, No. 4, pp. 9–22.

Acs, Z., Parsons, W. and Tracy, S. (2008), *High-impact firms: gazelles revisited,* Small Business Administration, Office of Advocacy, Washington.

Anyadike-Danes, M., Hart, M. and Du, J. (2015), 'Firm dynamics and job creation in the United Kingdom: 1998–2013', *International Small Business Journal*, Vol. 33, No. 1, pp. 12–27.

Audretsch, D. B. and Elston, J. A. (2006), 'R&D intensity and the relationship between firm size and growth in Germany', in Santarelli, E. (ed.), *Entrepreneurship, growth, and innovation. The dynamics of firms and industries*, Springer, Cham, pp. 134–148.

Banerjee, B. and Jesenko, M. (2014), 'Dynamics of firm-level job flows in Slovenia, 1996–2011', *Comparative Economic Studies*, Vol. 56, No. 1, pp. 77–109.

Bentivogli, C. and Pagano, P. (1999), 'Trade, job destruction and job creation in European manufacturing', *Open Economies Review*, Vol. 10, No. 2, pp. 165–184.

Bilkey, W. J. (1978), 'An attempted integration of the literature on the export behavior of firms', *Journal of International Business Studies*, Vol. 9, No. 1, pp. 33–46.

Birch, D. L. (1979), *The job generation process*, MIT Press, Cambridge, MA.

Birch, D. L. (1981), 'Who creates jobs?' *The Public Interest*, No. 65, pp. 3–14.

Bogas, P. and Barbosa, N. (2015), 'High-growth firms: what is the impact of region-specific characteristics?', in Baptista, R. and Leitão, J. (eds), *Entrepreneurship, human capital, and regional development*, Springer, Cham, pp. 295–308.

Brown, R. and Mawson, S. (2016), 'The geography of job creation in high growth firms: the implications of "growing abroad"', *Environment and Planning C*, Vol. 34, No. 2, pp. 207–227.

Casillas, J. C. and Moreno-Menéndez, A. M. (2014), 'Speed of the internationalization process: The role of diversity and depth in experiential learning', *Journal of International Business Studies*, Vol 45, No. 1, pp. 85–101.

Chetty, S. and Campbell-Hunt, C. (2004), 'A strategic approach to internationalization: a traditional versus a "born-global" approach', *Journal of International Marketing*, Vol. 12, No. 1, pp. 57-81.

Cieślik, J. (2017), *Entrepreneurship in emerging economies: enhancing its contribution to socio-economic development*, Springer, Cham.

Coviello, N. (2015), 'Re-thinking research on born globals', *Journal of International Business Studies*, Vol. 46, No. 1, pp. 17–26.

Coviello, N. E. and Munro, H. J. (1995), 'Growing the entrepreneurial firm: networking for international market development', *European Journal of Marketing*, Vol. 29, No. 7, pp. 49–61.

Davis, S. J. and Haltiwanger, J. (1992), 'Gross job creation, gross job destruction, and employment reallocation', *Quarterly Journal of Economics*, Vol. 107, No. 3, pp. 819–863.

Davis, S. J., Haltiwanger, J. and Schuh, S. D. (1996), 'Small business and job creation: dissecting the myth and reassessing the facts', *Small Business Economics*, Vol. 8, No. 4, pp. 297–315.

de Morais Sarmento, E. and Nunes, A. (2015), 'Entrepreneurship, job creation, and growth in fast-growing firms in Portugal: is there a role for policy?' in Baptista, R. and Leitão, J. (eds), *Entrepreneurship, human capital, and regional development*, Springer, Cham, pp. 333–386.

Decker, R., Haltiwanger, J., Jarmin, R. and Miranda, J. (2014), 'The role of entrepreneurship in US job creation and economic dynamism', *Journal of Economic Perspectives*, Vol. 28, No. 3, pp. 3–24.

Decker, R. A., Haltiwanger, J., Jarmin, R. S. and Miranda, J. (2016), 'Where has all the skewness gone? The decline in high-growth (young) firms in the U.S.', *European Economic Review*, Vol. 86, pp. 4–23.

Dencker, J. C., Gruber, M. and Shah, S. K. (2009), 'Individual and opportunity factors influencing job creation in new firms', *Academy of Management Journal*, Vol. 52, No. 6, pp. 1125–1147.

Ellis, P. and Pecotich, A. (2001), 'Social factors influencing export initiation in small and medium-sized enterprises', *Journal of Marketing Research*, Vol. 38, No. 1, pp. 119–130.

Eurofound (2012), *Born global: the potential of job creation in new international businesses*, Publications Office of the European Union, Luxembourg.

Eurofound (2016), *Job creation in SMEs: ERM annual report 2015*, Publications Office of the European Union, Luxembourg.

Faggio, G. and Konings, J. (2003), 'Job creation, job destruction and employment growth in transition countries in the 90's', *Economic Systems*, Vol. 27, No. 2, pp. 129–154.

Francioni, B., Vissak, T. and Musso, F. (2017), 'Small Italian wine producers' internationalization: the role of network relationships in the emergence of late starters', *International Business Review*, Vol. 26, No. 1, pp. 12–22.

Glaister, A. J., Liu, Y., Sahadev, S. and Gomes, E. (2014), 'Externalizing, internalizing and fostering commitment: the case of born-global firms in emerging economies', *Management International Review*, Vol. 54, No. 4, pp. 473–496.

Hagen, B. and Zucchella, A. (2014), 'Born global or born to run? The long-term growth of born global firms', *Management International Review*, Vol. 54, No. 4, pp. 497–525.

Haltiwanger, J. (2012), 'Job creation and firm dynamics in the United States', *Innovation Policy and the Economy*, Vol. 12, No. 1, pp. 17–38.

Haltiwanger, J. C. and Vodopivec, M. (2002), 'Gross worker and job flows in a transition economy: an analysis of Estonia', *Labour Economics*, Vol. 9, No. 5, pp. 601–630.

Haltiwanger, J. C., Jarmin, R. S. and Miranda, J. (2013), 'Who creates jobs? Small versus large versus young', *Review of Economics and Statistics*, Vol. 95, No. 2, pp. 347–361.

Henrekson, M. and Johansson, D. (2010), 'Gazelles as job creators: a survey and interpretation of the evidence', *Small Business Economics*, Vol. 35, No. 2, pp. 227–244.

Hohenthal, J., Johanson, J. and Johanson, M. (2014), 'Network knowledge and business-relationship value in the foreign market', *International Business Review*, Vol. 23, No. 1, pp. 4–19.

Huber, P., Oberhofer, H. and Pfaffermayr, M. (2017), 'Who creates jobs? Econometric modeling and evidence for Austrian firm level data', *European Economic Review*, Vol. 91, pp. 57–71.

Johanson, J. and Vahlne, J-E. (1977), 'The internationalization process of the firm: a model of knowledge development and increasing foreign market commitments', *Journal of International Business Studies*, Vol. 8, No. 1, pp. 23–32.

Johanson, J. and Vahlne, J.-E. (1990), 'The mechanism of internationalisation', *International Marketing Review*, Vol. 7, No. 4, pp. 11–24.

Jurajda, Š. and Terrell, K. (2008), 'Job reallocation in two cases of massive adjustment in Eastern Europe', *World Development*, Vol. 36, No. 11, pp. 2144–2169.

Kletzer, L. G. (2002), *Imports, exports, and jobs: what does trade mean for employment and job loss?* W. E. Upjohn Institute for Employment Research, University of California, Santa Cruz, Kalamazoo.

Knight, G. (2015), 'Born global firms: evolution of a contemporary phenomenon', in Zhou, S. Xu, H. and Shi, L. H. (eds.), *Advances in international marketing 25*, Emerald, Bingley, pp. 3–19.

Knight, G. A. and Cavusgil, S. T. (1996), 'The born global firm: a challenge to traditional internationalization theory', in Cavusgil, S. T. and Madsen, T. K. (eds), *Advances in international marketing 8*, Emerald, Bingley, pp. 11–26.

Knight, G. A. and Cavusgil, S. T. (2004), 'Innovation, organizational capabilities, and the born-global firm', *Journal of International Business Studies*, Vol. 35, No. 2, pp. 124–141.

Krillo, K. and Masso, J. (2010), 'The part-time/full-time wage gap in Central and Eastern Europe: the case of Estonia', *Research in Economics and Business: Central and Eastern Europe*, Vol. 2, No. 1, pp. 47–75.

Kuhn, J. M., Malchow-Møller, N. and Sørensen, A. (2016), 'Job creation and job types: new evidence from Danish entrepreneurs', *European Economic Review*, Vol. 86, pp. 161–187.

Landström, H. (2005), *Pioneers in entrepreneurship and small business research*, Springer, Cham.

Madsen, T. K. and Servais, P. (1997), 'The internationalization of born globals: an evolutionary process?' *International Business Review*, Vol. 6, No. 6, pp. 561–583.

Mason, C., Brown, R., Hart, M. and Anyadike-Danes, M. (2015), 'High growth firms, jobs and peripheral regions: the case of Scotland', *Cambridge Journal of Regions, Economy and Society*, Vol. 8, No. 2, pp. 343–358.

Masso, J., Eamets, R. and Philips, K. (2005), *Job creation and job destruction in Estonia: labour reallocation and structural changes*, IZA Discussion Paper No. 1,707, The Institute for the Study of Labor, Bonn.

McDougall, P. P., Oviatt, B. M. and Shrader, R. C. (2003), 'A comparison of international and domestic new ventures', *Journal of International Entrepreneurship*, Vol. 1, No. 1, pp. 59–82.

McKinsey and Company (1993), *Emerging exporters: Australia's high value-added manufacturing exporters*, McKinsey and Company and Australian Manufacturing Council, Melbourne.

Meriküll, J. (2016), 'Labor market transitions during the great recession in Estonia', In Kahanec, M. and Zimmermann, K. F. (eds), *Labor migration, EU enlargement, and the great recession*, Springer, Cham, pp. 347–365.

Mets, T. (2016), 'Is Estonia becoming better home for "born globals"?' In Smallbone, D., Virtanen, M. and Sauka, A. (eds), *Entrepreneurship, innovation and regional development*, Edward Elgar, Cheltenham, pp. 101–124.

Mettler, A. and Williams, A. D. (2011), *The rise of the micro-multinational: how freelancers and technology-savvy start-ups are driving growth, jobs and innovation*, Lisbon Council Policy Brief, Lisbon Council, Brussels.

Moen, O. and Servais, P. (2002), 'Born global or gradual global? Examining the export behaviour of small and medium-sized enterprises', *Journal of International Marketing*, Vol. 10, No. 3, pp. 49–72.

Morgan-Thomas, A. and Jones, M. V. (2009), 'Post-entry internationalization dynamics: differences between SMEs in the development speed of their international sales', *International Small Business Journal*, Vol. 27, No. 1, pp. 71–97.

Mudambi, R. and Zahra, S. (2007), 'The survival of international new ventures', *Journal of International Business Studies*, Vol. 38, No. 2, pp. 333–352.

OECD (2009), *OECD employment outlook 2009: tackling the jobs crisis*, OECD Publishing, Paris.

Oviatt, B. M. and McDougall, P. P. (1994), 'Toward a theory of international new ventures', *Journal of International Business Studies*, Vol. 25, No. 1, pp. 45–64.

Prashantham, S. and Young, S. (2011), 'Post-entry speed of international new ventures', *Entrepreneurship Theory and Practice*, Vol. 35, No. 2, pp. 275–292.

Rennie, M. (1993), 'Born global', *McKinsey Quarterly*, No. 4, pp. 45–52.

Rialp, A., Rialp, J. and Knight, G. A. (2005), 'The phenomenon of early internationalizing firms: what do we know after a decade (1993–2003) of scientific inquiry?' *International Business Review*, Vol. 14, No. 2, pp. 147–166.

Rialp, A., Rialp, J. and Knight, G. A. (2015), 'International entrepreneurship: a review and future directions', in Fernhaber, S. A. and Prashantham, S. (eds), *The Routledge companion to international entrepreneurship*, Routledge, New York, pp. 7–28.

Romanello, R. and Chiarvesio, M. (2016), 'Turning point: when born globals enter post-entry stage', *Journal of International Entrepreneurship*, in press.

Sleuwaegen, L. and Onkelinx, J. (2014), 'International commitment, post-entry growth and survival of international new ventures', *Journal of Business Venturing*, Vol. 29, No. 1, pp. 106–120.

Stangler, D. (2010), *High-growth firms and the future of the American economy*, Kauffman Foundation, Kansas City, Missouri.

Stangler, D. and Litan, R. E. (2009), *Where will the jobs come from?* Kauffman Foundation, Kansas City, Missouri.

Tracy, S. L. Jr. (2011), *Accelerating job creation in America: the promise of high-impact companies*, US Small Business Administration, Office of Advocacy, Washington.

Vissak, T. (2007), 'The emergence and success factors of fast internationalizers: four cases from Estonia', *Journal of East-West Business*, Vol. 13, No. 1, pp. 11–33.

Vissak, T. and Masso, J. (2015), 'Export patterns: typology development and application to Estonian data', *International Business Review*, Vol. 24, No. 4, pp. 652–664.

Wagner, J. (1995), 'Firm size and job creation in Germany', *Small Business Economics*, Vol. 7, No. 6, pp. 469–474.

Welch, C. and Paavilainen-Mäntymäki, E. (2014), 'Putting process (back) in: research on the internationalization process of the firm', *International Journal of Management Reviews*, Vol. 16, No. 1, pp. 2–23.

Yazdanfar, D. and Öhman, P. (2015), 'Firm-level determinants of job creation by SMEs: Swedish empirical evidence', *Journal of Small Business and Enterprise Development*, Vol. 22, No. 4, pp. 666–679.

Zahra, S. A. and George, G. (2002), 'International entrepreneurship: the current status of the field and future research agenda', in Hitt, M. A., Ireland, R. D. Camp, S. M. and Sexton, D. L. (eds), *Strategic entrepreneurship: Creating a new mindset*, Blackwell, London, pp. 255–288.

Zhao, H. and Hsu, C.-C. (2007), 'Social ties and foreign market entry: an empirical enquiry', *Management International Review*, Vol. 47, No. 6, pp. 815–844.

7 Born globals and the medical technology cluster in the west of Ireland

Natasha Evers and Majella Giblin

7.1 Introduction

Born globals are a unique type of entrepreneurial venture and can be defined as 'business organisations that from inception have a global mindset and seek to derive significant competitive advantage from the use of resources and the sale of outputs in multiple countries spanning three economic trading Blocs of NAFTA, EU and Asia-Pacific' (Andersson *et al.*, 2013). Born global firms are typically internationally market driven from the outset and acquire at least 25 per cent of foreign sales from multiple foreign countries in the first year of trading (Evers, 2010; Hennart, 2014).

With radical scientific advancements in sectors such as life science and medical technologies, there is a greater urgency for small ventures in these sectors to rapidly exploit proprietary knowledge on international markets. A number of European based studies (Giblin and Ryan, 2012; Andersson *et al.*, 2013) have shown that born globals operating in the medical device industry clusters have been found to act as agents of industry change through their radical innovations. In recent years, European policy makers have begun to recognise born globals as dynamic job creators in Europe (Eurofound, 2012; 2016), in particular, in those regions peripherally located from the industrial centres of mainland Europe (O'Gorman and Evers, 2011). In light of the growing importance of born globals for European regional economic development (Eurofound, 2016), there is a need for policy makers and researchers to acquire further insights into the industry context in which born globals emerge and the economic impact they can potentially make to employment and revenues in peripheral regions of Europe.

Although much research has focused on the internal firm attributes investigating born global emergence (Terjesen *et al.*, 2016), more recently scholars have turned their attention to the external factors and context that have led to born globals' creation (Andersson *et al.*, 2014; Ryan *et al.*, 2015). The nature of the industry and the context in which the firm operates can have a significant impact on the firm's internationalisation path (Evers *et al.*, 2015). The industry context can influence a born global's internationalisation processes (Andersson *et al.*, 2014; Evers, 2010). However, the local industry environment in which born globals are created and their aggregate impact on the context itself have received limited attention in the field of international entrepreneurship (Zahra and George, 2002; Fernhaber *et al.*, 2007; Evers, 2010; 2011).

Although few, some studies have shown that born global venture formation can be directly linked to industry characteristics such as the industry life cycle (embryonic, growth or mature), the degree of industry internationalisation (Evers, 2010; Fernhaber *et al.*, 2007) or the level of industry concentration in the form of regional industry clusters (Andersson *et al.*, 2013; Evers *et al.*, 2012). In particular, the role of industry clusters has received limited attention in born global research (Andersson *et al.*, 2013; Evers *et al.*, 2015), and no study has yet examined the role born global firms may play in generating job creation in an industry cluster.

Clusters have been traditionally defined as 'geographic concentrations of interconnected companies, specialised suppliers, service providers, firms in related industries, and associated institutions (for example universities, standards agencies, and trade associations) in particular fields that compete but also co-operate' (Porter, 1998). More recent definitions also acknowledge clusters as regional concentrations of related industries, including private business, suppliers and service providers, entrepreneurs as well as government agencies and other institutions which provide education, information, research and technical support to a regional economy (Slaper and Ortuzar, 2015). Industrial clusters have proved to be an important instrument of macroeconomic policy for national and regional governments. Governments, social partners and industry stakeholders have recognised industrial clusters as vital economic growth platforms creating and reviving regions in Europe (European Commission, 2012; Ketels *et al.*, 2012). For example, clusters have been identified as key facilitators of smart, sustainable and inclusive economic growth within the EU Framework Programme for Research and Innovation, Horizon 2020, and National/Regional Research and Innovation Strategies for Smart Specialisation (European Commission, 2012; European Cluster Policy Group, 2010).

Recent empirical research continues to endorse the importance of specialised industry clusters for regional economic development and for housing large tenant multinationals, driving productivity and job creation in the region (European Cluster Policy Group, 2010; Porter, 1998). High performing high tech industry clusters indicate strong job growth, higher levels of start-up activity, strong multinational presence, knowledge spill-overs, and economic productivity and export output (Ketels and Memedovic, 2008; Delgado *et al.*, 2014). In terms of job creation and innovation, Delgado *et al.* (2014) found that strong industry clusters record higher employment and innovation patenting growth with a strong complementarity between employment and innovation performance in regional clusters. Clusters can create multiple types of externalities, including knowledge, skills, and input–output linkages that improve regional performance (Delgado *et al.*, 2014; Delgado and Zeuli, 2016).

Other evidence on the economic impact of clusters found that clusters employ more than 50 per cent of the workforce and contribute a higher portion to GDP in post-industrial countries like the UK and the US (Choe and Roberts, 2011). Clusters rapidly increase levels of innovation, in terms of new product development, as they have been reported to account for 87 per cent of all patents within the US (Delgado *et al.*, 2014). The above results in greater industry contribution to a country's national GDP, employment and regional prosperity (European Commission, 2012; OECD, 1999; Sölvell *et al.*, 2003).

In terms of new firm creation, Fernhaber *et al.* (2007) propose the higher the level of concentration in the local industry, the greater the number of born global ventures created. Despite the positive employment effects delivered by industry clusters and born global ventures (Eurofound, 2016), research has been too brief on the employment effects of born globals in the context of regional industry cluster settings (Giblin and Ryan, 2012; Eurofound, 2016).

This chapter presents case evidence on the relationship between born global ventures and industry clusters as key drivers of job creation in small peripheral open economies such as Ireland. Drawing on extant evidence, it brings together key insights into the important role that the Galway medical technology industry cluster and indigenous born global entrepreneurship play in job creation in the western region of Ireland. It also examines the regional economic implications of this relationship for job creation in the Galway medtech cluster. According to a recent report on the Irish Medtech Industry (Cunningham *et al.*, 2015), Galway, a city in the west of Ireland, is the fourth most important location in the world for manufacturing of medical devices and employs one-third of the national workforce (approximately 9,000) in the Irish medical sector. Since the early 2000s the Galway cluster has developed into a globally competitive industry cluster in medical technologies (Giblin and Ryan, 2012). Research has shown that the medical technology (medtech) sectors have become highly internationalised through multinational corporations (MNCs) and have further catapulted rising numbers of rapidly internationalising medtech small- and medium-sized enterprises (SMEs) (Weigel, 2011). In recent years, studies have begun to pay particular attention to medtech sectors to explore born global ventures (Evers *et al.*, 2012; Andersson *et al.*, 2013).

This chapter follows with a review of the literature specifically on cluster theory and a review of studies examining born globals and industrial clusters. The Irish medical device cluster is then presented, followed by findings of case examples of born global emergence and implications on the cluster. The chapter concludes with a discussion of findings with insights for policy makers.

7.2 Literature review

7.2.1 Cluster theory

The literature on clusters, innovation systems, industrial districts and innovative milieu has focused on permanent geographical proximity or the co-location of various actors in a particular region that produces external economies and enhances their innovative capacity and competitiveness. Zaheer and George

(2004) empirically show that firms gain by developing linkages both within and outside geographical clusters. Other empirical investigations of clusters reveal a significant prevalence of firms accessing global linkages and emphasise the importance of such linkages and the circumstances under which they are most likely to occur (Andersson *et al.*, 2013).

In their cluster classification framework, Rugman and Verbeke (2003) identified clusters having geographic locus which can be either (1) with a strong domestic market and industry orientation – which resembles a local economy with no multinational corporations (MNCs) or trans-border connectivity; or (2) with an international or trans-border orientation, for example, hosting an influential MNC. In the latter case, foreign direct investment (FDI) attraction is based on 'the scope of activities and quality of the inter-linkages among activities in the cluster' (Birkinshaw, 2000). The World Bank Group and the OECD have advised that cluster policy should focus on the following three areas: locational focus (in terms of rural renewal and revival of lagging regions); sectoral development, i.e. sectors identified as strategically important for government investment and attracting FDI, such as the Marine Institute's project, supervised by National University of Ireland, Galway for the development of maritime and shipping services hub (IMDO, 2015); and actors, such as MNCs, universities, SMEs, research centres, cluster support organisations, etc. (Innovation Policy Platform, 2016).

7.2.2 *Born globals and industry clusters*

It has been found (Evers, 2010) and suggested (Andersson *et al.*, 2014) that peculiarities of some industry contexts can spur the creation of born global ventures. The nature of industry can determine the internationalisation path of firms in industry clusters (Evers *et al.*, 2012). The industry dynamics embedded between industry actors, particularly in high technology industry clusters, have been considered relevant for born globals' creation and development. Empirical evidence on born globals has been mainly set in high technology industry contexts. Technological capability has been recognised as a critical resource endowment of born global creation with technological strengths more easily accepted by global markets through their differentiated product offerings (Zahra *et al.*, 2006). Hence, new ventures also more likely display early internationalisation behaviour due to the role of knowledge in developing unique technologies (Oviatt and McDougall, 1994), the knowledge intensity of the sector they operate in (Autio *et al.*, 2000) and rapid technological learning (Zahra *et al.*, 2000).

Extant research suggests that born globals located in high tech clusters such as in medical technologies have rapidly internationalised, aided by their industry context and industry network members (Evers *et al.*, 2012). Studies have shown that new venture companies in high growth and innovation-based industries, such as the medical technology industry, agglomerate in cities and regions where they can benefit from local knowledge networks (Audretsch, 1998; Florida,

2002). Local institutions (e.g. governmental actors, hospitals and universities) are typically co-geographically located and, thus, offer an attractive infrastructural base for new medtech ventures (Al-Laham and Souitaris, 2008; Stuart and Sorenson, 2003).

Such local network connections generate benefits for the cluster actors, such as labour pooling, access to specialised suppliers and 'knowledge spillovers', which describe the transmission of sticky, non-articulated, tacit forms of knowledge between firms (Batheld *et al.*, 2004). In their study examining the influence of local and international networks on born global ventures in the Rhone-Alpes medtech cluster in France, Andersson *et al.* (2013) found that the highly internationalised medtech cluster facilitated the development of their born global case firms. Local networks in the cluster were important for influencing the internationalisation of medtech born global firms at inception. They also noted that local research institutions and their connections abroad helped born globals both to develop and internationalise their innovations rapidly in the global marketplace. Rapid internationalisation was found to be directly supported by born globals' close relationships with local research institutions, universities, specialised suppliers, hospitals and venture capital firms located in the regional cluster (Lechner and Leyronas, 2012; Andersson *et al.*, 2013). Co-location of industry actors in clusters can strengthen the relationships and networks embedded within them (Van Geenhuizen, 2008).

Medtech products are considered to experience short life cycles due to growing public and private investments as well as rapid developments in biosciences and biotechnologies. Collaboration between business actors and third level research entities has been recognised as advantageous for local industry development and renewal in regional clusters (Waluszewski, 2004). Product innovation processes in the medtech companies typically involve close cooperation with locally based university hospitals which have strong international links with research institutions (Weigel, 2011; Andersson *et al.*, 2013). Cooke and Huggins (2003) find that university links to national and international levels of industry are often much stronger than links to local industry. They also indentify a cluster's networks to engage successfully in product innovation and gain product synergies (Cooke and Huggins, 2003). Regional industry clusters that build productive links to organisations located outside their home region gain competitive advantages necessary to maintain or renew development trajectories (Kaufmann and Tödtling, 2000).

7.2.3 The cluster life cycle

Extant studies have reported on the emergence, growth and decline of industrial clusters (Giblin, 2011; Malmberg and Maskell, 2002; Tappi, 2005; Bergman, 2008). In this analysis, we refer to the cluster type denoting a strong MNC presence with an international orientation (Rugman and Verbeke, 2003). Due to rapid developments in technology and short product life cycles, high technology industry clusters also have life cycles and need to be managed to avoid their stagnation and decline (Malmberg and Maskell, 2002; Feldman *et al.*, 2005; Maskell and Kebir, 2006; Jenkins and Tallman, 2010). Technology 'clusters can rise or decline' (Jenkins and Tallman, 2010), when also exposed to local and regional economic shocks. Menzel and Fornahl (2009) have identified many conditions and factors appropriate to sustain each stage of the cluster life cycle for its successful development and performance. In the mature stage of the cluster life cycle, overdependence on its technology specialisation and excessive standardisation can result in 'lock-in' to technological capabilities (Hassink and Dong-Ho, 2005; Malmberg and Maskell, 2002), and organisational inertia (Narula, 2002), exposing it to potential technological obsolescence, exhaustion and to the cluster 'hollowing-out' or even its extinction. Cluster 'hollowing out' occurs when the higher profitability of overseas production reduces the relative importance of the cluster's core industrial base (Tomlinson and Cowling, 2003). This eventually leads to decline of production, FDI and entrepreneurial activity in the cluster. In particular, researchers have noted that factors such as knowledge 'lock-in', lack of entrepreneurial innovation, and overdependence on product specialisation can lead to cluster exhaustion and 'hollowing out' (Maskell and Kebir, 2006; Giblin and Ryan, 2012). To avoid clusters entering the decline stages and innovation inertia, Narula and Dunning (2010) suggest that industry clusters should leverage benefits that flow from local subsidiary MNC's external linkages with their parent company. A continuous flow of entrepreneurial radical and incremental innovations must be encouraged for cluster renewal and to strengthen knowledge embeddedness amongst MNC tenants, SMEs and local research infrastructure (Clancy *et al.*, 2013). Similarly, small enterprises have been found to adapt well to cyclical developments in technological innovation, thus supporting cluster development (Audretsch and Feldman, 1996; Giblin, 2011).

7.3 Irish medical technology industry

Up until the 1960s, Ireland had been a primarily agriculturally dependant, closed economy with high levels of unemployment, illiteracy and poverty (O'Rourke, 2016). From the 1960s and 1970s, led by the Secretary of Department of Finance, T. K. Whitaker, Irish economy policy began to aggressively pursue open trade agreements, promotion of competition and enterprise to generate industrial activity in emerging sectors. Ireland's EU membership in 1972, its introduction of fiscal incentives and substantial investment in third level education from 1980s onwards, enabled the government to successfully attract needed FDI into sectors that were deemed emerging with high-growth, high-performance potential (e.g. ICT, medical technology and pharmaceuticals).

Today Ireland has developed world-class industry specialisation in areas such as medical devices, technology, digital, IT, pharmaceuticals and financial services. Ireland has been acknowledged as world leader in attracting high value FDI projects (IBM, 2016) with its capital Dublin ranked third in by the Financial Times FDI's rankings as European City of the Future 2016/2017 (Financial

Times, 2016). There are currently over 174,000 people employed within foreign owned companies in Ireland, representing one in ten workers (IDA, 2015). It is well documented that high-technology activity in the Irish economy developed predominantly as a result of attracting inward foreign investment and therefore transferring knowledge from abroad. Within such sectors, specific multinational corporations were strategically targeted and enticed to set up operations in Ireland through a dedicated state sponsored industrial development agency called Industrial Development Agency (IDA) Ireland.

The medical technology sector was one such sector targeted by IDA Ireland and has been a major recipient of inward FDI. Fifteen of the top twenty medical technology companies globally have operations in Ireland, including Medtronic, Boston Scientific, Abbott, and Johnson & Johnson. Due primarily to these investments, medical devices and diagnostics now account for 8 per cent of total merchandise exports in Ireland, making the country the second largest exporter of medical technology products in Europe (IDA, 2016). There are currently approximately 400 companies in the sector in Ireland (indigenous and foreign-owned; includes supplier companies) employing 27,000 people (DJEI, 2016).

Between 2006 and 2015, the medical instruments and supplies sector was one of the top four leading sectors within Irish manufacturing in terms of employment growth (see Figure 7.1). While employment in many manufacturing sectors fell during this period – that includes the economic crisis – employment in the medical instruments industry grew by 34 per cent (DJEI, 2016).

Despite the strong MNCs presence, 90 per cent of companies in the sector are SMEs (Cunningham *et al.*, 2015). Foreign firms employ 96 per cent of the 27,000 employees in the sector (DJEI, 2016). However, the indigenous base of

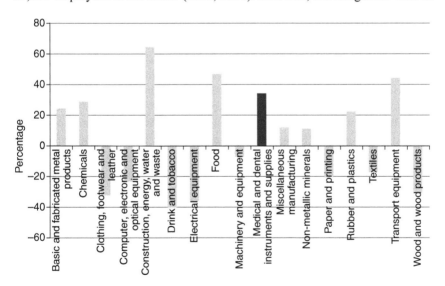

Figure 7.1 Manufacturing employment change by sector, 2006–2015.
Source: DJEI (2016).

companies in the sector is expanding in terms of employment and, although it is still comparatively very small, it is growing faster than the foreign-owned base. From 2006 to 2015, employment in Irish owned medical technology companies grew by 261 per cent (from 290 to 1,047 employees), while employment in foreign-owned counterparts grew by 16.9 per cent (from 22,307 to 26,087 employees) (DJEI, 2016).

To gain more insights into the character and contributions of the indigenous base within the Irish medical technology sector, the next section focuses on a regional cluster case.

7.3.1 The medical technology cluster in the west of Ireland

Emulating the characteristics of the medical technology sector nationally, a cluster of activity has emerged at a regional level in the west of Ireland, particularly around Galway city and county (Giblin and Ryan, 2012; 2015). Galway has been recognised as a 'focal point for many device firms' (Stommen, 2005) and 'one of Europe's leading industrial clusters' (Brown, 2005). The economic regional impact of Galway medtech cluster in the west of Ireland has been significant, employing one third of Ireland's 27,000 medical device employees and accounting for 39 per cent of regional distribution of medical devices (DJEI, 2016).

Employing approximately 4,500 people between them, two US owned subsidiaries – Boston Scientific and Medtronic – are considered anchors in the cluster playing a significant role in its development (Giblin and Ryan, 2012). In particular, the region has built a specialisation in the area of cardiovascular devices as those two large MNCs produce drug-eluting stents from their sites in Galway.

Interestingly, the Galway-based cluster has grown and developed organically as a successful internationalised and export-driven cluster without any formal leadership of cluster director or manager as seen in clusters in other EU regions. The origins that drove the organic growth were first the establishment of foreign investment in the 1980s and 1990s, more specifically the arrival of CR Bard in 1982 (this division and facility was later acquired by Medtronic) and Boston Scientific in 1994. Prior to these facilities there was little by way of medical technology activity in Galway; just one foreign-owned diagnostics company existed and a couple of indigenous supplier-service firms had set up to meet the needs of this company.

Since their establishment in Galway, the CR Bard/Medtronic and Boston Scientific sites have been involved in the production of stents and have evolved from solely manufacturing facilities to product design and development of next generation devices, so that R&D activity now resides along with manufacturing (Giblin and Ryan 2012; 2015). The Boston Scientific and Medtronic subsidiaries have become significant sites within their respective corporate environments earning titles and associated investments from the headquarter such as Customer Innovation Centre in 2013 (CR Bard/Medtronic) and Centre for Excellence in

Drug Eluting Stents in 2012 (Boston Scientific). Further, the anchor presence of MNCs have transformed the Galway cluster into a magnet for FDI and have strengthened the medtech cluster eco-system further to stimulate rapid spread of indigenous entrepreneurship in the form of service supply and born-global driven as discussed below.

The presence of the MNC tenants has influenced the technology trajectory of the cluster. In 2015, 71 medical technology companies were identified in the cluster, of which 34 per cent were foreign-owned and 66 per cent indigenous. As a result of the presence of foreign-owned firms as well as their transition from solely manufacturing to higher value added activities, the indigenous sector has also been influenced. The cluster produces cardiology-related products (e.g. hypotubes, balloon catheters, filters and guidewires) as well as other products in the areas of muscle and nerve stimulators, soft tissue implants and pulmonary drug delivery systems.

As shown in Figure 7.2, the cluster is highly internationalised, first by the presence of foreign owned companies which has also led to international and export market orientation of firms emerging in the cluster. International knowledge embeddedness has also occurred through engagement in networks with specialised suppliers, strategic partners, distributors and internal sales offices on a global level. The end-users for many of the medical devices produced by firms

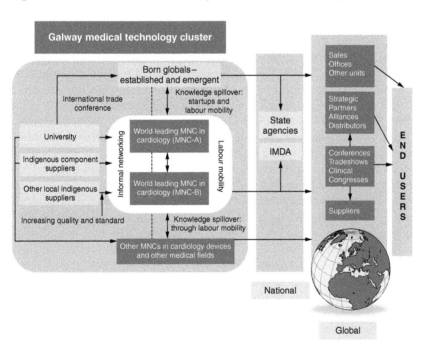

Figure 7.2 The industry actors in the Galway medtech cluster.

Source: Lucerna Report, NUIG (2010). Accessible at: www.nuigalway.ie/whitakerinstitute/research/lucerna.html.

in the Galway cluster are international. The knowledge infrastructure and commercial activity in the medical device cluster in Galway is underpinned by university-industry linkages, a continuous development of a skilled labour pool, international reputation through the success of Boston Scientific and Medtronic, the growth of supplier firms and knowledge transfers establishing new start-ups.

The international reputation of local research infrastructure of researchers and medical professionals at the National University of Ireland, Galway (NUIG) and public and private hospital institutions are sources of knowledge and offer international connections to research institutions abroad. Such end-users can provide feedback on a device in terms of its usability, any changes that are needed and the type of instrumentation required for the latest procedures or medical issues. Therefore, accessing such end-users and particularly the internationally leading ones is reported as important for the firms. As a senior manager from one MNC states:

> We use people in Ireland but the way the industry works, the way the sector works, is that there are a number of physicians that are well-respected internationally and we would work with those internationally-respected ones as well as the local ones.
>
> (Giblin, 2011)

7.3.2 Indigenous entrepreneurship in the cluster

There are two forms of indigenous activity that have emerged from the cluster. One form consists of locally focused suppliers, that is, firms set up as suppliers to service predominantly the foreign-owned companies locally (at least initially). The other can be categorised as born globals (as defined earlier) operating in the medtech sector: these companies were established with the intention of developing their own medical device, component to a device, materials or software product in the medical technology sector for an international marketplace; included in this definition are also firms that supply design and development services (e.g. R&D) locally to fund the development of the their own devices/components. The 'locally focused suppliers' category of indigenous activity was first to emerge in the early 1980s, in the early stages of the cluster's development, following investments by foreign-owned corporations (the first such foreign investment was in 1973). As Figure 7.3 illustrates, the number of these suppliers continued to rise steadily in the 1990s and first half of 2000s. However the number reached peak by 2010 and began to decrease in more recent years.

In contrast, born global firms emerged later in the growth stages of the cluster's development and grew quite sharply from the late 1990s to early 2000s, with a continued upward trend. The number of born globals began to level to just under 30 firms from 2012 onwards. Similarly, to coincide with this growth in the cluster and FDI, in 1998 the Irish born global firm Creganna Medical Group relaunched itself fully into medical device production. Creganna Medical Group has become a leading Irish indigenous global supplier located in the

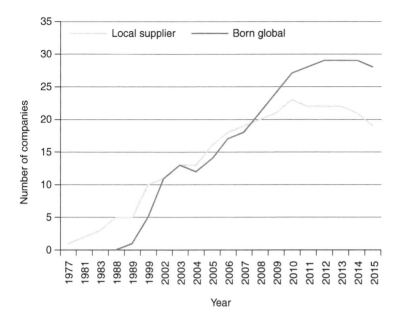

Figure 7.3 Number of indigenous suppliers and born global firms in the Galway medical technology cluster between 1980 and 2015.

Source: adapted and updated from Giblin and Ryan (2015).

cluster and has grown from a born global device venture in the 1980s to a full producer of medical devices in the late 1990s as cluster specialisation grew. In the last decade, a smaller base of indigenous firms has developed, and other foreign-owned companies have been attracted to the region. Creganna Medical Group had been acknowledged on the Europe Top 500 list for growth in job creation with 800 in the Galway plant and 2,000 worldwide during the period 1998 to 2004 (IMDA, 2016) Just over six years after Creganna transitioned solely into the medical device sector, it was awarded Europe's Top 500 high growth companies for job creation.[1]

The role of Irish serial entrepreneurs in born global development

These born global firms have certain characteristics that demonstrate the significance of their role in the cluster. First, while they are relatively small in terms of employment-size (all of the born globals in the cluster have been micro or SME size[2]) compared to the foreign-owned MNC counterparts, there is a trend of founders of born globals becoming serial entrepreneurs in the cluster and establishing sequentially multiple born globals in the region. Previous research has shown that many of the born globals' founders are ex-employees of the large-sized foreign-owned MNCs in the cluster: in 2011, over 50 per cent of the born global firms in existence were founded by ex-employees of the local MNC sub-sidiaries (Giblin and Ryan, 2015).

When taking on the role of serial entrepreneurs, these ex-MNC employees also become investors or mentors in other born globals establishing in the cluster. Examples of this phenomenon are displayed in Figure 7.4. The shaded boxes in the figure represent examples of born global firms established in the region. Three ex-employees of the foreign-owned MNC, CR Bard, established the firm Mednova in Galway in 1996, which was one of the first born globals in the cluster. This firm was set up to design and develop an endovascular-related filter device aimed at the international marketplace. Mednova was acquired by the foreign-owned MNC Abbott in 2005 (which also had operations in Galway at this time). Two of the co-founders subsequently established Veryan Medical and Novate Medical in 2003 and 2006 respectively. More recently, one of the founders also became an investor in, and chairman/director of, other born globals in the region – for example, Bluedrop Medical, established in 2014, and Embo, established in 2012 and later acquired by a foreign-owned MNC. Similarly, the third co-founder of Mednova co-founded another born global (Neuravi) and became a chairman of another born global in the region (Cambus Medical). In an interview conducted in 2010 with the Chairman and co-founder of Cambus Medical, he said: 'We're now 3 years old, we have over 40 customers in 20 countries, over 20 countries actually now so we're, we're already kind of well global at this stage'. When asked if they supply to local market or local multi-nationals, he responded: 'No, oh god no, no it's a global industry!'

These findings show that the born global community of the Galway medtech cluster is characterised as being well networked locally with some entrepreneurs founding multiple companies while also investing or acting in an advisory and executive management capacity as chairpersons or directors to other new born

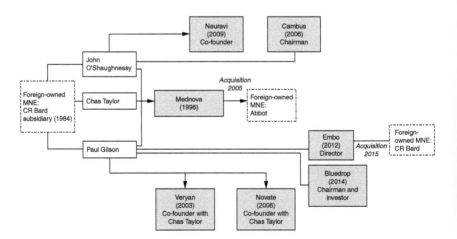

Figure 7.4 Illustration of the role of serial entrepreneurs in the creation of multiple born global firms with diverse innovations in the Galway medtech cluster.

global firms in the cluster. The significance of inter-firm networking activities for knowledge flows and thus the innovativeness and competitiveness of firms and the cluster alike are well documented in the cluster literature (e.g. Andersson *et al.*, 2013; Bell 2005, Breschi and Malerba, 2005) and in this respect the born global entrepreneurs of the Galway medtech cluster play an important role.

Born globals in cluster innovation and technology diversity

The second significant characteristic of the born globals in the cluster is their engagement in related and unrelated technological areas to the core cluster specialisation of producing cardiovascular stents used in angioplasty procedures. Giblin and Ryan's (2012) study of the Galway medtech cluster found that the anchor subsidiaries – Boston Scientific and Medtronic – did not cooperate on product development (to guard against unintentional knowledge spill-over); yet both of these leading subsidiary MNCs shaped the cluster's technological trajectory in vascular devices, resulting in the concentration in few medical devices (i.e. interveinal cardiology). Further, they have jointly influenced university provisions in the locality and the advancement of supplier capabilities. This specialisation – particularly in the endovascular area – evolved due to the significant presence of the foreign-owned MNCs, namely CR Bard, Medtronic and Boston Scientific, among others. Such behaviour in the cluster could reduce the risk of 'technological lock-in' and product over-dependencies. However, it can be indicated that it is indigenous activity locally that has helped drive technological diversity in the cluster. Giblin and Ryan (2015) reveal that, by 2011, 82 per cent of the companies engaging in additional technological areas to what existed in the cluster in 1990 or 2000 were indigenous.

Further analysis of the 28 born globals that were identified in 2015 reveals that 10 of these companies can be classified as being primarily engaged in developing devices, components or materials specifically in the vascular space (cardiovascular, endovascular). The output from these firms can be recorded as being of a 'related variety' nature to the core cluster specialisation as these born globals are not necessarily developing full stents but rather have identified niche areas to pursue related to the vascular space (e.g. biomaterial solutions, materials for catheter-based medical devices). The other 18 born globals can be categorised as involved in activities that are of a more 'unrelated variety' nature to the core cluster specialisation, such as connected healthcare for drug delivery systems and for use in diagnostics/detection; gastroenterology intelligent systems; devices for urology, pulmonary, gynaecology and respiratory; and medical software.

Further, the cluster's eco-system has also created opportunities for convergent technologies between biopharma and medical device firms by developing and investing in product capabilities. Medical device ventures are identifying opportunities by combining mainstream product innovation capabilities in medical devices to ally with the biopharma sector to deliver advanced technology in drug delivery to patients (Evers *et al.*, 2012). For example, Irish born global medical device firms such as Aerogen have extended their products to deliver total technological solutions by partnering with biopharma companies to integrate drugs into their own medical devices to offer innovative solutions. A recently established Galway based born global venture called Nortev was created by developing a currently sold medical device technology into a device for the global equine and veterinary markets.

7.4 Discussion

From this study, a number of observations emerge. First, this study concurs with the view that the greater the intensity of global integration in an industry sector, the higher the likelihood for additional born globals to emerge in the sector (Evers, 2010; Andersson et al., 2013; Evers et al., 2015). The global dynamics of the Galway medtech industry driven by technology and MNC acquisitions further suggest that structural factors can necessitate firms to embrace global strategies early in their life cycle (i.e. high product development cost and niche products with limited home market demand) and a multi-domestic strategy (i.e. different regulations in different countries).

Second, extant entrepreneurship research has suggested that, during the growth stages of an industry cluster's development, larger tenant firms tend to collude against new entry of new ventures. This behaviour assumes that new venture creation is thus discouraged during a cluster's growth phase by the likelihood of being forced abroad to chase opportunities for survival or alternatively be wiped out by domestic larger players (Oster, 1999). Consequently, this chapter's findings show that during the growth phases of the cluster's development (late 1990s onwards), new ventures emerged as born globals and equally important agents of change through innovations they created (Giblin, 2011). By acting as a conduit of the requisite knowledge, MNC behaviour in the cluster embraced born global entrepreneurial behaviour, rather than prohibiting it as prompted above (Oster, 1999). Further, the Galway cluster's MNCs recognised that born globals can influence their global business trajectories as generators of innovation and international product strategies (Vapola et al., 2008). Combining local knowledge held in the technological cluster with international knowledge and technologies gained from MNC affiliates facilitated a variation of activities around the global value chain's higher order needs. Vapola (2012) supports this view and introduces the idea of a global innovation constellation, referred to as a set of MNCs and start-ups in a loose, nonequity, innovation alliance in a particular competitive domain, which eventually leads to enhanced innovation performance for the whole economy. Hence, traditional MNCs learnt from born globals about new technological and market opportunities, while the born global benefitted by accessing international markets.

Figure 7.5 depicts the antecedents driving the emergence of born globals in the Galway medtech cluster. It captures the components underpinning local cluster's eco-system such as skills development generated by local MNCs. Figure 7.5 also identifies the highly globalised nature of the medtech industry and its network connections which are important for the cluster in born global creation.

The antecedents for serial and first time entrepreneurship are the prior MNC experience that acquire in the form of typically ex-employees of MNC in the cluster itself who decide to create their own venture. Serial entrepreneurs (as shown in Figure 7.4) and first time entrepreneurs in Creganna Medical Group and Aerogen for example drive indigenous globally orientated entrepreneurship in the cluster and serve as employment generators through diverse lines of medtech innovation. Clancy *et al.* (2013) argue that diversity can come about in two ways: first, MNC subsidiaries move into new development areas through internal sources (i.e. intrapreneurship); and second, they do so externally, in more novel technologies, through collaboration with external actors in the clusters. The analysis in this chapter aligns with the view that collaboration between traditional MNCs in regional industry clusters and entrepreneurial behaviour is advantageous for local industry development and renewal.

This study finds that entrepreneurs who drive the establishment of born globals either directly as founders or in executive capacity on boards of management are essential in driving job creation and growth in specialised sectors of the medtech industry. In particular those entrepreneurs that pursue acquisition as an exit strategy after a relatively short period of time trading, typically do not just establish one born global but rather multiple numbers of firms; creating jobs in each of these over the life span of a cluster.

The case study on the medtech cluster eco-system in the Galway region has demonstrated that the cluster has served as antecedent to the creation of the born global firms with cutting edge technologies (Figure 7.5). Thanks to indigenous born global innovation activity, the cluster has benefited from renewal and diversity of innovation specialisation which has led to greater employment for the region. It can be argued that large MNC subsidiaries in a cluster are mainly driven by scale and hence specialise in a small number of particular product areas. This batch specialisation is often conferred on the Galway based MNC subsidiaries by their US-based headquarters of parent subsidiaries, and therefore its local employees are highly specialised in these product technologies. The born global ventures, on the other hand, rather than competing with larger MNCs, have mainly undertaken product development activities in areas that are often more market niche and arguably more technologically novel (e.g. converging technologies in new ways and applying university-based research to the creation of new products). As a result, born globals have played an important role in developing the local human capital and specialised lines of employment driven by the innovation they create. Hence born globals have added to the diversity of skills and technical exposure of actors in the cluster.

To extend the growth phase of a cluster, and avoid a technological lock-in and therefore evade exhaustion, a cluster needs to continuously renew itself through technological diversification (Martin and Sunley, 2011; Malmberg and Maskell, 2002). Specialisation is required at least initially for cluster growth but a balance of specialisation and diversification is needed to extend the cluster life cycle. The findings of the research on the Galway medtech cluster strengthen empirical support in the literature on cluster extension. Another positive impact

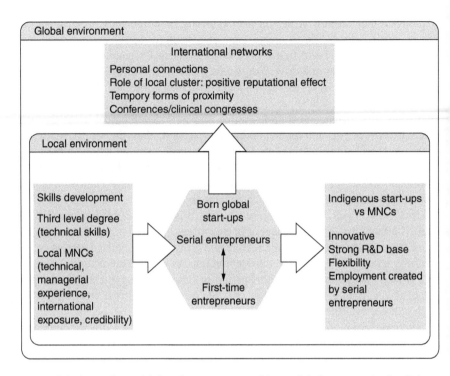

Figure 7.5 Antecedents driving the emergence of born global ventures in the Galway medtech industrial cluster eco-system.

of born globals' innovation behaviour on job creation in the cluster is that it has helped create job categories under new lines of innovation and further helped prevent the hollowing-out effect on the cluster. Born globals created by serial entrepreneurs identified specialised and novel technologies in both mainstream product categories and also diversified into emergent categories outside the cluster's specialisation. This contributed to prevention of cluster hollowing-out and over-specialisation in mainstream product categories (Clancy *et al.*, 2013). Born globals are flexible, innovative and risk-taking entities but also generate technological diversification needed for the cluster's technological renewal.

At the same time, the case of the Galway medtech cluster reveals that the presence of large organisations alone does not inevitably stimulate such a clustering effect and emphasises that appropriate characteristics and conditions need to be in place, namely entrepreneurial activity and local research infrastructure such as universities. Certain stages of the innovation process require actors to meet for the effective transfer of knowledge and, therefore, geographical proximity in a temporary form 'remains essential' (Torre, 2008). The findings indicate the importance of the interaction between local and international actors for innovation. Such findings align with a study on Norway's Urban High Tech Cluster which stressed that:

Interaction through MNC and SME global pipelines was as much as four times more powerful than local interaction when it came to radical innovation ... The idea about global pipelines has become quite prominent in research over the past few years but you don't see much of a policy impact yet.

(Fitjar and Rodríguez-Pose, 2011)

Hence, the region has served as a magnet for MNC investment to stimulate and refuel needed resources for accelerating markets for indigenous innovation through born globals.

In line with Vapola (2012), the traditional MNC are cognisant of entrepreneurial innovation in the Galway medtech cluster. MNCs acknowledge that their performance and employment potential was facilitated by entrepreneurial innovations through a continuous flow of innovation with global demand potential. As new ventures need resources to be able to exploit internationalisation (Preece *et al.*, 1999), many resource opportunities exist for new firms in the growth stage of an industry cluster life cycle, resulting in somewhat lessened competitive pressures (Fernhaber *et al.*, 2007). Hence, as evidenced from the case study of the Galway medtech cluster, the growth stage of cluster life cycle has benefited from born global creation and vice versa. In the case of the medical technology cluster, the study shows that, when large firms enact a leading role by influencing the technology trajectory of the region and stimulate the local dynamic in the form of born global activity, they can generate agglomerative effects, thereby enhancing the economic performance and sustainability of clusters. In line with extant research (Andersson *et al.*, 2013), this study supports the view that leading organisations can act as an important facilitator in connecting the global and local dimensions of clusters even in the absence of extensive local formal linkages.

7.5 Conclusions

Drawing on extant evidence, this chapter brings together key insights of the relationship between the Galway medical technology cluster and indigenous born global entrepreneurship. It also examines the regional economic implications of this relationship for job creation, through cluster renewal and sustainability. As the example of the Galway medtech cluster shows, born global nascent ventures can propel economic regional development in cluster locations.

First, the economic role of the highly internationalised medtech cluster in Galway has proved itself as a national employment and wealth creator for the Irish economy. Employment and export growth has not only been driven by FDI through MNCs but also through indigenous supply based entrepreneurship through service supply base and at a more strategic level through globally-orientated entrepreneurship. Born globals enact a dynamic role with the cluster as a key agent of innovation and firm creation. The born globals may well have emerged from the cluster but in exchange have adopted a multifaceted role by strengthening capabilities in innovation enabling sustainability, renewal and re-invention of the cluster eco-system. Hence, the potential contribution of born globals to employment and job creation may often be misjudged by policy-makers who may focus on the number of jobs created by firms in existence at a particular point in time. It may be prudent for researchers and policy makers to focus on the serial entrepreneurs founding these born globals and their role in job creation as well as shaping human capital development over a number of years as a cluster evolves. In this respect, a significant issue to be addressed is how the exit strategies often employed by serial entrepreneurs may subsequently impact jobs and labour expertise developed over time.

Second, in particular for policy makers, the importance of born global entre-preneurship in the cluster strengthens the Irish government's remit to focus on export-driven ventures. This study reinforces the policy line that new ventures at start-up and early growth stages should be provided with structurally embedded support and leadership programmes to ensure that they move into their growth stages and continue to generate greater security of employment. For a cluster in the early stages of the development, a stakeholder driven co-ordinated approach would be required from policy, for example in appointing a cluster co-ordination team represented by public and private stakeholders.

Third, this study points to the fact that born globals can play an important role in developing the local human capital by adding to the diversity of skills and technical exposure. Operating in a high knowledge-intensive sector such as medtech, born global founders are highly industry experienced and thus any future creation of born globals in the cluster would depend on high volumes of skilled human capital to create innovative ventures with global market impact. Hence, bottom-up initiatives at firm-level are needed, such as management and commercialisation training and support initiatives to stimulate innovation and entrepreneurship. This could help ensure a strong pipeline of new entrepreneur-ial managers who would lead the born global ventures and grow them into indi-genous medium- to large-scale global employers in the region.

Fourth, policy further needs to prioritise the certainty across Irish third-level education institutions in delivering a steadfast supply of educated and skilled human capital in areas required by clusters such as design and mechanical engi-neering, marketing, biomedical science and entrepreneurship. For example, the successful 'BioInnovate programme' at National University of Ireland (Galway) is based on the 'Biodesign model' at Stanford University.[3]

Finally, the case study presented illustrates that the cluster eco-system has been instrumental in breeding born globals which can co-create both new product and areas of human expertise to support this innovation. However, from the Galway medtech case it can be noted that, once the technology in born globals has been fully commercialised, the born global founders tend to opt for foreign MNC acquisition rather than growing them independently as born global firms. In light of the significant public investment in R&D and in local public research infrastructure, national policy needs to develop to incentivise born global entrepreneurs to grow the venture internationally or employ a manager who can do it for them. Such incentives may help the region reduce high dependency upon the main sources of employment in the cluster – namely MNCs. Hence, policy needs to provide incentives to born global start-ups not to sell off technology early in the firm's life cycle but rather collaborate with the aim of growing into an indigenous global SME or large scale enterprise, following the path of the flagship Irish medtech company Creganna Medical Group.

Notes

1 www.creganna.com/creganna-receives-innovation-of-thc-year-award/ (accessed 27 February 2017).
2 The EU definition of Small and Medium sized Enterprises (SMEs) is categorised into three types of enterprises (1) micro firms (0–9 employees); (2) small firms (10 to 49 employees); and (3) medium firms (50–249 employees).
3 www.bioinnovate.ie.

References

Al-Laham, A. and Souitaris, V. (2008), 'Network embeddedness and new-venture internationalization: analyzing international linkages in the German biotech industry', *Journal of Business Venturing*, Vol. 23, No. 5, pp. 567–586.

Andersson, S., Evers, N. and Griot, C. (2013), 'Local and international networks in small firm internationalisation: cases from the Rhône-Alpes medical technology regional cluster', *Entrepreneurship and Regional Development*, Vol. 25, Nos. 9 and 10, pp. 867–888.

Andersson, S., Evers, N. and Kuivalainen, O. (2014), 'International new ventures: rapid internationalisation across different industry contexts', *European Business Review*, Vol. 26, No. 5, pp. 390–405.

Audretsch, D. B. (1998), 'Agglomeration and the location of innovative activity', *Oxford Review of Economic Policy*, Vol. 14, No. 2, pp. 18–29.

Audretsch, D. B. and Feldman, M. P. (1996), 'Innovative clusters and the industry life cycle', *Review of Industrial Organization*, Vol. 11, No. 2, pp. 253–273.

Autio E, Sapienza, H. and Almeida, J. (2000), 'Effects of age at entry, knowledge intensity and imitability on international growth', *Academy of Management Journal*, Vol. 43, No. 5, pp. 909–924.

Batheld, H., Malmberg, A. and Maskel, P. (2004), 'Clusters and knowledge: local buzz, global pipelines and the process of knowledge creation', *Progress in Human Geography*, Vol. 28, No. 1, pp. 31–56, 314.

Bell, G. G. (2005), 'Clusters, networks and firm innovativeness', *Strategic Management Journal*, Vol. 26, No. 3, pp. 287–295.

Bergman, E. (2008), 'Cluster life-cycles: an emerging synthesis', in Karlsson, C. (ed.), *Handbook of research on cluster theory*, Edward Elgar, Cheltenham, pp. 114–132.

Birkinshaw, J. (2000), 'Upgrading of industry clusters and foreign investment', *International Studies of Management & Organization*, Vol. 30, No. 2, pp. 93–113.

Breschi, S. and Malerba, F. (eds) (2005), *Clusters, networks and innovation*, Oxford University Press, Oxford.

Brown, J. M. (2005), 'Industry clusters: Galway gets to the heart of the matter', *Financial Times*, 11 February.

Choe, K. A. and Roberts, B. H. (2011), *Competitive cities in the 21st century: cluster-based local economic development*, Asian Development Bank, Mandaluyong City, Philippines.

Clancy, J., Ryan, P. and Giblin, M. (2013), 'High technology clusters, flagship MNE subsidiaries, and mothership ecosystems', *35th DRUID celebration conference 2013*, Barcelona, 17–19 June.

Cooke, P. and Huggins, R. (2003), 'High technology clustering in Cambridge', In Amin, A., Goglio, S. and Sforzi, F. (eds), *The institutions of local development*, IGU, London, pp. 51–74.

Cunningham, J., Dolan, B., Kelly, D. and Young, C. (2015), *Medical device sectoral overview*, Galway City and County Council Industrial Baseline Publication, Galway.

Delgado, M., Porter, M. E. and Stern, S. (2014), 'Clusters, convergence, and economic performance', *Research Policy*, Vol. 43, No. 10, pp. 1785–1799.

Delgado, M. and Zeuli, K. (2016), 'Clusters and regional performance: implications for inner cities', *Economic Development Quarterly*, Vol 30, No. 2, pp. 117–136.

DJEI (2016), *Annual employment survey 2015*, Department of Jobs, Enterprise and Innovation, Dublin.

Eurofound (2012), *Born global: the potential of job creation in new international businesses*, Publications Office of the European Union, Luxembourg.

Eurofound (2016), *Job creation in SMEs, ERM annual report 2015*, Publications Office of the European Union, Luxembourg.

European Cluster Policy Group (2010), *European Cluster Policy Group final recommendations: a call for policy action*, Brussels. Available at: www.theairnet.org/v3/publications-2/.

European Commission (2012), *Restructuring and anticipation of change: what lessons from recent experience?* EUR-Lex, COM(2012) 7 final, Brussels.

Evers, N. (2010), 'Factors influencing internationalisation of new ventures: an exploratory study of the Irish aquaculture industry', *Journal of International Entrepreneurship*, Vol. 8, No. 4, pp. 392–416.

Evers, N. (2011), 'International new ventures in low-tech sectors: a dynamic capabilities perspective', *Journal of Small Business and Enterprise Development*, Vol. 18, No. 3, pp. 502–528.

Evers, N., Andersson, S. and Hannibal, M. (2012), 'Stakeholders and marketing capabilities in international new ventures: evidence from Ireland, Sweden and Denmark', *Journal of International Marketing*, Vol. 20, No. 4, pp. 46–71.

Evers, N., Kuivalainen, O. and Andersson, S. (2015), 'Industry factors influencing international new ventures' internationalisation process', in Konara, P., Ha, Y., McDonald, F., Wei, Y., Pettit, C. P. C. and Dunleavy, P. (eds), *The rise of multinationals from emerging economies*, Palgrave Macmillian, London, pp. 226–242.

Feldman, M. P., Francis, J. and Bercovitz, J. (2005), 'Creating a cluster while building a firm: Entrepreneurs and the formation of industrial clusters', *Regional Studies*, Vol. 39, No. 1, pp. 129–141.

Fernhaber, S., McDougall, P. and Oviatt, B. (2007), 'Exploring the role of industry structure in new venture internationalization', *Entrepreneurship Theory and Practice*, Vol. 31, No. 4, pp. 517–542.

Financial Times (2016), *European cities and regions of the future 2016/2017*, fDi Intelligence. Available at: www.fdiintelligence.com.

Fitjar, R. D. and Rodríguez-Pose, A. (2011), 'When local interaction does not suffice: sources of firm innovation in urban Norway', *Environment and Planning A*, Vol. 43, No. 6, pp. 1248–1267.

Florida, R. (2002), *The rise of the creative class, and how it is transforming work, leisure, community and everyday life*, Basic Books, New York.

Giblin, M. (2011), 'Managing the global-local dimensions of "lead" organizations: the contrasting cases of the software and medical technology clusters in the west of Ireland', *European Planning Studies*, Vol. 19, No. 1, pp. 23–42.

Giblin, M. and Ryan, P. (2012), 'Tight clusters or loose networks? The critical role of inward foreign direct investment in cluster creation', *Regional Studies*, Vol. 46, No. 2, pp. 245–258.

Giblin, M. and Ryan, P. (2015), 'Anchor, incumbent and late entry MNEs as propellants of technology cluster evolution', *Industry and Innovation*, Vol. 22, No. 7, pp. 553–574.

Hassink, R. and Dong-Ho, S. (2005), 'The restructuring of old industrial areas in Europe and Asia', *Environment and Planning A*, Vol. 37, No. 4, pp. 571–580.

Hennart, F. (2014), 'The accidental internationalists: a theory of born globals', *Entrepreneurship Theory and Practice*, Vol. 38, No. 1, pp. 117–135.

IBM (2016), *Global location trends report 2016.* Available at: www-935.ibm.com/services/us/gbs/thoughtleadership/gltr2016/.

IDA (2015), *Winning: foreign direct investment 2015–2019*, Dublin.

IDA (2016), *Irelands knowledge development box*, Dublin.

Innovation Policy Platform (2016), *The innovation policy platform.* Available at: www.innovationpolicyplatform.org/.

Irish Marine Development Office (IMDO) (2015), *E-ZINE newsletter*, November 2015. Available at: http://imdo.newsweaver.ie/newsletter/1n8d0q5b4qe?a=1&p=49532808&t=16488724.

Irish Medical Devices Association (IMDA) (2016), *Medtech rising 1916–2016*, Dublin. Available at: www.irishmedtechassoc.ie.

Jenkins, M. and Tallman, S. (2010), 'The shifting geography of competitive advantage: clusters, networks and firms', *Journal of Economic Geography*, Vol. 10, No, 4. pp. 599–618.

Kaufmann, A., and Tödtling, F. (2000), 'System of innovation in traditional industrial regions: the case of Syria in a comparative perspective', *Regional Studies*, Vol. 34, No. 1, pp. 29–40.

Ketels, C., Lindqvist, G. and Solvell, O. (2012), *Strengthening clusters and competitiveness in Europe: the role of cluster organizations*, The Cluster Observatory and Stockholm School of Economics, Stockholm.

Ketels, C. and Memedovic, O. (2008), 'From clusters to cluster-based economic development', *International Journal of Technological Learning, Innovation, and Development*, Vol. 1, No. 3, pp. 375–392.

Lechner, C. and Leyronas, C. (2012), 'The competitive advantage of cluster firms: the priority of regional network position over extra-regional networks – a study of a French high-tech cluster', *Entrepreneurship & Regional Development*, Vol. 24, Nos. 5–6, pp. 457–473.

Malmberg, A. and Maskel, P. (2002), 'The elusive concept of localization economics: Towards a knowledge-based theory of spatial clustering', *Environment and Planning*, Vol. 34, No. 3, pp. 429–449.

Martin, R. and Sunley, P. (2011), 'Conceptualizing cluster evolution: beyond the life cycle model?' *Regional Studies*, Vol. 45, No. 10, pp. 1299–1318.

Maskell, P. and Kebir, L. (2006), 'What qualifies as a cluster theory?' in Asheim, B., Cooke, P. and Martin, R. (eds), *Clusters and regional development: critical reflections and explorations*, Routledge, London and New York, pp. 30–49.

Menzel, M. and Fornahl, D. (2009), 'Cluster life cycles: dimensions and rationales of cluster evolution', *Industrial & Corporate Change*, Vol. 19, No. 1, pp. 205–238.

Narula, R. (2002), 'Innovation systems and "inertia" in R&D location: Norwegian firms and the role of systemic lock-in', *Research Policy*, Vol. 31, No. 5, pp. 795–816.

Narula, R. and Dunning, J. H. (2010), 'Multinational enterprises, development and globalisation: some clarifications and a research agenda', *Oxford Development Studies*, Vol. 38, No. 3, pp. 263–287.

OECD (1999), *Boosting innovation*, OECD Publishing, Paris.

O'Gorman, C. and Evers, N. (2011), 'Network intermediaries in the internationalisation of new firms in peripheral regions', *International Marketing Review*, Vol. 28, No. 4, pp. 340–364.

O'Rourke, K. (2016), *Independent Ireland: a comparative perspective*, UCD Centre for Economic Research WP16/20, Dublin.

Oster, S. M. (1999), *Modern competitive analysis*, Oxford University Press, New York.

Oviatt, B. M. and McDougall, P. P. (1994), 'Toward a theory of international new ventures', *Journal of International Business Studies*, Vol. 25, No. 1, pp. 45–64.

Porter, M. E. (1998), 'Clusters and competition: new agendas for companies, governments and institutions', in Porter, M. E. (ed.), *On competition*, Harvard Business School, Boston, MA.

Preece, S. B., Miles, P. and Baetz, M. C. (1999), 'Explaining international intensity and global diversity of early stage technology-based firms', *Journal of Business Venturing*, Vol. 14, No. 3, pp. 259–281.

Rugman, A. M. and Verbeke, A. (2003), 'Multinational enterprises and clusters: an organizing framework', *Management International Review*, Vol. 43, No. 3, pp. 151–169.

Ryan, P., Evers, N. and Smith, A. (2015), 'Born global networks: a study of the Irish digital animation sector', in Larimo, J. and Nummela, N., *Handbook of international alliances and networks*, Routledge, London.

Slaper, T. and Orutzar, G. (2015), 'Industry clusters and economic development', Indiana Business Review, Vol 90, No. 1, pp. 7–9.

Sölvell, Ö., Lindqvist, G. and Ketels, C. H. M. (2003), *The cluster initiative greenbook*, Ivory Tower, Stockholm.

Stommen, J. (2005), 'Growth of med-tech sector is a boon to Ireland's economy', *Medical Device Daily*, Vol. 9, No. 72, pp. 1–2.

Stuart, T. and Sorenson, O. (2003), 'The geography of opportunity: spatial heterogeneity in founding rates and the performance of biotechnology firms', *Research Policy*, Vol. 32, No. 2, pp. 229–253.

Tappi, D. (2005), 'Clusters, adaptation and extroversion: a cognitive and entrepreneurial analysis of the Marche music cluster', *European Urban and Regional Studies*, Vol. 12, No. 3, pp. 289–307.

Terjesen, S., Hessels, J. and Li, D. (2016), 'Comparative international entrepreneurship: a review and research agenda', *Journal of Management*, Vol. 42, No. 1, pp. 299–344.

Tomlinson, P. R. and Cowling, K. (2003), 'The problem of regional "hollowing out" in Japan: lessons for regional industrial policy', in Sugden, R., Cheung, R. and Meadows, R. (eds), *Urban and regional prosperity in a globalised new economy*, Edward Elgar, Cheltenham, pp. 33–58.

Torre, A. (2008), 'On the role played by temporary geographical proximity in knowledge transmission', *Regional Studies*, Vol. 42, No. 6, pp. 869–889.

Van Geenhuizen, M. (2008), 'Knowledge networks of young innovators in the urban economy: biotechnology as a case study', *Entrepreneurship & Regional Development*, Vol. 20, No. 2, pp. 161–183.

Vapola, T. J. (2012), 'Battleship strategy for managing MNC-born global innovation networks', in Gabrielsson, M. and Kirpalani, V. H. M. (eds), *Handbook of research on born globals*, Edward Elgar, Cheltenham, pp. 161–184.

Vapola, T. J., Tossavainen, P. and Gabrielsson, M. (2008), 'The battleship strategy: the complementing role of born globals in MNC's new opportunity creation', *Journal of International Entrepreneurship*, Vol. 6, No. 1, pp. 1–20.

Waluszewski, A. (2004), 'A competing or co-operating cluster or seven decades of combinatory resources? What's behind a prospering biotech valley?' *Scandinavian Journal of Management*, Vol. 20, No. 1, pp. 125–150.

Weigel, S. (2011), 'Medical technology's source of innovation', *European Planning Studies*, Vol. 19, No. 1, pp. 43–61.

Zaheer, A. and George, V. (2004), 'Reach out or reach within? Performance implications of alliances and location in biotechnology', *Managerial and Decision Economics*, Vol. 25, Nos. 6/7, pp. 437–452.

Zahra, S. and George, G. (2002), 'International entrepreneurship: the current status of the field and future research agenda', in Hitt, M., Ireland, D., Sexton, D. and Camp, M. (eds), *Strategic entrepreneurship: creating an integrated mindset*, Blackwell, Oxford.

Zahra, S. A., Ireland, R. D. and Hitt, M. A. (2000), 'International expansion by new venture firms: international diversity, mode of market entry, technological learning, and performance', *Academy of Management Journal*, Vol. 43, No. 5, pp. 925–950.

Zahra, S. A., Sapienza, H. J. and Davidsson, P. (2006), 'Entrepreneurship and dynamic capabilities: a review, model and research agenda', *Journal of Management Studies*, Vol. 43, No. 4, pp. 917–955.

8 More than job creation

Employee engagement in knowledge sharing and learning advantages of newness

María Ripollés, Andreu Blesa,
*Miguel A. Hernández and Iñigo Isusi**

8.1 Introduction

Until the late 1990s, Spanish companies concentrated on their domestic markets with little or no international projection, but in less than a decade everything changed. The number of Spanish companies going into international markets increased significantly. The majority of them were SMEs with fewer than 200 employees. Although Spanish research focused on born globals is still scarce, the contribution of these kind of firms to the Spanish rate of internationalisation is becoming increasingly more recognised (Consejo Económico y Social, 2016). There is no univocal criterion to define born globals, but there seems to be some consensus on this term referring to firms that meet the following requirements: to start the international activity within a period of no more than five years after their creation; to realise 25 per cent of their sales in foreign markets during at least two years; to have foreign activity in two or more countries; to be run by a top management with a global vision of the market; and to offer innovative products/services with high market potential or new technologies or designs regardless of the industry in which they operate (Rialp *et al.*, 2005; Ripollés and Blesa, 2017).

Empirical research has shown a positive direct and indirect effect of Spanish new venturing on employment growth (Arauzo *et al.*, 2008). From 2008 to 2012, new businesses were responsible for the creation of 2,455,900 jobs, nearly 40 per cent of the total number of jobs created during that period (Consejo Económico y Social, 2016). Born globals are expected to contribute to these figures and, despite the lack of specific quantitative data, it is increasingly appreciated that born globals do not only operate in markets with high growth potential, but also have potential for rapid growth in those markets (Gabrielsson *et al.*, 2008) when constraints in resources and market legitimacy are exacerbated (Oviatt and McDougall, 2005). Far from being anecdotal, it is supposed that these ventures make a significant contribution to the economic and social progress of any community. According to data from the Global Entrepreneurship Monitor, almost one-fifth of young European enterprises can be considered born globals, and these firms are characterised by, on average, higher employment figures (which is expected to continue) than domestically oriented young firms (Eurofound, 2012).

The growing recognition of the social and economic importance of these firms has been accompanied by a corresponding increase in research (see Jones *et al.*, 2011, for a review), with some scholars appreciating that born globals enjoy some 'learning advantages of newness', which offset their lack of resources and market legitimacy. Learning advantages of newness are related to the born globals' ability to quickly and proactively develop new knowledge for the rapid commercialisation of their products (Autio *et al.*, 2000). Factors such as social networks (Prashantham and Young, 2011; De Clercq *et al.*, 2012) or the entrepreneur's international experience, vision, commitment, innovativeness or entrepreneurial orientation (Li *et al.*, 2009; Cavusgil and Knight, 2015) are deemed to play a facilitating role.

Understanding the human resource management practices contributing to born globals' learning advantages of newness is key for the consolidation of this research area, but these factors remain under-researched (Glaister *et al.*, 2014). This dearth of studies raises difficulties because the role of human resources cannot be overlooked to explain how born globals develop and expand their knowledge base (Minbaeva, 2013; Voorde *et al.*, 2016). This chapter seeks to fill this important gap and considers it essential to focus on how born globals attract employees who are engaged in knowledge sharing (that is, their education, experiences and information) with other employees. Job engagement has been suggested to be important in knowledge development (Cabrera and Cabrera, 2005; Wang and Noe, 2010). While scholars have discussed a multitude of human resource practices that can enhance employee engagement (Andreeva and Sergeeva, 2016), this chapter will focus on two individual-level human resource practices that seem to be the ones that work best to assist born globals in ensuring that their employees engage in knowledge sharing: staff recruitment and training (Kuvaas *et al.*, 2012; Swart and Kinnie, 2013; Chowhan, 2016). Born globals differ from other internationalised firms (Jones *et al.*, 2011) and, therefore, it is necessary to explore how research embedded in the human resource management tradition accommodates to their reality. A greater understanding of these mechanisms will allow a better comprehension of how born globals develop learning advantages of newness and succeed in foreign markets.

As there is hardly any empirical research on this subject, the approach followed in this study is exploratory and serves the objective of initially mapping the field. After carrying out a review of the most relevant literature on employees' engagement in knowledge sharing and the individual human resource practices that can promote it, the chapter takes six cases of Spanish born globals to describe the processes applied during job creation and the characteristics of the jobs created. This analysis will reveal the importance of born globals as employers and the problems they have, not only when it comes to engaging employees but also to holding onto their human resources. Following from this, the chapter then analyses the influence of staff recruitment, training and employee engagement to nurture the born global's ability to expand its knowledge base.

8.2 Learning advantages of newness

Drawing on knowledge-based theory, Autio *et al.* (2000) suggested that new enterprises which internationalise quickly, and hence born globals, enjoy some 'learning advantages of newness' when compared to firms that follow slower internationalisation processes. Learning advantages of newness represent a competitive advantage for born globals in foreign markets (Autio *et al.*, 2000). Oviatt and McDougall (2005) pointed out that 'the learning advantages of newness represent a counterpoint to the widely accepted concept that there is a liability of newness for young firms ... and deserve additional empirical testing and conceptual development'. On the same lines, Zahra (2005) stated that 'the concept of learning advantages of newness opens the black box that appears to exist in theorising about the advantages that INVs [international new ventures] might reap from internationalisation'.

Learning advantages of newness are related to born globals' ability to create value by expanding their knowledge-based resources (Nonaka, 1994), in which absorbing new knowledge plays a decisive role. Born globals' knowledge base tends to be narrow and focused on a chosen market niche (Zahra and Filatotchev, 2004). As a result, their capacity to cultivate new knowledge and nurture its evolution is limited.

Absorbing new knowledge involves the unlearning of old knowledge and routines (Nonaka, 1994). Firms that internationalise at a later stage may have developed political, cognitive and relational impediments that could diminish their capacity to absorb new knowledge (see Chapter 4; Cohen and Levinthal, 1990; Eriksson *et al.*, 1997). The longer managers have been building a domestic strategy, the more reluctant they will be to shift the attention of their firms to fully-fledged efforts in foreign markets, and the more likely they will be to focus their attention on the negative aspects of those options. Similarly, the more time they have devoted to building relationships and reciprocal loyalties and obligations with domestic business partners, the more likely they will be to continue to treat domestic partners as their first priority (Autio *et al.*, 2000). These impediments do not work in born globals (Autio *et al.*, 2000) due to their limited engagement in domestic markets and their young age. Additionally, scholars have recognised the importance of several factors in promoting learning advantages of newness, namely, the international experience, vision, commitment, innovativeness, entrepreneurial orientation (Li *et al.*, 2009; Cavusgil and Knight, 2015) or social networks (Prashantham and Young, 2011; De Clercq *et al.*, 2012) of the born globals' entrepreneurs. However, and taking into account research on human resource management, it can be proposed that employees' engagement in knowledge sharing is also an important element in nurturing born globals' learning advantages of newness (Foss *et al.*, 2010; Minbaeva, 2013), which has been systematically ignored in the specialised theory. Additionally, employee engagement is increasingly regarded as a key priority by managers, as it is claimed to be crucial for organisational success (MacLeod and Clarke, 2009), and for individual wellbeing. Employee engagement is linked to lower levels of work-related stress and burnout, and to higher levels of employee satisfaction (Demerouti *et al.*, 2001; Britt *et al.*, 2005). Nevertheless, scholars have neglected it both in their research on born globals and, more specifically, on the learning advantages of newness.

8.3 Employee engagement in knowledge sharing

A number of studies have suggested that employee engagement is the key to achieving the desired attitudes and behaviours of employees (Macey *et al.*, 2009; Crawford *et al.*, 2010). Employee engagement can be defined as 'a positive, fulfilling, work-related state of mind that is characterised by vigour, dedication and absorption' (Schaufeli *et al.*, 2002). Vigour implies high levels of energy and mental resilience while working, the willingness to invest effort in one's work, and persistence even in the face of difficulties. Dedication refers to being strongly involved in one's work and experiencing a sense of significance, enthusiasm, inspiration, pride and challenge. Absorption is characterised by being fully concentrated and deeply engrossed in one's work, whereby time passes quickly and one has difficulties with detaching oneself from work. A multitude of human resource practices have been suggested to enhance employee engagement in knowledge sharing and can be grouped into three main categories, that is, those fostering employees' motivation, enhancing their abilities in knowledge sharing, and providing opportunities (Andreeva and Sergeeva, 2016).

According to the classic theory of reasoned action, the intention to engage in a specific behaviour is determined by motivations towards that behaviour as well as by perceptions of social norms (Fishbein and Ajzen, 1975). Motivation is influenced by beliefs on and assessments of the outcomes of the behaviour. Subjective norms refer to beliefs and to the existence of social expectations regarding behaviour. When applied to knowledge sharing, this theory predicts a link between motivation and subjective norms about knowledge sharing, intentions to share knowledge and actual sharing of knowledge (Cabrera and Cabrera, 2005). Davenport and Prusak (1998) outlined some of the perceived expected benefits that may regulate behaviour, namely, future reciprocity, status, job security or promotional prospects. Consequently, knowledge sharing will be positively affected when individuals trust that their behaviour will be reciprocated with some benefit in the future. Therefore, employees must be willing and motivated to exchange their experiences, training and information with other employees in order to collaborate with them to solve problems, develop new ideas or implement new policies and procedures (Nonaka and Takeuchi, 1995; Cabrera and Cabrera, 2005; Wang and Noe, 2010).

Similarly, to share knowledge with colleagues, in addition to motivation, employees have to possess certain skills in order to be able to effectively explain and transfer what they know (Cohen and Levinthal, 1990). Scholars discuss the wide array of individual characteristics as elements of the ability to share knowledge (Andreeva and Sergeeva, 2016). These include, for example, the capability to find a common language with colleagues (Nahapiet and Ghoshal, 1998), the capability to learn and acquire new knowledge (Cohen and Levinthal, 1990) or the capability to verbalise and externalise one's own knowledge (Andreeva and Sergeeva, 2016). According to the classic theory of reasoned action, knowledge sharing self-efficacy – a belief in one's own ability to share – is also important (Fishbein and Ajzen, 1975).

Additionally, organisations should provide employees with appropriate opportunities to apply their skills and motivation (Kaufman, 2015), for example, by organising knowledge sharing-focused meetings and workshops, providing time at work for sharing, implementing employee rotation, and improving job or workspace designs that allow for teamwork and free communication (Andreeva and Sergeeva, 2016).

Next, an analysis of two human resource management practices that influence motivation, ability and organisation is presented: selective recruitment and training.

8.3.1 Selective recruitment

Selective recruitment refers to the processes by which born globals recruit skilled employees according to the characteristics of the work setting (Zacharatos *et al.*, 2005). It involves acquiring the minimum of suitable and productive staff to do the required tasks (Pfeffer, 1998). The importance of having employees that possess not only suitable technical but also learning capabilities has been highlighted as a fundamental requirement to make knowledge sharing in organisations easier (Markos and Sridevi, 2010; Messersmith and Wales, 2013). Since selection of the right candidate, that is, one who, among other elements, shares the perception of knowledge sharing applied in the company, is of high priority, the recruitment methods deployed should enable the firm to attract those with an inclination towards knowledge sharing. The selection process should be carefully designed to ensure validity and reliability when selecting the pro-knowledge sharing employee (Fong *et al.*, 2011).

The literature about hiring recommends a systematic five-stage process consisting of an assessment of whether the vacancy needs to be filled, a job analysis, a job description, a person specification (Carroll *et al.*, 1999) and a screening process (Larquier and Marchal, 2016). The screening phase seeks to check the fit between employer's needs and the applicant's characteristics by using methods such as curriculum vitae examination, interviews, tests and simulation of job tasks (Larquier and Marchal, 2016).

Additionally, the recruitment process can be either formal or informal (Greenidge *et al.*, 2012). The formal recruitment process consists of established procedures that help firms to speed up the processing of a considerable number of applications and the filling of multiple job positions (Barber *et al.*, 1999). Formal recruitment processes often utilise public or private employment agencies (Sabatier, 2010; Pellizzari, 2011) and resource-intensive advertising methods, such as newspapers, radio, television or promotional events (Beardwell *et al.*, 2004). Informal processes, in contrast, are usually carried out by the owner without delegating, using less resource-intensive methods, such as the 'word of mouth' (Kotey and Sheridan, 2004). The popular media has reported an increase in the number of cases in which companies, in both formal and informal processes, hire professionals in an attempt to find out more detailed information about job applicants from social networking sites such as Facebook or LinkedIn (Brown and Vaughn, 2011). If the company has deficiencies in its hiring capabilities, informal processes are less appropriate to ensure the hiring of employees with the ability and motivation to engage in knowledge-sharing activities.

8.3.2 Training

Training is an important driver of knowledge transfer (Kaše *et al.*, 2009). The influence of training practices on employee outcomes could be moderated by the employees' perceptions of these activities (Brown, 2005; Colquitt *et al.*, 2000). Employees become more motivated to share knowledge if they perceive the activities carried out to train them in their job as valuable experiences (Colquitt *et al.*, 2000).

Training practices for engagement in knowledge sharing may include training in the ability to learn, communication skills, self-reflection, team working or mentoring (Jackson *et al.*, 2006). In essence, these practices influence their vigour, dedication and absorption in knowledge-sharing activities (Bandura, 1977). Moreover, extensive training may familiarise employees with the internalisation of values, norms and schemata for sharing knowledge (Cabrera *et al.*, 2006). Training practices contribute to employees' positive attitudes towards the organisation and evoke a reciprocal willingness to do their best, even if the training and developmental activities are perceived as organisational demands and when controlling for the more general perception of role overload (Kuvaas *et al.*, 2012). Additionally, training is important, as training sessions offer employees an opportunity to share information and knowledge (Ipe, 2003; Rhodes *et al.*, 2008). In essence, training practices influence their vigour, dedication and absorption in knowledge-sharing activities (Bandura, 1977).

Training can be formal or informal (Greenidge *et al.*, 2012) and both types have a significant impact on employee engagement in knowledge sharing (Shuck *et al.*, 2010; Shuck and Rocco, 2014). Formal training usually includes an off-the-job setting such as an educational institution, while informal training is unplanned, not documented and largely unstructured (Valentin, 2014). Moreover, training programmes provide a platform for employees to interact and, therefore, they will provide advancement opportunities that contribute to the creation of a knowledge sharing environment (Grimshaw and Miozzo, 2009). Besides formal training, informal training is equally important in knowledge sharing, as knowledge transfer could occur via suppliers when employees undergo training on how to use a new piece of equipment or when they teach customers (Ramirez and Li, 2009).

8.4 Primary evidence from six Spanish case studies

8.4.1 Sample

In order to explore the relationships among selective recruitment, training, employee engagement and born globals' capacity to expand their knowledge base, six Spanish case studies were selected from different industries. The key principle used to select the cases was their relevance to the research question rather than representativeness: firms including a wide range of human resource practices and approaches were chosen to illustrate core elements that foster learning advantages of born globals. Data collection took place from February 2015 to November 2016.

Semi-standardised face-to-face interviews were conducted with both the entrepreneur/general manager and some employees. Interviews were recorded, transcribed and then sent to the interviewees to be checked and confirmed. With the purpose of triangulating the collected data (Yin, 2014), additional information was gathered from the websites of the companies, companies' publicly available annual reports and on-site observation by the interviewer.

A brief description of each case study is presented in the following:

- *Case study Alpha:* Alpha was founded in 2011 by two entrepreneurs – one local (Spanish) and one Dutch – with wide experience in the footwear sector. The company is dedicated to the production of anatomic accessories for shoes, which are sold in 13 countries across the five continents (Australia, China, Saudi Arabia, India, Canada, Chile, Peru, the Netherlands, Germany, France, United Kingdom, Luxembourg and Norway). Since its conception, the company has aimed to export the whole production in a business-to-costumer relationship. Moreover, Alpha imports 30 per cent of the raw materials it needs to produce the goods. The company employed eight workers at the time of the interview, and 100 per cent of its turnover came from foreign markets.
- *Case study Beta:* Beta was set up in 2011 by two young entrepreneurs in their mid-thirties, who 'joined forces' to form the company based on the idea of combining what each of them had acquired during their education, as one of the partners was specialised in management and the other in software. The enterprise provides mobile software applications and consultancy services, which are produced on demand. At the time of the interview, 35 per cent of its income was based on export sales, with its own delegations in The Netherlands, Italy and Panama. Apart from that, the organisation also has partnership agreements in Colombia and Argentina. Beta employed 55 workers at the time of the interview and expected to grow steadily in the coming years.
- *Case study Gamma:* Gamma was founded in 2013 and is specialised in the production of sports safety equipment, which it began to sell in the second year after its foundation. The whole range of accessories is produced in a

foreign country and imported to Spain, where an assembly process is applied in order to obtain the final product. The aim of the company was to expand dynamically in order to be present in every possible country and thus avoid imitations of their products. At the time of the interview, Gamma exported 70 per cent of its production to 72 countries under the business-to-consumer formula, and to 15 countries by business-to-business. The percentage of their turnover coming from international clients is 70 per cent and the mean rate of sales increased sharply between 2014 and 2016 due to the high opinion of the products that it manufactures. The company employed nine people at the time of the interview.

- *Case study Delta:* Delta was founded in 2008 and is specialised in the design, development and execution of complex (heating, ventilation and air conditioning) engineering projects in the industrial sector, delivering turnkey projects to clients, as well as maintenance service activities for these installations. The company was founded by a 36-year-old engineer who, after several years of experience as an employee in various engineering companies, decided to set up his own company with two employees. The firm, employing 35 people at the time of the interview, has achieved a wide client portfolio, including national and international multinational engineering companies. Approximately 60–70 per cent of the total turnover of the enterprise comes from international projects, both in the European Union and beyond, and it has two delegations (one in Israel and the other in Algeria).

- *Case Study Epsilon:* Epsilon was set up in 2011. The company was founded by three former telecommunications engineering students to commercially exploit the PhD thesis developed by one of them. The company has developed a patented cryptography solution that enables effective and secure protection of digital communications. Epsilon employed 24 people at the time of the interview (including the management board members). Due to the 'double-use' nature of the firm's products, its main clients work in both the military and civilian spheres (both public and private). Around 30–40 per cent of its turnover comes from international clients located in European Union and non-European Union countries (Colombia, Ecuador, the US, Saudi Arabia), and this percentage is expected to increase substantially in the coming years. The company also has an office in Silicon Valley, in the US.

- *Case Study Zeta:* Zeta was set up in 2013 and is specialised in the development of eye-tracking-based techniques that allow eye movement to be used as a substitute for a conventional computer mouse for people with very severe mobility limitations (for instance people affected by Amyotrophic Lateral Sclerosis or Cerebral Palsy). The company was originally founded to commercially exploit a technology developed by a local technology centre, although at the time of interview the company operates independently from this centre. *Zeta* is a micro company and employed five people at the time of the interview, including the chief executive officer. Approximately 60 per cent of the company's turnover comes from foreign markets, including European and non-European countries (France, Greece, Ireland, Argentina, Venezuela, the US, Turkey, etc.), and major clients include amyotrophic lateral sclerosis associations and individual users affected by major mobility problems.

8.4.2 Description of the jobs created

The six case studies analysed have realised employment creation during their years of existence, which was more important in the cases of Delta, Epsilon, Gamma and Beta than in Zeta and Alpha.

The diverse productive specialisation of the six case studies analysed explains the different composition of their workforce, with a relatively high presence of medium skilled blue-collar workers in the case of Delta in comparison to an overwhelming presence of university graduate white-collar employees in Epsilon, Zeta and Beta. In Alpha and Gamma, the jobs offered were blue and white collar, as both born globals are active in the manufacturing sector.

The six case studies share a number of common characteristics in terms of the employment created and the associated working conditions.

To start with, the six case studies suggest that there is a high interest in having a stable and well-trained workforce, resulting in a very high presence of full-time and indefinite/permanent employees (with percentages that in many cases exceed 70 per cent of the workforce). These data are remarkable considering that, according to the data from the fourth trimester of 2016 of the Spanish Labour Survey, the percentage of full-time indefinite employment is around 54 per cent of the total Spanish workforce.

Second, all the born globals analysed have a preference for young highly qualified workers, which is reflected in the fact that the average age of company staff is below 30 in all cases (often the founders are the oldest people in the companies), while the average age of the active population in Spain for 2016 is 40 and the percentage of employees under 30 is 17.6 per cent, according to the Spanish Institute of Statistics. Additionally, knowledge of foreign languages is usually a must, especially as far as English is concerned, but also other languages in the case of more specific job positions.

Third, enterprises face strong difficulties in being able to offer high salaries. This is due, among other reasons, to a very strict company salary policy intended to keep fixed costs as low as possible in the initial stages of the company, and also as a consequence of the economic crisis that the country is undergoing. These limited salary possibilities are considered an obstacle to attracting highly qualified professionals.[1] In order to somehow offset them, four of the six born globals analysed have developed variable incentive schemes that depend on the accomplishment of enterprise and/or individual goals (open to all employees or only for some specific groups).

Fourth, the born globals analysed suggest that these limited salary possibilities are somehow balanced by a number of advantageous working conditions that are intended to secure long-standing working relationships with employees (especially with the critical ones). Examples include high levels of autonomy for individuals/groups to organise their work, flexible working time arrangements, time compensations for extra working hours, teleworking practices in some of the companies (such as Epsilon and Beta) or, finally, attention paid to the development of flat structures as well as continuous communication and dialogue practices between management and the workforce. Incidentally, none of the six born globals analysed have any collective workers' representative structure or works council, and neither managers nor employees have taken any initiative in this direction. In fact, none of them are required to have any according to the Spanish legislation on the issue, which states that the threshold to constitute these councils is 50 workers. As a consequence of this requirement only 11 per cent of Spanish SMEs have a works council.

8.4.3 Employees' engagement in knowledge sharing

The born globals studied generally employ a modest number of employees, which means that each employee has to be versatile: an employee can handle very different tasks, as there is usually no specific department to cope with a specific matter. Therefore, the information that an employee manages can be very rich, so it is important that this worker shares the information and the knowledge generated from the different tasks effectively with his or her colleagues and the rest of the company. Not only is the employee feeding information and knowledge, but at the same time, he/she is also receiving feedback from other members of the company, thus activating the employee learning process (Cohen and Levinthal, 1990). The information and knowledge does not only refer to the born global's activity, but also to personal affairs that can be relevant for the born global. These personal affairs could be related to employees' labour burnout or their satisfaction with the current tasks. In this way, the entrepreneur gets feedback from the employee about the employee's work and personal situation, which can be used to take decisions regarding the management of the business but also regarding appropriate human resource practices to be implemented. For example, employees in Beta offer the entrepreneur proposals about the training necessary for each post or even the appropriate new candidate to be hired.

The knowledge that the employee can deliver to the born global or to the entrepreneur is highly valued, as it refers not only to external information about the market, but also to internal processes, improvements, innovations, ideas for new businesses, etc. This knowledge constitutes an important source for expanding born globals' knowledge-base and can contribute to nurture their learning advantages of newness, and to support the firm's sustainability, competitiveness and growth.

One Beta employee shared with the entrepreneur his personal interest in creating a spin-off starting with his own business idea. Moreover, employees share their knowledge with their workmates, who can benefit from fresh creativeness and different points of view to solve a problem, or job experiences that enrich the born global's knowledge pool.

The process of knowledge sharing among employees is very dynamic and takes place continuously, even if the interlocutor is not physically present. Knowledge sharing is favoured by born globals through several human resource practices at firm level. For example, reduced status distinctions among employee, manager and entrepreneur (as in the case of Alpha); fostered communication practices through work teams (as in the case of Beta); technical means of communication available (i.e. telephone, email, web servers, instant messaging such as written, voice or video chat) (as in the case of Alpha); absence of closed office cabinets; favourable working atmosphere (as in the case of Gamma); socialising processes or regular meetings to perform knowledge sharing (as in the case of Beta). This is echoes the work of Autio *et al.* (2000), which suggests that born globals' workspace is designed to allow employee engagement in knowledge sharing activities.

8.4.4 *Recruitment and employee engagement in knowledge sharing*

One challenge that confronts born globals is their need for highly motivated and skilled staff. While this is a problem often encountered by SMEs, it can be even more acute for born globals (Eurofound, 2012). Each case study follows its own procedures when recruiting employees. Notwithstanding, regarding the relationship between recruitment and employee engagement in knowledge sharing, all six case studies share a number of common elements.

To start with, all case studies follow a formalised, systematic and standardised recruitment and induction procedure, developed by the entrepreneur of the companies after a learning process that has been refined over the first years of the company. For instance, in case study Delta, the entrepreneur posits that recruitment procedures had been gradually formalised during the last few years, whereas the initial recruitment processes were more on an ad-hoc/improvised basis. For his part, the entrepreneur from Beta stated that in the early days they were 'shooting in the dark' and doing things with the best of intentions, which were sometimes perceived by the employees with some doubt.

The identification of the need for additional human resources is usually performed by the entrepreneur, in all cases assisted by key personnel in the companies. It is interesting to underline that all the born globals studied have a very rigorous and accurate recruitment policy, so hiring only takes place if very specific and clear needs are detected, and following the guidelines established in the business plans of the different companies. In terms of the characteristics that they consider to be the most significant when it comes to recruiting new staff, the companies interviewed highlighted the importance of the candidates being committed to life-long learning and team work. Both characteristics facilitate their commitment to knowledge sharing (Markos and Sridevi, 2010; Messersmith and Wales, 2013). For instance, Beta aims to have workers that may show certain attitudes and behaviours that suggest their devotion, commitment, desire and responsiveness towards learning and the improvement of their abilities. In all the case studies analysed, new entrants are first offered temporary contracts.

This trial period, running from six months to two years, is regarded as particularly valuable and relevant to test and identify those candidates who will finally remain in the company.[2] These temporary contracts have become common in the Spanish labour market, where the numbers of indefinite contracts and temporary contracts have been growing at a rate of 1.5 per cent and 5.9 per cent, respectively, since 2013. In this trial/induction period, new temporary entrants are usually assigned a company mentor who assists them in their day-to-day activities in the company, and may even train them on-the-job. If they are given a positive final evaluation, they are offered a permanent job in the company.

All the case studies analysed make use of different external tools to identify and attract suitable job candidates, among which social networks developed by the entrepreneur over the years play a decisive role. Although born globals' networks are made up of different types of ties depending on their origin (Ripollés and Blesa, 2017), ties with incubators and third-party institutions such as universities or vocational schools in the surrounding region are frequently utilised for recruitment purposes. For instance, Beta's entrepreneur pointed out that collaboration with different lecturers at the university where he studied was essential, especially the fact that he participated in some of their sessions which raised students' interest in working for the company while at the same time allowing the entrepreneur a first assessment on the students' fit to his company.

Gamma incorporates new employees into the company as students doing their internship so that they can complete their university final project. After that, the candidate is hired on the basis of an apprenticeship contract, where he/she is trained for about a year. Finally, the candidate is given a standard labour contract. This new employee is what the company considers a 'basic profile' of worker, a worker without labour experience but with the basic knowledge provided by his/her degree, and with a favourable attitude towards learning. Delta and Epsilon also have formal agreements with the regional university and some local vocational schools to identify suitable candidates. These candidates may join the company through apprenticeship contracts. Again, a need to hire candidates committed to learning activities is relevant for Delta and Epsilon.

In Alpha, the entrepreneur positively values their network ties with other companies located in the same incubator. Hiring employees from that network made it easy for employees to engage in knowledge sharing activities inside the firm. The same applies for Gamma, whose entrepreneur places great value on the location of the company in an incubator. This offers networking opportunities that generate confidence among the firms within the incubator, and that in turn facilitates the information and knowledge sharing process among their employees. The entrepreneur considers that the incubators play a fundamental role in creating a culture that fosters the exchange of information and knowledge among all companies located there and among their employees. The mutual trust derived from the joint experiences gained from being part of the same incubator could minimise the potential risks associated with employees' possible opportunistic behaviour, such us spreading sensitive information with external organisations, accelerating the process of knowledge transfer.

Furthermore, Delta, Epsilon and Zeta make increasing use of online job search engines (for instance LinkedIn, Jobandtalent, Infojobs, etc.) to both identify suitable candidates and/or advertise job offers. This is especially the case when looking for very specific job profiles that are not necessarily available in the region. Unsolicited applications (curricula vitae sent from potential candidates without a prior vacancy note or job advertisement published by the company) are also taken into account by all the case study enterprises, although most of the candidates are of no interest to the companies. By way of contrast, only Beta uses consultancy and human resources companies to identify suitable candidates, which can probably be explained by the aim of the others to keep hiring costs to a minimum.

The selection of the candidates is usually based on the identification of the best curricula vitae and carrying out a face-to-face interview with the top manager(s) assisted by key personnel. Elements of the interview usually include technical skills, soft skills and personality traits, potential to learn and progress, previous (if any) working experience, and command of foreign languages, among other elements. With all this information, the final decision is rather informal and mainly based on the 'gut feelings' of the manager(s) and the other personnel involved.

From the analysis of the six cases a common pattern for recruitment of skilled staff can be detected. All analysed born globals seem to overcome their resource and legitimacy constraints by turning to their networks as their principal source of recruitment. This practice is in line with the network theories. Brass (1995) suggested the utilisation of networks as a more effective means to recruit people who fit the organisation better as compared to traditional practices. In fact, Leung (2003) showed that rather than recruiting from their social networks, entrepreneurs tend to utilise their business networks, mostly built around the firms' activities, to scout their talents. As candidates are expected to identify themselves with the company's vision and culture, and be motivated to join because they see the potential of the company, entrepreneurs still mostly draw on their business networks to recruit.

In the specific case of born globals, Jones *et al.* (2011) pointed out the importance of networks as providers of new employees. Although past research has not explicitly considered the specific type of network ties that are involved in the hiring of employees, networks with third-party organisations like incubators and universities seem to play an important role in staff recruitment. Lechner *et al.* (2006) suggested that the main goal pursued by firms in this kind of ties is to attain legitimacy and market reputation. Benefits of such ties may include preferential access to valuable market information, referral, fewer bureaucratic delays in response to customer needs, monetary and non-monetary incentives, and protection from external threats to a firm's credibility (Ripollés and Blesa, 2017). In born globals, a new role seems to be associated with this type of networks: the staff provider.

8.4.5 Training and employee engagement in knowledge sharing

From the analysis of the selected cases, it becomes obvious that in born globals formal training is not a human resource practice that is commonly used, with the exception of English language training, which is regularly offered by Alpha and Beta. Born globals' entrepreneurs' and employees' knowledge of foreign languages is a distinguishing characteristic which facilitates the building of global networks and engaging in international operations (Eurofound, 2012). In fact, the entrepreneur in Alpha recognises that there is a lack of training in his company. Although new employees are highly qualified, due to the cutting-edge technology used by the company, they require specific training to perform their tasks properly. In born globals, training is often provided because of a request from the worker, and not suggested by the entrepreneur, and is mainly focused on technical aspects. For example, in Beta it is the employees who request or signal their need for specific training to be able to perform their tasks. Later, the entrepreneur carefully studies those requests, which are then approved or declined based on several indicators, such as significance for the company, alignment with business objectives, as well as the entrepreneur's subjective opinion. Training usually takes place outside the company in official institutions, and is financed by the company. Examples of training can be specialised courses in some disciplines or languages, as well as academic postgraduate courses.

Nevertheless, there are also examples for informal training. Once, Gamma had to redesign the organisation's website and nobody had the knowledge to do it. One of the workers coached himself by looking for information, mainly from the internet, in order to carry out the task. This self-training was carried out willingly and because of the engagement he felt with his job.

The aim of training is for the worker to acquire more skills and thus do his/ her job better, but also for the born global to update their knowledge base. For instance, one of the employees in one of the lower positions at Beta proposed to the entrepreneur the idea of attending an academic postgraduate course and he has now become the current project and sales market manager, and demonstrating excellent performance in his job. Beta's entrepreneur is open towards training as a way of supporting the employees in giving their best.

However, in Gamma and Alpha employees are trained from recruitment, because they are usually lacking in-work experience. The employee's inexperience obliges the entrepreneur to monitor their work and teach them the right way to do things. The entrepreneur uses this process of supervision as a way to train the employees to engage in knowledge sharing activities. For example, they have to draw up weekly written reports about their tasks and deliver a brief presentation to the rest of their workmates.

Interestingly, in all cases it can be observed that the entrepreneurs emphasise the need for employees who have undergone training to share what they have learnt with their workmates, because (1) as born globals are working with state-of-the-art technology for which no training outside the company is available, self-training is common for employees in these firms in order to obtain specific knowledge; (2) the company can save money on training; and (3) it fosters a sense of cohesion among the staff, as well as their engagement. With this purpose in mind, entrepreneurs usually hold informal meetings with their employees with the aim of sharing and developing possible actions – strategic or tactical – that could derive from the training received. Training in born globals not only contributes to improve the capacity of employees to acquire new information and knowledge, but also reinforces their motivation to learn and create an atmosphere in which to share their new knowledge. This human resource practice is not common in traditional SMEs.

8.5 Conclusions: uncovering the role of human resource practices in promoting born globals' learning advantages of newness

The joint analysis of the six cases seems to indicate that employees play an important role in explaining born globals' learning advantages of newness. For born globals it is crucial to ensure that their employees will be engaged in knowledge sharing activities in order to overcome their narrow market knowledge resulting from their liabilities of newness, smallness and foreignness. In spite of born globals' resource constraints and lack of market legitimacy, their employees seem to have the motivation and the abilities needed to engage in knowledge sharing with other employees. The results suggest that to better understand born globals' learning advantages of newness it is necessary to incorporate human resources management factors into the explanatory models. Moreover, if the focus is on how entrepreneurs deploy their human resources, early international entry and growth can be better understood.

Two human resource practices play a determining role in fostering born globals' knowledge development, and this relationship seems to be mediated by individual characteristics such as employee engagement in knowledge sharing. In fact, a pattern seems to emerge in terms of born globals' recruitment and training practices. First, networks – especially with universities, vocational schools, incubators and third-party organisations – are the main source of new employees. Second, the entrepreneur is involved in the process of selecting staff and does not outsource it to external agencies. Third, except for key managerial posts, there is no need for previous work experience, but on the other hand the educational profile of recruits is high. Therefore, the average age of the workers is very low and – at least in the analysed cases – they are mostly hired under apprenticeship contracts. Moreover, born globals mainly prefer to recruit inexperienced individuals so that the company can train them in a certain organisational culture in which sharing knowledge is a priority. Through training, entrepreneurs also ensure their employees develop the needed skills. In other words, born globals aim to shape employees in an idiosyncratic way, according to their culture and needs. Finally, the influence of formal training practices in promoting knowledge sharing among employees is limited. More generally, on the job training, in this type of firms the training

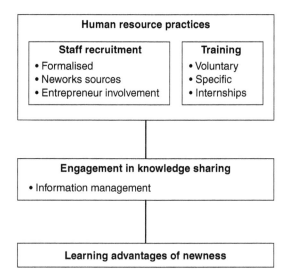

Figure 8.1 Influence of job engagement on the learning advantages of newness of born globals.

process is developed as a part of the recruitment process through the use of internships. When needed, employees are enrolled in external specific/technical educational programmes. Figure 8.1 summarises the theoretical conclusions of the analysis of this chapter.

Notes

* Authors are grateful for the financial support from the Spanish Ministry of Economy and Competitiveness (Ministerio de Economía y Competitividad. Programa Estatal de Fomento de la Investigación Científica y Técnica de Excelencia. 2013–2016. Referencia ECO-2013–44027-P).
1 In the case of Gamma, in particular, the company fully respects the existing wage conditions established in the regional sectoral collective agreement (which can probably be explained by the manufacturing specialisation of the company).
2 In some cases, and depending on the characteristics of the candidates, the enterprise may also benefit from existing public support (via subsidies for social security contributions) when transforming these temporary contracts into permanent ones.

References

Andreeva, T. and Sergeeva, A. (2016), 'The more the better … or is it? The contradictory effects of HR practices on knowledge-sharing motivation and behavior', *Human Resource Management Journal*, Vol. 26, No. 2, pp. 151–171.
Arauzo, J. M., Liviano, D. and Martín, M. (2008), 'New business formation and employment growth: Some evidence for the Spanish manufacturing industry', *Small Business Economics*, Vol. 30, No, 1, pp. 73–84.

Autio, E., Sapienza, H. J. and Almeida, J. G. (2000), 'Effects of age at entry, knowledge intensity, and imitability on international growth', *Academy of Management Journal*, Vol. 43, No. 5, pp. 909–924.

Bandura, A. (1977), 'Self-efficacy: Toward a unifying theory of behavioral change', *Psychological Review*, Vol. 84, No. 2, pp. 191–215.

Barber, A. E., Wesson, M. J., Roberson, Q. M. and Taylor, M. S. (1999), 'A tale of two job markets: Organizational size and its effects on hiring practices and job search behaviour', *Personnel Psychology*, Vol. 52, No. 4, pp. 841–868.

Beardwell, I., Holden, L. and Claydon, T. (2004), *Human resource management: A contemporary approach*, 4th ed., Financial Times Prentice Hall, Harlow.

Brass, D. J. (1995), 'A social network perspective on human resource management', in Ferris, G. (ed.), *Research in personnel and human resource management*, Vol. 13, pp. 39–79, JAI Press, Greenwich, CT.

Britt, T. W., Castro, C. A. and Adler, A. B. (2005), 'Self-engagement, stressors, and health: A longitudinal study', *Personality and Social Psychology Bulletin*, Vol. 31, No. 11, pp. 1,475–1,486.

Brown, K. G. (2005), 'An examination of the structure and nomological network of trainee reactions: A closer look at "smile sheets"', *Journal of Applied Psychology*, Vol. 90, No. 5, pp. 991–1001.

Brown, V. R. and Vaughn, E. D. (2011), 'The writing on the (Facebook) wall: The use of social networking sites in hiring decisions', *Journal of Business and Psychology*, Vol. 26, No. 2, pp. 219–225.

Cabrera, A., Collins, W. C. and Salgado, J. F. (2006), 'Determinants of individual engagement in knowledge sharing', *The International Journal of Human Resource Management*, Vol. 17, No. 2, pp. 245–264.

Cabrera, E. F. and Cabrera, A. (2005), 'Fostering knowledge sharing through people management practices', *The International Journal of Human Resource Management*, Vol. 16, No. 5, pp. 720–735.

Carroll, M., Marchington, M, Earnshaw, J. and Taylor, S. (1999), 'Recruitment in small firms: Processes, methods and problems', *Employee Relations*, Vol. 21, No. 3, pp. 236–250.

Cavusgil, S. T. and Knight, G. (2015), 'The born global firm: An entrepreneurial and capabilities perspective on early and rapid internationalization', *Journal of International Business Studies*, Vol. 46, No. 1, pp. 3–16.

Chowhan, J. (2016), 'Unpacking the black box: Understanding the relationship between strategy, HRM practices, innovation and organizational performance', *Human Resource Management Journal*, Vol. 26, No. 2, pp. 112–133.

Cohen, W. M. and Levinthal, D. A. (1990), 'Absorptive capacity: A new perspective on learning and innovation', *Administrative Science Quarterly*, Vol. 35, No. 1, pp. 128–152.

Colquitt, J. A., LePine, J. A. and Noe, R. A. (2000), 'Toward an integrative theory of training motivation: A meta-analytic path analysis of 20 years of research', *Journal of Applied Psychology*, Vol. 85, No. 5, pp. 678–707.

Consejo Económico y Social (2016), *La creación de empresas en España y su impacto en el empleo*, Consejo Económico y Social España, Madrid.

Crawford, E. R., LePine, J. A. and Rich, B. L. (2010), 'Linking job demands and resources to employee engagement and burnout: A theoretical extension and meta-analytic test', *Journal of Applied Psychology*, Vol. 95, No. 5, pp. 834–848.

Davenport, T. H. and Prusak, L. (1998), *Working knowledge: How organizations manage what they know*, Harvard Business School Press, Boston, MA.

De Clercq, D., Sapienza, H. J., Yavuz, R. I. and Zhou, L. (2012), 'Learning and knowledge in early internationalization research: Past accomplishments and future directions', *Journal of Business Venturing*, Vol. 27, No. 1, pp. 143–165.

Demerouti, E., Bakker, A. B., Nachreiner, F. and Schaufeli, W. B. (2001), 'The job demands-resources model of burnout', *Journal of Applied Psychology*, Vol. 86, No. 3, pp. 499–512.

Eriksson, K., Johanson, J., Majkgård, A. and Sharma, D. D. (1997), 'Experiential knowledge and costs in the internationalization process', *Journal of International Business Studies*, Vol. 28, No. 2, 337–360.

Eurofound (2012), *Born global: The potential of job creation in new international businesses*, Publications Office of the European Union, Luxembourg.

Fishbein, M. and Ajzen, I. (1975), *Beliefs, attitudes, intention and behaviour: An introduction to theory and research*, Addison-Wesley, Reading, MA.

Fong, C. Y., Ooi, K. B., Tan, B. I., Lee, V. H. and Yee-Loong Chong, A. (2011), 'HRM practices and knowledge sharing: An empirical study', *International Journal of Manpower*, Vol. 32, No. 5/6, pp. 704–723.

Foss, N. J., Husted, K., and Michailova, S. (2010), 'Governing knowledge sharing in organizations: Levels of analysis, governance mechanisms, and research directions', *Journal of Management Studies*, Vol. 47, No. 3, pp. 455–482.

Gabrielsson, M., Kirpalani, V. M., Dimitratos, P., Solberg, C. A. and Zucchella, A. (2008), 'Born globals: Propositions to help advance the theory', *International Business Review*, Vol. 17, No. 4, pp. 385–401.

Glaister, A. J., Liu, Y., Sahadev, S., and Gomes, E. (2014), 'Externalizing, internalizing and fostering commitment: The case of born-global firms in emerging economies', *Management International Review*, Vol. 54, No. 4, pp. 473–496.

Greenidge, D., Alleyne, P., Parris, B. and Grant, S. (2012), 'A comparative study of recruitment and training practices between small and large businesses in an emerging market economy: The case of Barbados', *Journal of Small Business and Enterprise Development*, Vol. 19, No. 1, pp. 164–182.

Grimshaw, D. and Miozzo, M. (2009), 'New human resource management practices in knowledge-intensive business service firms: The case of outsourcing with staff transfer', *Human Relations*, Vol. 62, No. 10, pp. 1521–1550.

Ipe, M. (2003), 'Knowledge sharing in organizations: A conceptual framework', *Human Resource Development Review*, Vol. 2, No. 4, pp. 337–359.

Jackson, S. E., Chuang, C.-H., Harden, E. E. and Jiang, Y. (2006), 'Toward developing human resource management systems for knowledge-intensive teamwork', in Martocchio, J. J. (ed.), *Research in personnel and human resources management, vol. 25*, Emerald Group publishing, Bingley.

Jones, M. V., Coviello, N. and Tang, Y. K. (2011), 'International entrepreneurship research (1989–2009): A domain ontology and thematic analysis', *Journal of Business Venturing*, Vol. 26, No. 6, pp. 632–659.

Kaše, R., Paauwe, J. and Zupan, N. (2009), 'HR practices, interpersonal relations, and intrafirm knowledge transfer in knowledge-intensive firms: A social network perspective', *Human Resource Management*, Vol. 48, No. 4, pp. 615–639.

Kaufman, B. E. (2015), 'Theorising determinants of employee voice: An integrative model across disciplines and levels of analysis', *Human Resource Management Journal*, Vol. 25, No. 1, pp. 19–40.

Kotey, B. and Sheridan, A. (2004), 'Changing HRM practices with firm growth', *Journal of Small Business and Enterprise Development*, Vol. 11, No. 4, pp. 474–485.

Kuvaas, B., Buch, R. and Dysvik, A. (2012), 'Perceived training intensity and knowledge sharing: Sharing for intrinsic and prosocial reasons', *Human Resource Management*, Vol. 51, No. 2, pp. 167–187.

Larquier, G. and Marchal, E. (2016), 'Does the formalization of practices enhance equal hiring opportunities? An analysis of a French nation-wide employer survey', *Socio-Economic Review*, Vol. 14, No. 3, pp. 567–589.

Lechner, C., Dowling, M. and Welpe, I. (2006), 'Firm networks and firm development: The role of the relational mix', *Journal of Business Venturing*, Vol. 21, No. 4, pp. 514–540.

Leung, A. (2003), 'Different ties for different needs: Recruitment practices of entrepreneurial firms at different developmental phases', *Human Resource Management*, Vol. 42, No. 4, pp. 303–320.

Li, Y. H., Huang, J. W. and Tsai, M. T. (2009), 'Entrepreneurial orientation and firm performance: The role of knowledge creation process', *Industrial Marketing Management*, Vol. 38, No. 4, pp. 440–449.

Macey, W. H., Schneider, B., Barbera, K. M. and Young, S. A. (2009), *Employee engagement: Tools for analysis, practice, and competitive advantage*, Wiley-Blackwell, Chichester.

MacLeod, D. and Clarke, N. (2009), *Engaging for success: Enhancing performance through employee engagement*, Department for Business, Innovation and Skills, London.

Markos, S. and Sridevi, M. S. (2010), 'Employee engagement: The key to improving performance', *International Journal of Business and Management*, Vol. 5, No. 12, pp. 89–96.

Messersmith, J. G. and Wales, W. J. (2013), 'Entrepreneurial orientation and performance in young firms: The role of human resource management', *International Small Business Journal*, Vol. 31, No. 2, pp. 115–136.

Minbaeva, D. B. (2013), 'Strategic HRM in building micro-foundations of organizational knowledge-based performance', *Human Resource Management Review*, Vol. 23, No. 4, pp. 378–390.

Nahapiet, J. and Ghoshal, S. (1998), 'Social capital, intellectual capital, and the organizational advantage', *Academy of Management Review*, Vol. 23, No. 2, pp. 242–266.

Nonaka, I. (1994), 'A dynamic theory of organizational knowledge creation', *Organization Science*, Vol. 5, No. 1, pp. 14–37.

Nonaka, I. and Takeuchi, H. (1995), *The knowledge-creating company: How Japanese companies create the dynamics of innovation*, Oxford University Press, New York.

Oviatt, B. M. and McDougall, P. P. (2005), 'Defining international entrepreneurship and modeling the speed of internationalization', *Entrepreneurship Theory and Practice*, Vol. 29, No. 5, pp. 537–554.

Pellizzari, M. (2011), 'Employers' search and the efficiency of matching', *British Journal of Industrial Relations*, Vol. 49, No. 1, pp. 25–53.

Pfeffer, J. (1998), *The human equation: Building profits by putting people first*, Harvard Business Press, Boston, MA.

Prashantham, S. and Young, S. (2011), 'Post-entry speed of international new ventures', *Entrepreneurship Theory and Practice*, Vol. 35, No. 2, pp. 275–292.

Ramirez, M. and Li, X. (2009), 'Learning and sharing in a Chinese high-technology cluster: A study of inter-firm and intra-firm knowledge flows between R&D employees', *New Technology, Work and Employment*, Vol. 24, No. 3, pp. 277–296.

Rhodes, J., Lok, P., Hung, R. Y. Y. and Fang, S. C. (2008), 'An integration model of organizational learning and social capital on effective knowledge transfer and perceived organizational performance', *Journal of Workplace Learning*, Vol. 20, No. 4, pp. 245–258.

Rialp, A., Rialp, J. and Knight, G. A. (2005), 'The phenomenon of early internationalizing firms: What do we know after a decade (1993–2003) of scientific inquiry?', *International Business Review*, Vol. 14, No. 2, pp. 147–166.

Ripollés, M. and Blesa, A. (2017), 'Influence of network ties on inter-firm network management activities: A comparative study between international new ventures and international mature firms', *Canadian Journal of Administrative Sciences*, in press.

Sabatier, M. (2010), 'Filling vacancies: Identifying the most efficient recruitment channel', *Economics Bulletin*, Vol. 30, No. 4, pp. 3355–3368.

Schaufeli, W. B., Salanova, M., González-Romá, V. and Bakker, A. B. (2002), 'The measurement of engagement and burnout: A two sample confirmatory factor analytic approach', *Journal of Happiness Studies*, Vol. 3, No. 1, pp. 71–92.

Shuck, B. and Rocco, T. S. (2014), 'Human resource development and employee engagement', in Truss, C., Delbridge, R., Alfes, K., Shantz, A. and Soane, E. (eds), *Employee engagement in theory and practice*, Routledge, New York, pp. 116–130.

Shuck, B., Rocco, T. S. and Albornoz, C. A. (2010), 'Exploring employee engagement from the employee perspective: Implications for HRD', *Journal of European Industrial Training*, Vol. 35, No. 4, pp. 300–325.

Swart, J. and Kinnie, N. (2013), 'Managing multidimensional knowledge assets: HR configurations in professional service firms', *Human Resource Management Journal*, Vol. 23, No. 2, pp. 160–179.

Valentin, C. (2014), 'The extra mile deconstructed: A critical and discourse perspective on employee engagement and HRD', *Human Resource Development International*, Vol. 17, No. 4, pp. 475–490.

Voorde, K., Veldhoven, M. and Veld, M. (2016), 'Connecting empowerment-focused HRM and labour productivity to work engagement: The mediating role of job demands and resources', *Human Resource Management Journal*, Vol. 26, No. 2, pp. 192–210.

Wang, S. and Noe, R. A. (2010), 'Knowledge sharing: A review and directions for future research', *Human Resource Management Review*, Vol. 20, No. 2, pp. 115–131.

Yin, R. K. (2014), *Case study research: Design and methods*. 5th ed., SAGE Publications, London.

Zacharatos, A., Barling, J. and Iverson, R. D. (2005), 'High-performance work systems and occupational safety', *Journal of Applied Psychology*, Vol. 90, No. 1, pp. 77–93.

Zahra, S. A. (2005), 'A theory of international new ventures: A decade of research', *Journal of International Business Studies*, Vol. 36, No. 1, pp. 20–28.

Zahra, S. A. and Filatotchev, I. (2004), 'Governance of the entrepreneurial threshold firm: A knowledge-based perspective', *Journal of Management Studies*, Vol. 41, No. 5, pp. 885–897.

9 Conclusions

Policy relevance of born globals for job creation in Europe

Irene Mandl

9.1 Why focus on job creation in born globals?

In a time of recovery from the most severe economic downturn for decades, European policy debate intensively discusses options to cope with the high levels of unemployment resulting from the crisis in most Member States of the European Union. Quite naturally, the issue of job creation is in the centre of these discussions, and policy-makers have realised that it is companies, notably small and medium-sized enterprises (SMEs), who need to be targeted to ensure employment growth. Both at European and national levels, several support mechanisms are available to assist SMEs in their economic advancement which, in turn, is assumed to lead to some job creation. Examples are initiatives to reduce administrative burden and allow companies to better concentrate on their core business, to ensure better access to finance (for example, loans, grants or subsidies) for product development and innovation, production and service provision or marketisation (including internationalisation) or demand-side oriented measures targeting the customers of specific sectors to foster a stable level of orders and workload within the firms. In parallel, specific instruments exist that directly incentivise SMEs to hire additional staff, such as employment subsidies for specific labour market groups or sectors, the reduction of non-wage labour costs or the provision of training measures that are (better) aligned to the skills needs of the companies.

Against this background it is somewhat surprising that there is little discussion about the fact that not all (types of) SMEs equally contribute to employment growth in Europe – or even want to do so. From a policy perspective, these differences justify the need for a more differentiated approach. Targeting those (types of) SMEs that have a higher potential of creating jobs with specific instruments results in a better resource efficiency and effectiveness, something highly relevant considering that several Member States experience public budget cuts. However, for such a targeted approach, more information on the characteristics of those SMEs which are more promising as regards job creation, the external framework conditions that need to be in place to allow them to grow and their public support needs, are required.

Based on Eurofound (2016a), this book has considered the factors which determine the job creation effort in SMEs. As a result, born globals (that is, young companies which quickly after their inception intensively engage in international activities, and thereby follow an 'untraditional' business development and internationalisation pathway) have been identified as potentially dynamic job creators in Europe. This assessment is based on the fact that the business model of born globals includes a large number of the elements identified as fostering job creation in SMEs. However, and while born globals have been the subject of academic research now for about two decades, little data and information is available on employment issues related to this company type. By compiling this available information and giving it further consideration, this book aims to contribute to a currently highly relevant policy debate – and to stimulate a shift in focus from a broader discussion on employment growth in SMEs to job creation in a specific business model.

9.2 Development pathways of born globals

In contrast to academia, which has been researching the business model of born globals long before the latest recession, policy-makers in Europe seem to show interest in this company type only recently. This is not very surprising, taking into account that the business model of born globals differs from more traditional forms of entrepreneurship, and awareness about the existence of born globals is not that widespread. Furthermore, the unique characteristics of born globals result in a wide array of specific challenges they are confronted with – which influences the emergence and sustainability – and hence overall spread – of this type of business. Accordingly, the share of born globals is limited within the European economy. As shown in this book (see Chapter 3), it is estimated that about 12 per cent of young companies (up to 3.5 years) and 2.5 per cent of all European SMEs are born globals. Available national data for Austria (see Chapter 5) and Sweden (see Chapter 4) show similar levels.

Accordingly, even if born globals are an interesting business model which has promising employment growth potential (see Sections 9.3 and 9.4), they must not be seen as the 'silver bullet' that could solve all labour market problems currently experienced in Europe (Eurofound, 2012; Mettler and Williams, 2011). As has already been indicated, this is even more the case since literature on born globals highlights the numerous challenges these businesses are confronted with – and which go beyond the common issues all SMEs typically experience in their daily activities. These challenges are mainly caused by the coincidence of liabilities of newness, smallness and foreignness at the same time, which is deemed to make born globals especially vulnerable. Taking into consideration that a favourable and sustainable business performance has been identified as one of the key determinants for job creation (see Chapter 2), it becomes obvious that born globals' survival and economic development are an essential factor for their job creation dynamism.

Interestingly, however, the issue of born globals' survival is hardly discussed in research and policy debate at the present time. A few authors have tried to shed light on this subject, but came to different results. Mudambi and Zahra

(2007), for example, find a lower survival rate for British born globals compared to firms using a different internationalisation mode. In contrast, Sui (2009) finds that, for Canadian companies, being a born global has a significant effect on their survival capacity compared with enterprises going global more gradually, and Halldin (2011) shows that, for Sweden, born globals have a higher survival rate than other young firms. Within this book, it was also highlighted that, for Estonia (see Chapter 6), born globals are more likely to survive than other exporters and non-exporters.

As regards born globals' resilience to economic shocks – a topic that is highly relevant when discussing their economic and employment contribution during and in the aftermath of the recent recession – anecdotal evidence hints towards born globals having the potential of being more sustainable in those circumstances, but that fewer new born globals emerge during such phases (Eurofound, 2012; Piva *et al.*, 2012).

For those born globals that succeed in remaining in the market, again little is known as regards their development pathways. Eurofound (2012) uses financial data to illustrate that French born globals are more profitable and financially sustainable than other young firms. Other authors show that being a born global increases competitiveness (Blesa *et al.*, 2008) and sales growth (Mascherpa, 2012). In contrast, Piva *et al.* (2012) cannot empirically establish a relationship between international expansion (of a sample of mainly young firms) and firm growth.

From these considerations it can be concluded that the development pathway of born globals is far from straightforward, and it can be assumed that there is some heterogeneity among them as regards the continuity, direction and level of their economic performance. Eurofound (2012) derived four theoretical models of born globals' development (see Figure 9.1). 'Dynamic born globals' are the ones which are able to realise the ideal development pathway of quickly reaching a high level of international activity, which is then continued over time. Also 'steady born globals' quickly achieve a high internationalisation level. However, after a while this dynamism slows down and stabilises – but still allows the company to benefit from the advantages of well-performing international activities. 'Volatile born globals' realise high levels of international activities during some part of their early growth phase, but also experience drops in international orders over and over again. Hence, their economic development is unstable and probably cannot be fully influenced by the company itself. Such a 'random' development path might raise some concerns within the management, which also influences their employment plans. The last potential development pathway describes 'decreasing born globals'. These are young enterprises with initial high levels of internationalisation which, however, voluntarily or involuntarily decrease their international business throughout their life course. Taking into consideration that a general characteristic of born globals is that they provide products or services for niche markets at global level, there is a high potential that domestic market demand is not sufficient for the business to prosper, or maybe even survive. Accordingly, the job creation potential of decreasing born globals is assumed to be low.

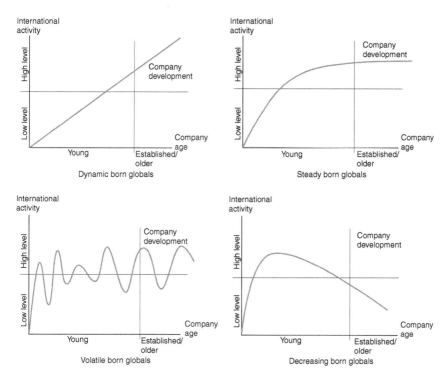

Figure 9.1 Potential economic development pathways of born globals.
Source: Eurofound, 2012.

From a policy perspective, policy-makers should aim at supporting born globals to follow the first two potential development pathways, as these are the most promising ones as regards contribution to the overall economy and the labour market. At the same time, the latter two groups should not be neglected. Companies in those groups are characterised by a combination of promising features – otherwise they would not have been able to become a born global in the first place. However, they probably face some internal or external challenges which prevent them from realising a steadier growth pathway. These challenges should be identified and addressed to better take advantage of the opportunities of born globals.

While such information on specific challenges for the individual (theoretical) types of born globals is not yet available, some general policy pointers can be derived on how to (better) support the establishment and performance of young international businesses (Eurofound, 2012). First, as born globals cannot yet take advantage of a good international reputation themselves due to their newness, public initiatives to foster the reputation of the home country or sector abroad ('branding') are assumed to be beneficial for born globals' continuous and sustainable international activities. Second, while across Europe a wide range of start-up support is available, early-phase support (that is, more ongoing advice in the first years after inception, going beyond the start-up phase, to cover the first critical years in business development) is rare and should be enhanced. Thereby, advisors must: be made aware that internationalisation is also an option for very young firms; be informed of the specific characteristics and needs of born globals; and be provided with the relevant knowledge to assist them in their globalisation pathway. Such early-phase instruments should also involve psychological support, since it is very likely that born globals do not experience immediate success (or experience some success mixed with some failures). Hence, they might need some 'soft support' in terms of confidence in the potential of their approach, to keep the business going and avoid strong frustrations deriving from setbacks. Third, most SMEs, and born globals even more so, are challenged by securing sufficient capital to finance their activities. In addition to traditional instruments like favourable credit or subsidies, the provision of and access to a broader range of non-traditional financing options (such as public seed money, business angels or venture capital) seems to be particularly important for born globals (Gabrielsson *et al.*, 2004; Liesch *et al.*, 2007).

9.3 Specific public support for job creation in born globals

The contributions to this book cover a variety of countries, sectors, methodological approaches and specific research questions. Nevertheless, they all have in common the discussion on employment effects of born globals. Although the share of born globals in the European economy and their company size are limited – hence the small scale of their absolute contribution to the labour market – the various authors agree that born globals must not be neglected in public debate and policy on job creation. These types of companies are not only very ambitious to grow (which is identified as one of the key determinants for job creation, see Chapter 2), but the scattered data available show that they do just that. At EU level, GEM data (see Chapter 3) highlights that they are bigger and plan to hire more additional staff in the years to come than other young companies. The same is also found at individual country level for Sweden (Chapter 4) and Austria (Chapter 5). The available data for Estonia (see Chapter 6) show that the net job creation rate (that is, the difference between job destruction and job creation) of born globals is higher than for non-exporters and older exporters. Furthermore, there are some indications that the jobs created by born globals are, in general, comparatively stable and sustainable as well as of high quality (see, for example, Eurofound, 2012; Estonian data in Chapter 6; anecdotal evidence from Austrian case studies in Chapter 5).

However, the employment dynamism of born globals must not be taken 'as a given'. Important preconditions (see Chapter 2) and challenges (see Chapters 3–7) related to job creation in born globals have been identified in this book. These should be addressed by public policy to take full advantage of the employment potential of this company type.

First, due to their newness and smallness, born globals are confronted – probably more so than other young or small companies – with the challenge of attracting staff. This becomes even more difficult if they are looking for highly skilled specialists (which is very probable, taking into account the high degree of innovation and orientation in niche products/services characterising born globals). In this respect, the issues are: recommendations for policy focus on public measures that ensure a better visibility of born globals as potential employers and improve their employer branding; initiatives that support them in approaching a higher number of suitable candidates (for example, access to specialised recruitment platforms free of charge or through encouraging higher education providers to cooperate with born globals in terms of giving them access to their graduates); or instruments increasing their attractiveness as employer (such as wage subsidies or reductions in social security contributions which allow them to offer higher remunerations).

One aspect which is striking in the various contributions to this book is that, in spite of the strong international orientation of born globals and their requirement of foreign language coverage by their staff, international recruitment seems to be rather limited. Accordingly, and notably for the EU-level, it is recommended that better cross-national job vacancy and mediation/matching services are fostered, which also includes a highly skilled and specialised workforce and enables easy, quick and cheap access to such for born globals. In another area, exchange of good practices of and cooperation between respective national instruments should be fostered.

In Chapter 8 of this book, the Spanish experience shows the relevance of knowledge acquisition and sharing for the positive development of born globals, and hence their job creation performance. This also highlights the importance of access to information related to, for example, technical aspects of products, administrative and legal issues (including institutional aspects) as well as supply and demand in various markets (including cultural aspects) (Eurofound, 2012). In this context, the provision of and access to peer platforms informally exchanging knowledge might be particularly suitable for born globals as the anecdotal evidence shows the importance of informal entrepreneurial and managerial learning and social capital for this type of companies. Furthermore, the relevance of skills and knowledge sharing for born globals' success flags the issue of the education system. The education and training provided to those entering the labour market for the first time, but also to those who already belong to the active workforce, need to be aligned with the specific needs of born globals. This refers to occupational skills, transversal/social skills, but also to internationalisation skills (such as managerial, languages, cultural awareness and familiarity as well as knowledge about foreign markets). Taking into account the characteristics of born globals, such a provision of skills and knowledge needs to be very practical, in order for the new staff to immediately become operational rather than having to undergo a longer induction period during which they are not yet productive. Accordingly, theoretical education combined with practical training, also abroad, is recommended.

Finally, some anecdotal evidence (see, for example, Chapter 7 on Ireland) highlights the potential for born globals to be acquired by larger and older national or international ventures after their early phase, in order to merge their innovation capabilities into existing structures. While this should not be considered as a negative as such, it might limit the potential employment effects. A born global might be more inclined than the acquiring firm to hire additional staff to cope with the daily business activities, as the acquiring firm has already disposed of a large collection of internal resources. Hence, public policy might want to consider incentives for born global entrepreneurs to continue developing their business themselves rather than selling them after the start-up phase.

9.4 For future policy debate: job creation by born globals

In order to expand the discussion on employment effects of born globals, the future debate should go one step further and (also) focus on job creation *by* born globals (rather than just *in* born globals). The fragmented available evidence points towards born globals' role in international supply chains and their effects on other companies. Due to their innovative character, they have the potential for not only creating value-added for themselves, but also of fostering the innovation and competitiveness of their partner firms (Eurofound, 2012) – which, in turn, might result in employment growth in these companies linked to the born globals in their supply chains. Accordingly, enhancing networking skills and social capital in born globals might not only help these companies, but also result in job creation in other firms. In this context, Eurofound (2007) for example highlights the relevance of the regional level in terms of a shared vision of regional firms and commitment to jointly progress. This must be fostered by a regional key actor (such as the government, a regional development agency or a chamber of commerce) who could also act as a coordinator across companies and ensure relevant communication and information flows. This is needed to allow mutual trust to develop between the companies, which is an important precondition for social capital and networking. At the same time, this coordinator should encourage cooperation pathways, which must fairly quickly result in some initial positive outcomes for the involved firms, as otherwise their confidence in the collaboration might decrease and they might become reluctant to engage in networking.

Furthermore, incentives for companies to jointly engage in product development and marketisation could foster the sustainability, competitiveness and growth of all involved companies (born globals and nationally-oriented ones). Respective examples are tax incentives for joint R&D or the requirement of cooperation in public tenders (Eurofound, 2012). Such initiatives might be more effective if targeted at companies that have already shown some interest in collaborating with others, for example through their involvement in business clusters.

Chapter 7 discusses the embeddedness of born globals in local business clusters on an Irish example and highlights favourable outcomes in terms of economic and employment growth and innovation levels for the involved companies, the cluster and the host region as such. A few years ago, the European Commission (2012) recognised the importance of business clusters as intermediaries to help SMEs in their internationalisation activities and launched some support programmes to facilitate cluster internationalisation. Such instruments (both at EU and national levels) should be further encouraged and scrutinised as regards their suitability and effectiveness for born globals and their partner companies.

Notably in relation to job creation, it should be highlighted that it does not necessarily need to be realised by a single company in the business cluster, but it could result from joint action from several enterprises. In this context, a new employment form has been identified as emerging in a few EU Member States, defined as 'strategic employee sharing' (Eurofound, 2015). It refers to a situation in which different regional companies have a fragmented, but recurring and well predictable, specific HR demand. Rather than offering part-time or fixed-term contracts or outsourcing these services, the employers jointly hire one or several workers who work in the participating companies on a rotating basis, satisfying the individual HR needs of the firms. The workers are offered a permanent full-time contract and the affiliated employers have a joint and several liability towards them. While still not well known and hence small in scale, this employment model is assumed to have a positive labour market potential as it provides companies with the labour flexibility they need while creating stable and good quality employment for the workers (Eurofound, 2016b). Strategic employee sharing seems to be particularly interesting for born globals active in regional business clusters as it could solve some of their challenges related to staff recruitment, and could result in additional jobs at regional level through cross-organisational HR cooperation between born globals and other local firms. Such a job creation would not occur by the participating companies acting exclusively in isolation. However, this employment form does not come into existence on its own but requires some impetus and favourable framework conditions that should be supported by public policy (Eurofound, 2016b). Next to a legal framework that allows for the implementation of this employment form, companies need to be made aware of its existence and implications and actively approached to get involved in it. Furthermore, there should be a so-called 'resource centre' which provides information as well as theoretical advice and practical support to the establishment, implementation and operation of strategic employee sharing models. Such resource centres need to be financially supported by public funds.

To conclude, international business incubators have been identified as effective support instruments for born globals (Eurofound, 2012) as they do not only offer them low-cost workspace but also networking and peer review opportunities. In this context it can be assumed that the exchange with others and the mutual learning (also see Section 9.3) does not only benefit the born globals, but also the (more nationally oriented) firms hosted by the incubator, hence encouraging employment growth in those.

References

Blesa, A., Ripollés, M., Monferrer, D. and Nauwelaerts, I. (2008), 'The effect of early international commitment on international positional advantages in Spanish and Belgian international new ventures', *Journal of International Entrepreneurship*, Vol. 6, No. 4, pp. 168–187.

Eurofound (2007), *Social capital and job creation in rural Europe*, Publications Office of the European Union, Luxembourg.

Eurofound (2012), *Born global: The potential of job creation in new international businesses*, Publications Office of the European Union, Luxembourg.

Eurofound (2015), *New forms of employment*, Publications Office of the European Union, Luxembourg.

Eurofound (2016a), *ERM annual report 2015: Job creation in SMEs*, Publications Office of the European Union, Luxembourg.

Eurofound (2016b), *New forms of employment: Developing the potential of strategic employee sharing*, Publications Office of the European Union, Luxembourg.

European Commission (2012), *New initiatives to assist small enterprises go international*, Press release, MEMO/12/225, 28 March, Brussels. Available at: http://europa.eu/rapid/press-release_MEMO-12-225_en.htm.

Gabrielsson, M., Sasi, V. and Darling, J. (2004), 'Finance strategies of rapidly growing Finnish SMEs: Born internationals and born globals', *European Business Review*, Vol. 16, No. 6, pp. 590–604.

Halldin, T. (2011), 'Born global firms in knowledge intensive business services (KIBS): What do we know of their performance?', *Cesis Working Paper*, Royal Institute of Technology, Stockholm.

Liesch, P., Steen, M., Middleton, S. and Weerawardena, J. (2007), *Born to be global: A closer look at the international venturing of Australian born global firms*, Australian Business Foundation, Sydney.

Mascherpa, S. (2012), *Born global companies as market driven organisations: An empirical analysis*, PhD thesis, Università degli Studi di Milano Bicocca, Milan.

Mettler, A. and Williams, A. D. (2011), *The rise of the micro-multinational: How freelancers and technology-savvy start-ups are driving growth, jobs and innovation*, Lisbon Council Policy Brief, Lisbon Council, Brussels.

Mudambi, R. and Zahra, S. (2007), 'The survival of international new ventures', *Journal of International Business Studies*, Vol. 38, No. 2, pp. 333–352.

Piva, E., Colombo, M., Quas, A. and Rossi-Lamastra, C. (2012), 'How do young entrepreneurial ventures in high-tech sectors react to the global crisis?', *Innovation and competitiveness: Dynamics of organizations, industries, systems and regions*, DRUID Society conference 2012, Copenhagen Business School, 19–21 June.

Sui, S. (2009), *Born global, gradual global, and their determinants of exit from exporting*, Carleton University, Toronto.

Index

Page numbers in *italics* denote figures, those in **bold** denote tables.

 # Taylor & Francis eBooks

Helping you to choose the right eBooks for your Library

Add Routledge titles to your library's digital collection today. Taylor and Francis ebooks contains over 50,000 titles in the Humanities, Social Sciences, Behavioural Sciences, Built Environment and Law.

Choose from a range of subject packages or create your own!

Benefits for you

>> Free MARC records
>> COUNTER-compliant usage statistics
>> Flexible purchase and pricing options
>> All titles DRM-free.

 Free Trials Available
We offer free trials to qualifying academic, corporate and government customers.

Benefits for your user

>> Off-site, anytime access via Athens or referring URL
>> Print or copy pages or chapters
>> Full content search
>> Bookmark, highlight and annotate text
>> Access to thousands of pages of quality research at the click of a button.

eCollections – Choose from over 30 subject eCollections, including:

Archaeology	Language Learning
Architecture	Law
Asian Studies	Literature
Business & Management	Media & Communication
Classical Studies	Middle East Studies
Construction	Music
Creative & Media Arts	Philosophy
Criminology & Criminal Justice	Planning
Economics	Politics
Education	Psychology & Mental Health
Energy	Religion
Engineering	Security
English Language & Linguistics	Social Work
Environment & Sustainability	Sociology
Geography	Sport
Health Studies	Theatre & Performance
History	Tourism, Hospitality & Events

For more information, pricing enquiries or to order a free trial, please contact your local sales team: www.tandfebooks.com/page/sales

 Routledge
Taylor & Francis Group

The home of
Routledge books

www.tandfebooks.com

For Product Safety Concerns and Information please contact our EU
representative GPSR@taylorandfrancis.com
Taylor & Francis Verlag GmbH, Kaufingerstraße 24, 80331 München, Germany

www.ingramcontent.com/pod-product-compliance
Ingram Content Group UK Ltd.
Pitfield, Milton Keynes, MK11 3LW, UK
UKHW020949180425
457613UK00019B/613